The Vampire of Reason

V

The Vampire of Reason

An Essay in the Philosophy of History

RICHARD JAMES BLACKBURN

VERSO

London · New York

First published by Verso 1990
© R.J. Blackburn 1990
All rights reserved

Verso
UK: 6 Meard Street, London W1V 3HR
USA: 29 West 35th Street, New York, NY 10001-2291

Verso is the imprint of New Left Books

British Library Cataloguing in Publication Data

Blackburn, Richard James
The vampire of reason : an essay in the philosophy of history.
1. History
I. Title
900

ISBN 0-86091-257-4
ISBN 0-86091-972-2 pbk

US Library of Congress Cataloging-in-Publication Data

Blackburn, Richard James, 1943–
The vampire of reason : an essay in the philosophy of history /
Richard James Blackburn.
p.   cm.
Includes bibliographical references.

ISBN 0-86091-257-4 — ISBN 0-86091-972-2 (pbk.)
1. History—Philosophy.   2. Historical materialism.
3. Geopolitics—Philosophy.   4. Intellectual life—History.
I. Title
D16.8.B54   1990
901—dc20

Typeset in September by Leaper & Gard, Bristol, England
Printed in Great Britain by Bookcraft (Bath) Ltd

Contents

Preface

The following essay has been written with two main objectives in mind. The first is to put forward a new perspective on a subject that had until recently fallen into disrepute; the philosophy of history. In the course of this proposal, a possible synthesis beyond Marxist theory is suggested which trespasses on the equally neglected domain of geopolitics. The second is to outline in the essay's later section an approach to understanding the long interplay between ideas and material forces, for which the initial discussion of Marxism is of double relevance, as both a chief actor in the drama and a leading candidate for its interpretation.

This requires a brief introduction, establishing the starting-point of the train of thought, to which, in the second chapter, a geopolitical critique of Marxism forms a counterpart. The third chapter gives a preliminary account of the synthesis in question. It is not until the beginning of the fourth chapter that it is possible to specify the structure and particulars of what is to follow.

While the philosophy of history underwent a decline in the postwar period, interest in the subject has, for several reasons, revived in the last few years. The emergence of a long growth crisis from 1974 has vindicated those espousing the long wave theory of capitalist development, such as Kondiatieff and Schumpeter, who, half a century before, had predicted just such an eventuality (and the probability of a further long boom beyond it). Indeed, forewarnings that an even longer-term *ecological* crisis was being prepared by present forms of economic growth have in recent years been strongly corroborated by various misfortunes befalling the environment. In the political sphere, the revelations made under Deng Xiaoping and now Gorbachev coming after those of Khrushchev have reminded many that the socialist revolutions of the century have confirmed the forebodings of Luxemburg and the young

Trotsky that Leninist party organizations would recapitulate the Jacobin phase of the French Revolution and reinvigorate autocratic traditions, notably with Stalinism and Maoism and their echoes of Ivan the Terrible, Peter the Great and the First Emperor of Ch'in. A reconsideration of the present in the light of the past has in these cases proved highly pertinent to assessing future trends, and certain alternatives within them, in economic and political life.

As for that not inconsiderable body of contemporary opinion which finds the whole enterprise of the philosophy of history redundant and antipathetic, the excellent remarks on the subject by two recent writers[1] render it unnecessary for me to dwell for long upon the justification of a new attempt in the genre.

As Hall points out, well-known opponents of the philosophy of history, such as Aron, Berlin and Popper, have more or less equated the subject with the tendencies of communism and Nazism, to which they have had a strong aversion, and whose successes they have ascribed to the power of their ideas, namely Marxism and a racial geopolitics. For Popper social life is so complex and the growth of scientific ideas, with all their immense impact for good or ill upon it, so unpredictable that its future course remains in principle impossible to foresee. Alleged sciences, such as Marxism and geopolitics, which depreciate or fail to admit these facts, are thus both spurious and dangerous: hence the anathema pronounced on all attempts at a theory of history.

Such an argument, as Hall says, presupposes its own philosophy of history, one that considers ideas to be the prime movers of historical change. This is an outlook with a long ancestry to be found latterly in Hegel, Weber and Toynbee, as well as Popper. In its twentieth-century liberal form, its rivals have been precisely Marxism and, for a spell in the Anglo-Saxon world and in Germany, geopolitics. The former has stressed the role of material, especially economic, development and of class struggle over its fruits in determining the structure and history of economic and social organization, of politics and of ideology. The latter has placed emphasis upon the struggle between states and their peoples for security and yet for scarce territory and resources, whether in diplomacy or warfare, in deciding their history and fate. It will be argued in this work that a further perspective is required in the light of which it can be seen that the Marxist theory of history, by far the most influential of recent years, needs to be corrected by geopolitics; but that any attempt to

---

1. John Hall, *Powers and Liberties: The Causes and Consequences of the Rise of the West*, Basil Blackwell, Oxford 1985; and George Dennis O'Brien, 'Does Hegel Have a Philosophy of History?', *Hegel*, edited by Michael Inwood, Oxford University Press, 1985, pp. 174–98.

combine them leads inexorably to a recognition of a considerable moment of truth in the original idealist theory itself. The three initial theories can be related in an alembic capable of resolving their antinomies and discarding their illusions, while preserving their respective moments of insight.

The philosophy of history can be interpreted as consisting of either a speculative or a critical enquiry, that is either a theory of the meaning of history itself or a critical review of works of historiography. As O'Brien points out, just as any philosophy of science presupposes ontological assumptions needing to be elucidated and defended, so, one can argue, a critical philosophy of history requires its own presuppositions to be endorsed by a speculative theory. To confine one's purview to criticism and evaluation of historians' work while eschewing any examination of one's assumptions, is to fail to do justice to the requirements of criticism itself. Nevertheless, a speculative theory divorced from a critical one would lack any exacting empirical trial. In the course of elaborating the present train of thought brief considerations will, therefore, be ventured of specific historical questions and of recent literature on them, to provide some checks upon this essay's claims.

In a sequel to this work an enquiry will be made into the range and validity of modes of argument concerning history, such as various forms of causal and functional explanation, relating them to the speculative theory elaborated here. In the light of these methodological considerations it will be possible to assess different historiographical debates, such as the decline of the Roman Empire and the character of feudalism and absolutist monarchy in the epoch of early capitalism; and to explore the impact of Marxism and socialism upon the world capitalist order created by the Industrial Revolution. This will render possible, it is hoped, an extended empirical 'testing' of several of the claims put forward here.

I would like to thank several readers of earlier drafts of the work for their comments and criticisms: Perry Anderson, Robin Blackburn, Marie-Françoise Golinsky, Roderick Grierson, Jon Halliday, Angus Hone and Garbor Shabert; each gave me at least one decisive stimulus for rethinking some aspect of the argument. I would also like to acknowledge a great debt to the late Nicholas Krasso, on whose anvil of criticism several of the following ideas were initially forged. Gerry Cohen, the supervisor of the D. Phil. thesis which formed the penultimate version of this work, gave me not only the benefit of his keen analytic acumen but also the encouragement I needed to persist in developing its main ideas. I had the further good fortune to receive a most perceptive critical commentary from John Torrance, one of my examiners. None of the former is of course in any way responsible for the errors and omissions which remain. I would like to conclude by thanking Sheila Tobun for her unfailing skill and good humour in retyping successive drafts of the text.

1

Introduction

The philosophy of history has come to be virtually expropriated by Marxism, contributing to the general disesteem in which the subject is now held by non-Marxists. Even its adversaries, such as Popper, define their positions primarily in relation to Marx's theory; much as Marx and his contemporaries defined theirs in relation to Hegel's.[1] Moreover, historical materialism has remained the monopoly of Marxists, whose possession of it nobody disputes. I want to argue here that the philosophy of history needs a further development of Marx's approach – one which goes beyond his own conclusions and those of his followers. The materialist correction of Hegel's idealist philosophy of history requires, as Marx understood, a transformation, not just an inversion, of its conceptions of historical development. I will argue that Marx only half fulfilled this project and that the introduction of several new themes, especially those of geopolitics and geoeconomics, is needed to complete it in order to achieve a genuinely materialist reordering of the philosophy of history. It will then be contended that such a radical departure beyond the Marxist version of materialism paradoxically implies that ideas and their development can play a decisive, indeed an increasingly decisive, role in human history; a partial vindication of Hegel's emphatic idealism as an instance of the unity of opposites. This, it will be argued, is the logical outcome of the materialist conception of history, desiderated, but not yet achieved, by Marxism. The aim indeed is not, as with Popper, to shave Marx's beard

---

1. Karl Popper, *The Open Society and its Enemies*, Routledge and Kegan Paul, London 1950, 2 vols. Popper's first volume is concerned with Plato, while his second begins with Hegel, but devotes far more time to Marx. Popper's successor work, *The Poverty of Historicism* (Routledge and Kegan Paul, London 1957), is mainly directed against Marx, whom he clearly regards as the most dangerous modern 'historicist'.

with Occam's Razor but rather to trim it with the blades of geopolitics so as to assure a continuation of its luxuriant growth.

Popper's other chief preoccupation, the recasting of the philosophy of science, can yield, however, a suggestion as to how to proceed. His subversion of verificationism with its contrary of falsificationism exemplifies the tenet of heuristic contrast. In the light of this principle it can be seen that Marx and Hegel before him expose to view the central role of production or creation to the neglect of the no less crucial role of destruction and disaster. In particular, Marx privileges material production, while disregarding the numerous forms of material destruction with which the former, and indeed every social level, is obliged to contend. He is thereby led to concentrate upon those dialectical processes that are closed and internal in character, disregarding those more comprehensive ones which are open to an active, and often hostile, external world.

An interplay between creation and destruction is the salient feature of dialectics. For Hegel and Marx, creative developments in history possess their own inherent contradictions, which eventually disrupt or devastate them from within. Thus, for Hegel, the development of an authoritarian, medieval Christendom inevitably provoked, and was disrupted by, the doctrines of Protestantism with their emphasis upon the individual and his free judgement, which ushered in the modern Germanic world. For Marx, the development of capitalism leads to the immanent emergence of the proletariat which at a certain moment devastates it by revolution. Destruction (that is either disruption or devastation of the form or the content) emanates here from the creative pole of social existence itself, the antithesis confronting the thesis and making possible a synthesis (or new thesis) by a perpetuation, yet transcendence, of the original thesis in an endlessly recurring pattern.

Both Hegel and Marx overlook here several considerations of fundamental importance. Firstly, creative development can be interrupted or terminated by environmental or external destruction from the outside world: this can arise in the shape of natural disaster, such as volcanic eruptions and floods; of more insidious forces, such as desertification and glaciation; or of foreign predators such as the Spaniards and the microparasites, which they brought with them, in conquering Meso-American societies. Secondly, this very set of possibilities entails that a society can survive only if it resists (and continues to resist) persistent and potentially lethal pressures stemming from its participation in nature and its relations with other societies. Thirdly, these external forces of destruction can vary widely in power and incidence through both time and space, depending upon the changing *historical* geography and human-cum-animal demography which underlie social existence.

If human communities are to persist, they are required to be pre-emptive of certain voracious types of destruction: starvation, exposure and entropy (as these threaten their individual members and their animate or inanimate possessions), by means of production of basic necessities; or invasion, by military capabilities; or disease and demographic extinction, by sexual reproduction, medicine and immunization against micropredators; or environmental degradation, by pollution control and ecological balance; or disintegration of the community itself, by group solidarity and cohesion. It is not merely the development of productive, or indeed military, capabilities which explains the social history of humankind, but in the first place the rapacious destructive forces which societies must avoid or mollify in order to survive. Some of these forces are volatile and others are relentlessly insistent, whether they stem from nature or from other societies. Any community is obliged to be prophylactic or recuperative of material destruction, where the damage in question emanates from those rife forces detrimental to its chances of survival. Indeed, as we shall see, many of the material forms of creative development and not a few of its cultural forms are undertaken in response to challenges or incipient realities of destruction which are posed by other societies or by human involvement with nature.

Social existence within nature is of course more rewarding than these remarks on their own imply. Humankind's environment is the source of its material creativity and, in a different sense, of its cultural creativity. The human species is the most creative outcome of natural evolution upon earth. Our planet, moreover, is singularly fortunate among the known planets – until recently only those of our solar system – for the encouragement which its atmospheric and geographical conditions have provided and continue to provide for the development and propagation of life. However, even upon earth, destructive forces are so common that an interplay between creation and destruction inevitably characterizes the history of its life-forms. The unusual creativity of homo sapiens with its forms of social organization and cultural inheritance has given rise to a novel mode of existence in which destructive forces are increasingly preempted or channelled into creative paths, notably so in the cases of fire and combustible energy. Our species's avoidance or taming of those lethal forces is more and more wide ranging, even as new threats to human existence are continually emerging, not least those which it engenders or precipitates itself. The Social Darwinists err, given these facts, in reducing social life to the play of the natural struggle for existence between individuals. Nonetheless, primitive and even civilized societies themselves remain subject to incessant destructive forces which are very similar, although not identical, to those of natural selection at large; in particular they face vulnerability to lack of food, to inclemency of the elements, to animal and human predators and to the problems of maintaining an ecological and demographic compatibility with their environment.

There are passages in Marx's works where he acknowledges some of these elementary facts, especially in his theory of the realm of necessity that exists in opposition to that of freedom. For the realm of necessity, it will be argued, is that sphere of activity in which societies are engaged in forestalling their destruction. The realm of freedom, on the other hand, comprises that sphere in which societies can be free of such constraint. The realm of necessity consists, in the first place, of the provision of necessaries – food, shelter, clothing and medicine – without which humankind would swiftly be destroyed. This insight is doubtless the one that so convinced Marx of the primacy of the economic over other social levels. Yet Marx fails to consider the full range of destructive forces at work in the human predicament. Had he done so, he would have had to assess not only the impact of disease, environmental degradation, entropy and demographic imbalance, as do geoeconomic studies, but also, more amply than he did, the impact of humanity on its own kind in the shape of warfare and violence which has been the especial pre-occupation of the geopolitical theorists. This involves exploring the possibility that the significant events in history include not only some that actually happen, but also many that do not happen because they are not permitted to do so, such as the Moslem occupation of Europe which feudalism pre-empted. It is not only forces of actual creation and destruction but also forms of avoidance of potential destruction which play a crucial role in history. Geopolitical theorists have been more sensitive than Marxists to this ambivalent dimension of social coexistence, as well as to the problems of actual wartime devastations; while environmentalists have been more sensitive to the uncertainties and dangers of human habitation of nature. It is to them, therefore, that it is now necessary to turn.

2

The Geopolitical Counter-Argument

It will prove helpful to the argument being put forward to pose in polemical terms a geopolitical counter-argument to historical materialism and then to outline a possible synthesis. As the introductory remarks already indicate, there are some prima facie objections to an exclusively geopolitical theory as well as to an exclusively Marxist one. The aim at the moment is to provide a sharp antithesis to Marxism, even if in exaggerated form, in order to clarify the issues involved in effecting an eventual synthesis. This requires an examination of the propositions of historical materialism from the perspective of geopolitics and then more comprehensively from that of geopolitics-cum-geoeconomics.

For Marx and Engels the 'history of all hitherto existing society is the history of class conflict';[1] class struggle and revolution occupy the central place on the historical stage. It is significant that Marx and Engels refer to society in the singular, rather than to the multiplicity of societies into which mankind, as a social species, is divided. Their analysis is, henceforth, conducted in abstraction from the vital being-for-others which all societies, as all individuals, are obliged to assume and negotiate. They distinguish between societies in time and postulate an order of their historical succession, but ignore their contemporary relations in space with all the profound implications which may be involved for their internal constitution.

It might be objected in opposition to them, for instance, that class collaboration has been far more characteristic of history than class conflict and that the history of all hitherto existing societies has been more one of individual or class collaboration within their mutual antagonism,

---

1. Karl Marx and Friedrich Engels, *The Communist Manifesto*, p. 1.

especially between their respective state powers. Group and national antagonism and warfare under a group or national allegiance have occupied the central place far more often than class struggle and revolution, even if the latter has increasingly been able to emerge from the wings and displace the former when it has led to collective humiliation and distress. 'State-power' is here defined with Weber to mean the political structure or grouping which 'successfully upholds a claim to the monopoly of the legitimate use of physical force in the enforcement of its order within a given territory';[2] its territorial ambiguity has been characteristically resolved within the field of force which defines a common region or zone of societies. In the initial stages of tribal or post-tribal social life the very existence of the community was in jeopardy from internal dissension or civil war, which was then characteristically exorcized by uniting against a common enemy. Civil wars gave way, often in external warfare and conflicts, to an internal regulation and pacification of social life. As a simple matter of historical fact external wars have been far more frequent than revolutions and have long antedated them as the main events of primitive societies and indeed of civilized societies through Roman times and the Dark Ages until at least the modern bourgeois epoch.

Similarly, the main focus of loyalty for nearly all societies has been not class, but the overall group, whether a tribe, a feudal community, or a nation. Its members acquire an attachment to its territory and customary institutions, including its state, endorsing the advantages of social pacification: everyone, even those in a subordinate class, benefits from minimization of dangers to person and individual or family property, an elementary fact slighted by Marxism. Moreover, the state, by its protection of the society against external aggression and encroachment and by its furtherance of general interests abroad, can usually benefit each member even more plainly and convincingly. For these material reasons, indeed precisely because of its monopoly of the legal use of violence, the state can receive a bedrock of support and legitimation in even highly exploitative social systems. Under such pressures nationalism or group loyalty has triumphed over class loyalties and inter-nationalism again and again in history.

It is not economic development and struggles over its fruits through class divisions of labour and ownership which have been ultimately determinant of most phases of history, as Marxism alleges, but rather the development of state power, whether group or national in character, and imperialist struggles between states for territory, resources, and booty (including slaves). The great epochs of history in varying zones or fields of

---

2. Max Weber, *The Theory of Social and Economic Organisation*, Free Press, New York 1966, p. 154.

force are distinguished from each other by the degree of security they offer their inhabitants, both internally and externally, and by their characteristic development of state power, imperialism and social pacification. Thus history has been primarily determined by the secular development of military technology and transport and other technology serviceable in war on the one hand, and by that of group loyalty and latterly nationalism on the other, rather than by techniques of production and class structures and struggles. The former, as the more urgent of the two, have determined the latter, not vice-versa.

The technology of civilian production stagnated for long historical periods, namely during the birth of civilization in Ancient Egypt, during the epoch of European antiquity and during the cyclical ages of many oriental despotisms, whereas military technology was perforce undergoing rapid development.[3] The eventual acceleration of technological development in industry and transport in Europe owed much to the stimulating effects of warfare and innovations in military technology which accompanied the formation of European nation-states from the late fifteenth century onwards.[4]

Often class differentiation has developed as the product of conquest or to meet the requirements of military activity, as in slave and feudal societies: economic advance has been a byproduct of power politics, promoting state power and military readiness, notably in the case of Japan's transition to capitalism; while in the form of trade either preparing the way for conquest or fostering mutual interdependence and so peace.[5]

It may be objected that warfare, unlike class struggle, has been only

---

3. See William McNeill, *A World History*, Oxford University Press, 1979, for an account of the overriding impact of new methods of warfare on successive civilizations – such as the chariot-based aristocratic empires of the Bronze Age (the Hyskos in Egypt, the Kassites in Mesopotamia and the Aryans in India), whose great mobility, armour and firepower eventually proved unavailing against the iron-clad and iron-weaponed infantry phalanxes of such states as the more democratic Greek city polities (Sparta and Athens) of the Iron Age; the nomadic cavalry empires of a later period and the stirruped and mounted cavalry of feudal Europe with its localized upkeep and sovereignty; and the artillery-based absolutist empires of the late fifteenth, sixteenth and seventeenth centuries in Europe, Asia and the Middle East, which could break down the castle and cavalry defences of local nobilities.

4. See William McNeill, *The Pursuit of Power*, Basil Blackwell, Oxford 1983.

5. Anthropologists since at least Mauss have recognized the vital significance attached by primitive societies to trade and the exchange of gifts as sureties of peace, which need not of course prevent them from being mutually beneficial in economic terms as well. See Marshall Sahlins, 'The Spirit of the Gift', Ch. 4, *Stone Age Economics*, Tavistock Publications, London 1974, pp. 149–84; and Marcel Mauss, *The Gift Forms and Functions of Exchange in Primitive Societies*, Routledge and Kegan Paul, London 1954, where Mauss says, 'although the prestations and counter-prestations (gifts and reciprocal gifts) take place under a voluntary guise they are in essence strictly obligatory and their sanction is private or open warfare', p. 3.

episodic in history and military preparations only interludes in otherwise peaceful, but still economically active, epochs. However, as Hobbes pointed out, the possibility of war can lend a quite different character to a whole period of time:

> For WARRE, consisteth not in batell only, or the act of fighting; but in a tract of time, wherein the will to contend by Battell is sufficiently known: and therefore the notion of Time is to be considered in the nature of Warre; as it is in the nature of Weather. For as the nature of Foule weather, lyeth not in a shower or two of rain, but in an inclination thereto of many dayes together; so the nature of Warre, consisteth not in actual fighting, but in the known disposition thereto during all the time there is no assurance to the contrary. All other time is PEACE.[6]

Hobbes's account refers here to the transition from the state of nature between individuals to civil society, not to interstate relations in a common field of force, although Hobbes considered them along similar lines elsewhere. Its aptness for the latter is scarcely to be disputed in our own epoch, which was until recently one of extended cold war. So far, indeed, the foregoing counter-argument may seem to be no more than a modern statement of pre-Marxist common sense and need scant support from geopolitics or political geography.

The development of state power and organization and so of class and other social forces can, however, be contended to be locally differentiated by reason of variations in the territory and population of the state in question. Mackinder has pointed out that political geography needs to be concerned with the relationship between man and geography in the sense of his varying environment. The relationship between man and nature or his overall environment is studied by physiology, biology and engineering among other disciplines: but political geography is 'the science whose main function is to trace that interaction of man in society and so much of his environment as varies locally'.[7] This definition is too broad, covering those activities of an economic character which it would be better to classify as geoeconomic ones. Geopolitics is better confined to study of political activities in the interaction between man in society and so much

---

6. Thomas Hobbes, *Leviathan*, Part 1, Ch. 13.

7. Sir Halford J. Mackinder, *On the Scope and Methods of Geography* and *The Geographical Pivot of History*, The Royal Geographical Society, London 1951; our quotation is from the former work, p. 14. Mackinder came to be esteemed among the German geopoliticians, who published the journal, *Zeitschrift für Geopolitik*, ed. Karl Haushofer. It was, doubtless, the Nazis' inclination towards geopolitics that led to this school of thought being generally discredited in the postwar world. A revival of geopolitics has been undertaken, however, in France by certain historians of the Annales school; see, for instance, Yves Lacoste, *Questions de Geopolitique, L'Islam, La mer, L'Afrique*, Le Livre de Poche, Paris 1988.

of his environment as varies locally, and to the study of interstate relations.

A dictionary definition is in some respects preferable: geopolitics is 'a study of the influence of such factors as geography, economics and demography on the politics and especially the foreign policy of a state'.[8] If it is to preserve its physicalist character, it is best to amend 'economics' to 'geoeconomics', where the latter refers to 'economic conditions or policies that are (directly) influenced by geographic factors and are international in scope'.[9]

In order to turn geopolitics into a properly historical discipline, moreover, 'geography' and 'demography' are best changed to 'historical geography' and 'historical demography' to refer to the historical territory and population of a country; for many of their features, contrary to a widespread misconception, are not constant, but capable of variation, having undergone continuous alteration in the course of history under the impact of independent natural forces and of geopolitic, and geoeconomic activities themselves. Geopolitics, then, is a study of the direct influence of historical geography, geoeconomics and historical demography upon the politics and especially the foreign relations of a state and of the influence in time of the latter activities upon the former. Geoeconomics is a study of economic conditions or relations that are directly influenced by and that secularly influence factors of historical geography (and demography) and are international as well as local in scope.

The more independent and perdurable features of historical geography and demography determine geopolitical and geoeconomic activities in a more formative way than the latter determine the former. For the character of a country's terrain, its territorial position and its resources and population size will heavily determine its military prospects and its rational mode of economic activity and so its entire social history. Some societies have a security against outside forces conferred on them by nature. Switzerland for example has been blessed with a mountainous inaccessibility and inhospitality that has both marginalized its political importance on the European continent and fostered egalitarian and demo-cratic forms of social organization in its isolated geopolity and for long primitive geoeconomic environment. France, Spain and Germany by contrast have had to endure the vulnerability to outside invasion of acces-sible and fertile land zones and a consequently class-divisive politics. The development of both a dynamic class society and economic activity is more common in temperate, close-knit, warlike zones, most notably western Europe, which has in succession spawned slave, feudal and capitalist societies, than in the empires of the Eurasian continent, the

8. *Webster's New Collegiate Dictionary*, Merriam, London 1974, p. 480.
9. Ibid.

Ming, Moghul and Ottoman empires in China, India and Turkey, let alone the tribal havens of pre-colonial Africa or Pacific islanders. History is the outcome of societies in conflict or unstable contact in a parturient environment: and class divisions are but an internal response.[10]

---

10. For another statement of the relevance of geopolitics and environmentalism see E.L. Jones, *The European Miracle: Environments, Economies and Geopolitics in the History of Europe and Asia*, Cambridge University Press 1981. His work forms a challenging pioneer attempt to integrate the concerns of environmentalism and geopolitics into economic history, in particular, into a comparative account of Europe's rise to pre-eminence. Jones focuses not only, as does Marxism, on the impact of changing technology, but also on that of fickle geography and demography and of warfare.

3

A Synthesis of Marxism and Geopolitics: The Dialectic of Creation and Destruction

The anti-Marxist perspective presented above is as astigmatic as that of Marx's historical materialism. They both contain an important measure of truth and need to be reconciled to each other's good points within a wider synthesis. For a dialectic of creation and destruction has underlain the course of history, taking a number of complex forms, the more significant of which we shall shortly attempt to delineate. It is not only the production of material life, but other ways of pre-empting destruction, such as the protection and reproduction of life and indeed of culture and society as a whole, which are vital in social existence. While Marxism elucidates one moment of this dialectic, that of material production, geopolitical and environmental studies do several others, capable of advancing historical materialism beyond its initial, strictly Marxist form. However, they each overlook further aspects of fundamental importance. An integration of their respective insights and a supersession of their mistakes and omissions within a wider framework of thought is by now overdue.

1. The Defects of Geopolitics

In the first place, geopolitical theory quite ignores the crucial significance of those long periods of Hobbesian 'PEACE'. The objectives of social existence are assumed to be primarily destructive or pre-emptive of manmade destruction, whether from internal or external violence. At worst this leads to the étatism and bellicism of Nazi doctrines. At best it underestimates the creativity and power of human societies outside the sphere of the state. It tends to underestimate in particular the significance of both economic production and culture.

Geopolitical and other advocates of interpreting history in terms of

11

wars and military preparations tend to single out the lust for power and victory as the mainspring of warfare. They consequently depreciate, to adopt their psychologistic vocabulary, the role of greed, or the economic advantages which normally accrue to the victors. Covetousness or economic aims, it can be argued, have been crucial in most instances of aggression in history whatever their ostensible purposes or pretexts. Commercial competition and acquisition of foreign property, tribute, slaves or plunder have seemingly motivated most warfare and imperialism in the West. McNeill in his latest book, *The Pursuit of Power*, provides many instances of this, contrary to the latitudinarian emphasis suggested by his title.[1]

A geopolitical theory which alludes to geoeconomic conditioning is less open to the charge of neglecting factors of economic significance. Indeed some societies, such as those of remote Pacific islanders, have developed in isolation from other human groups. Their social organization and history cannot be attributed to the exigencies of warfare or peaceful co-existence within foreign communities, while they clearly have to respond to those of their natural economy and situation. Yet economic activity cannot be reduced to the interaction between the productive system and the environment, important and underrated by economic theory as it may be. An economy needs to be comprehended as possessing a structure of production with a partly autonomous dynamic of its own, stemming from the property regime, the class structure and the system of allocating resources and income, a requirement which Marxist and other economic theories have made better attempts to fulfil. A depreciation of the structural and class-related features of political economy and politics is a common failing of geoeconomic and geopolitical studies.[2]

Thus geopolitics, while in this version of it comprehending geo-economic determination, still underestimates the significance of economic factors proper in history, most notably those appertaining to the property regime and socioeconomic system of production. In its original attempt to reduce international politics to conflicts between power blocs or individual states differentiated only by their geographical, demographic and technological endowments, it proves to be incapable of understanding the global dissension of our epoch, which in the central case of the Cold War has clearly possessed a wider dimension as a struggle between

---

1. William McNeill, *The Pursuit of Power*, Basil Blackwell, Oxford 1983.

2. For a critique of the 'geographisme' of Mahan and Mackinder see Yves Lacoste, *Questions de Geopolitique, L'Islam, La mer, L'Afrique*, Le Livre de Poche, Paris 1988, pp. 165–8. As Lacoste points out, the earlier geopolitical analyses revolve around allegories within which geographical entities become historical actors. With the Nazi geopoliticians these allegories took on a decidedly racialist hue.

contending socioeconomic systems. The integration of geopolitics with a class and economic analysis enables it, however, to be given a fuller explanatory power. Once it has been recognized that geopolitical rivalries coexist and sometimes coincide with conflicts between classes and are often the outcome of economic as well as geopolitical causes, their due relevance can in turn be admitted.[3]

2. The Defects of Marxism

Marxism, on the other hand, is dismissive of those destructive elements in history which do not issue from its constructive moments themselves. This purblindness is combined with a conflation in Marx himself of 'society' with 'societies' so that the spatial, as opposed to the temporal, distinctions between societies are depreciated by him. The qualifications of his followers to rectify these omissions have been introduced into a problematic generally recalcitrant to them. As a result, it will be seen, neither Marx nor Marxist philosophers and theorists have been able to account for the significance of nationalism and religion in history. Their productivist bias also explains their less often cited, because more widely shared, neglect of the role of environmental, demographic and other hazards and disasters in history. Indeed, these oversights have left Marxism unable to interpret class collaboration and social solidarity except as interruptions in class struggle or to apprehend the full force and significance of class conflict itself. Yet this productivist focus has its merits in explaining economic structures and economic and social upheavals, and, as we shall see, can help to elucidate the metamorphoses of class society.

Marx's productivism has a distinguished intellectual ancestry, stemming from both Hegel and 'political economy'. It has come to be taken as the hallmark of Marx's materialism, justifying, in conjunction with a historical perspective, his claim to found historical materialism. For Marxist productivism has involved an emphasis upon the development of material, rather than cultural, production as the explanans of historical changes in the last instance. It is not clear why an ultimately economic explanation of this type should be considered as more materialist than a military one that focuses on problems of material destruction and its avoidance, or why either should be more materialist than a geographical or even demographical one.

On the face of it, both geography and demography refer to forms of

---

3. For an incisive analysis of the Falklands War along these lines, see the last chapter of Yves Lacoste.

matter which are of fundamental relevance for any materialist theory of history – the local configurations of inanimate nature and of animal and human populations of it. Marxism has, nevertheless, remained as generally negligent of them as have more ostensibly idealist avenues of thought, such as Weber's sociology and most liberal historiography. This is doubtless due to the widespread conception of nature and its geographical and demographic conditions as constants or as merely cyclical (seasonal or generational) variables, undergoing long-run alterations only under the impact of social development itself. Economic development on the other hand is unmistakably a historical phenomenon, one which according to Marxism largely accounts for such long-term environmental and population changes as have taken place, as for wider social transformations generally.

One of the main purposes of this work is to argue that for several related reasons geographical and demographic conditions are of crucial significance in understanding historical development. It will be maintained that geography and more obviously demography are highly variable and historically active in ways that make them often autonomous, not merely dependent or background variables. The impact of *historical* geography and *historical* demography upon social change is frequently profound and pervasive; and, as will be seen, it is even the case that those aspects of historical geography which only change very slowly, such as mountains and coastlines, can in conjunction with technological invention inflect human societies in novel directions, as when landlocked environments were transformed by the spread of railway and motor transport in the nineteenth and twentieth centuries.

The development of knowledge has generally been characterized by the supersession of one set of problems by another, resolving the former at the price of opening up new perplexities. The replacement of one problematic by another characteristically involves, not a banal reversal of causal direction, as would be the case if, contrary to Marxism, the superstructures determined the economic base, but rather a realization that factors which had been considered as constants (in experimental sciences) or as original constraints or background noise (in historical sciences) are in fact capable of being autonomously variable in their potency and incidence; a famous instance is when Newton's absolute space and time became unified by Einstein into relative space–time. The Marxist explanation of social superstructures by the economic base and of the latter by the development of the productive forces assumes that geography and demography are given as background noise. In actuality, as we shall see, they are very far from being so; and they demand to be understood in their historical amplitude as creative and destructive variables of considerable, if not of course complete, independence, whose impact can deflect the course of social development in decisive ways. Only then can the phenomena which Marxism apprehends as superstructural, such as religion and nationalism, be viewed in sufficient depth. Historical materialism cannot live up to its name unless it appreciates the significance of the historicity of matter for that of social existence.

It is crucial instead for Marx to place primary emphasis upon the role of production. The concept of production is vested with enormous weight by both Marxist economics and historical materialism. Yet it has been given surprisingly little attention, let alone dialectical elucidation or definition, in the Marxist tradition itself.

A dialectical theory is normally concerned to relate the meaning of each of its concepts to that of its opposite and other allied notions, for only then can its further significance be revealed. The contrary to the concept of production, in the form of production of material goods and services, is commonly presumed in Marxist, as in other economic literature, to be that of consumption. Marxist economics, moreover, insists on the priority of production over consumption, not just in terms of chronology, but also in terms of explanatory power. The true contrary to the concept of production, as of creation, however, is not that of consumption, but that of destruction. Consumption is merely a peculiarly creative form of destruction: consumption of raw materials destroys them, at least their form, in order to create final goods, and consumption of final goods destroys them in order to reproduce or embellish life. But production can encounter other less creative forms of destruction, notably, as will be seen, disasters and gradual deterioration issuing from historical geography and demography.

The advocates and critics of historical materialism, by contrast, habitually oppose cultural activity to economic production. For the former, material production is more fundamental than cultural production, an axiom which the latter often contest. They both, however, remain within the problematic opposing materialism to idealism. It is this common preoccupation which tends to render their debates so sterile and difficult to resolve. The questions concerning the ultimately determinant level of social existence – whether such a level exists, whether indeed, it always consists of the economic level as Marxism alleges and whether it to some degree governs the development of the 'superstructures' – are incapable of resolution until the scope of the debate is enlarged.

It is necessary for this purpose to introduce at least one further pair of axes to that of idealism and materialism, namely that of creation and destruction. The latter pair of opposites cut across the former in ways which quite alter the significance of their respective moments. For materialism or the materialist moment of any realist theory remains incomplete until it recognizes the destructive as well as the creative properties of nature and man.

Nature is usually conceived, not least by Marxists, as a more or less munificent habitat for man, as Mother Nature. Marx pointed out on several occasions that goods and use-values are created not by labour alone, but by labour in conjunction with nature. He also ascribed early economic advance to the challenge posed by a less fecund environment, which spurs societies into finding creative solutions.[4] The emphasis remains, however, on the gradations of the creative properties of nature and its localized adversity to production rather than on its many-sided destructiveness. A more comprehensive appraisal of nature's destructive forces is required if a materialist theory, or at least the materialist moment of a realist theory, is to be properly elaborated. It is only necessary in this preliminary account of the synthesis in question to assess what are usually considered the most general forms of these destructive forces, those appertaining to economics, physiology and physics, sciences that take species-being and nature as their province. Discussion of what are usually considered to be the more particular and temporary forms of destruction can be delayed until a later chapter, when it will be seen that natural disasters and other contingent or fickle destructive forces studied by the historical sciences of nature, not only historical biology but also historical geography and demography, possess their own forms of ubiquity, permanence and, therefore, generality, which are relevant in understanding the history of the human species.

The most basic and universal physical constraint upon human society is often conceived to be scarcity, a deficiency of useful energy and material objects or properties of objects, such as oil, coal, mineral resources, fertile land, rainfall and water. Given the limitations variously imposed by exiguous nature and existing technology upon the transformation of matter and energy into products, scarcities of intermediate and final products themselves arise. The struggle against scarcity is often considered the rationale of both economic activity and human history in so far as it is governed by the dictates of economic activity. This conception underlies 'political economy' and certain schools of contemporary Marxism alike, notably in the latter's most wide-ranging engagement with social theory, Sartre's *Critique of Dialectical Reason*.

For Sartre, the fundamental datum of human existence is need, while that of history is scarcity. Scarcity 'is the basis of possibility of human history', although other conditions are also required for historical change to take place.[5] Matter, wherein scarcity is revealed, is considered the

---

4. Karl Marx, *Capital*, Vol. I, Moscow, pp. 512–4.
5. Jean-Paul Sartre, *Critique of Dialectical Reason*, Verso, London 1976, p. 125.

foundation of the 'practico-inert field', which is conceived as passively undergoing changes due to human activities or merely reactively, as in Sartre's case of Chinese agricultural cultivation and deforestation leading to a counter-finality of flooding and soil erosion in the struggle against scarcity. Need, scarcity and counter-finality of this sort, however, are not such fundamental forms of negativity confronting human societies as Sartre implies, being derivative on those that really are. Need, scarcity and counter-finality arise in the relationship of humanity as the consumer of and producer in nature. A more basic relationship is that of nature as the underlying producer of and perennial consumer of humanity. It is well known how homo sapiens emerged from the animal and plant world of life. It is appropriate to point out that in turn life arose from the far from inert or passive world of inorganic nature, which remains capable of destroying it.[6]

Nature of course has also produced the energy and wherewithal for our species to *reproduce* or sustain itself, even if often in only niggardly or scarce proportions, whether due to human depletion of resources and fertile land or, as we shall see, to its inexorable vicissitudes, such as micro-parasitic infestations, natural disasters or bad weather. Nature, far from composing an inert field, is the arena of perpetual creation and destruction by inanimate as well as animate forces, transforming things incessantly into each other and maintaining its zones in endless movement and suspense. Sartre in his concern to avoid the error of reifying humanity falls into the error of reifying matter.[7]

---

6. This emphasis has found expression in both Engels and more recently Timpanaro in his *On Materialism*, Verso, London 1975. Engels drew attention in *The Dialectics of Nature* to the historicity of nature, established by Darwin, in terms of its destructive as well as productive powers in relation to humankind. But the destruction of humanity, which Engels stressed, was that involved in the final end of the species as the sun and the solar system expire, a prevalent theme of late-nineteenth-century science. He was less concerned with the perennial consumption of human life that nature is responsible for, a theme which has been taken up with great verve and pungency by Timpanaro, who underlines the inherent biological frailty of life and the inevitability of individual death, disease and physical suffering, to some degree irrespective of the social order, whether it be capitalism or communism. Timpanaro's advocacy of the significance of the natural sciences, especially the historical sciences of nature, for understanding the human predicament and social life is similar to that attempted in this essay, albeit with the difference that a wider range of destructive forces will be considered here, not only death and suffering to our species and its members, but also those perennial forms of destruction of human beings and their societies and environments studied by physics and historical geography and demography, sciences whose relevance in this regard Timpanaro tends to ignore.

7. The ultimate reason for Sartre's conception of a prevalent inertia lies in his denial of any negativity and so determined totality and contradiction in nature except that which is engendered or experienced by organic beings. 'Negativity and contradiction come to the inert through organic totalization. As soon as need appears, surrounding matter is endowed with a passive unity, in that a developing totalization is reflected in it as a totality; matter revealed as passive totality by an organic being seeking its being in it – this is Nature in its

The very existence of human need arises from the fact that nature, while creating the possibility of life, also tends to destroy mankind and its possessions. Human beings and animals are victims of expenditure of energy and, along with inanimate objects, are prone to wear and tear, deterioration and ultimate disintegration under the impact of a variety of natural destructive forces. It is necessary for life that the effects of such forces be offset by the acquisition of energy, by regeneration and immuniz-ation and various other activities, the performance of each of which is a human need.

The possessions and environment of any society are subject to the perennially diverse motion of matter and energy, corrosive and destructive or fecund and creative as the case may be. It is to the restless motion of matter, so contrary to any conception of it as partaking of a practico-inert field, that Hobbes and Spinoza ascribe physical and even mental causation. In terms of modern physical science, this notion of the incessant transport and transformation of matter and energy has of course

---

initial form.' *Critique*, p. 81. This amounts to a denial of negativity in nature before the emergence of life. Sartre maintains 'that although in the *first instance* the material universe may make man's existence impossible, it is through man that negation comes to man and to matter ... There is no denying that matter passes from one state to another, and this means that change takes place. But a material change is neither an affirmation nor a negation; it cannot *destroy* anything, since nothing was *constructed*; it cannot *overcome resistances*, since the forces involved simply produced the result they had to', pp. 83–4. Sartre realizes here that the interplay between creation, preservation and destruction is crucial to dialectics. But his perspective remains akin to Kantianism, at least in regard to creation and destruction, or affirmation and negation, which are held to inhere in perception organizing being-in-itself into the world.

He is mistaken, however, in thinking that creation and destruction are relative to humanity. Any event in the physical world, such as the formation of a galaxy and its solar systems or the hunting and eating of animals, must be both creative and destructive, in these cases creation of suns or of food and destruction of the nebulae and gas clouds or animals, consumed in their creation. For sentient beings what is perceived as creative by the predator will be perceived as destructive by the prey. But this epistemological relativism implies no ontological one. It remains an objective fact of nature that predation, in general or in particular, is creative for the predator and destructive for the prey. The order of creation and destruction, whether of solar systems or animals, contain objective directions of negativity, albeit ones which will be recognized and valued as creative or destructive depending on the percipient in question.

Negativity, throughout Sartre's oeuvre, has its existence endowed upon it by the percipient or for-itself, either in the *négatités* of the world or in its constitution of conscious-ness as reflection or emptiness of being: its *esse est percipi* or its *esse est percipere*. While avoiding idealism in his conception of being-in-itself, Sartre falls into it in his conception of nothingness and so negativity. This is inadmissible if carried over into his project of constructing a materialist dialectic, particularly one which does not depend on, but does not deny the possibility of a dialectic of nature (*Critique*, pp. 32–3). For if one is prepared to grant such a possibility, then this dialectic, clearly older than life itself, would be incon-ceivable without an original negativity in nature. Such natural negativity may only be knowable to organic beings, but it would be a conflation of the epistemological and onto-logical orders, so lucidly undertaken by Berkeley, to infer from this that its existence relies upon perception of it.

been vindicated by quantum physics: yet matter is also always in motion and change at the macrolevel which we inhabit, due not just to the inherent molecular mobility of fluids, gases and liquids, but to the molecular vibrations and environmental alteration of solids. Gases, liquids and solids change under the common influence of each other, of gravity, of heat and of electro-magnetic forces: gases liquefy or ignite, liquids solidify, freeze, evaporate or boil and solids dampen, dehydrate, melt or ignite under certain atmospheric conditions and altitudes and at certain temperatures.

Changes in temperature are associated with alteration of the motion of matter and energy and of the entropy which is produced by the thermo-dynamics of irreversible processes in nature. Within any closed physical system, according to the laws of classical thermodynamics, its entropy or quantum of unavailable energy tends to increase. A closed system is very likely to change from the less probable configuration of order to the more probable one of disorder. An open system is also likely to do the same in the temporary absence of outside interference, although the possibility of a return to order is realised if the correct intervention takes place.[8] Hence, buildings, artifacts and other objects which are open to the environment tend to undergo deterioration and disintegration in a manner which can only be reversed by human work expended upon them. The disruptive powers of entropy and disasters such as fires and floods can only be avoided by the activities involved in disentropy, such as repair and maintenance of buildings, and the preservation of a modus vivendi with the environment.

The exceptions to this rule arise when entropy is countered by non-equilibrium mutations in nature, as a new structural order emerges out of disorder or chaos.[9] But these occasions are anomalous even in the sphere of biological reproduction. An asymmetry exists between the long periods of time required for order favourable to humanity to emerge, unassisted by it, from nature's disorder, as with fuel deposits from fossilization, and the brief, indeed often sudden, action of entropy, disasters and parasites, as with the decomposition of dead organisms into their environment. The climatic consequences of the onset of ice ages impose a new order of glaciation (associated with the 'residual entropy' of the irregular positions

---

8. See I. Prigogine, *The Thermodynamics of Irreversible Processes*, Interscience Publishers, Chichester 1967, chs I–III. Prigogine explores the possibilities of extending the classical equations of the basic laws of thermodynamics to irreversible non-linear, non-equilibrium processes such as are prevalent in the world at large.

9. Ilya Prigogine and Isabelle Stengers, *Order out of Chaos*, Bantam, USA 1984. This is a more accessible work for the general reader than Prigogine's specialist contributions, giving an account of the increasingly historical conceptions of modern physics and their implications for the study of living processes.

of hydrogen protons at low temperatures) or destroy fertile landscapes far more rapidly than they can reconstitute them out of deserts and wastes.

Sartre has an inkling of this more fundamental negativity of nature and its remorseless frustration of living creatures when he points out, 'to preserve its reality as a *dwelling* a house must be inhabited, that is to say looked after, heated, swept, repainted, etc.; otherwise it deteriorates. This vampire object constantly absorbs human action, lives on blood taken from man and finally lives in symbiosis with him.'[10] Sartre fails unfortunately to take this instance of disentropy contending with entropy as indicative of the starting-point required by his attempt to elaborate a materialist dialectic. Instead he recuperates it into his initial problematic of humanity struggling against material inertia and the passive perversity of matter deflecting praxis from its original goals in the context of the prevalent scarcity which has characterized it, that is into the problematic of humanity as the producer in and the consumer of a recalcitrant nature: 'the synthetic unification of a habitat is not merely the labour which has produced it but also the activity of inhabiting it; reduced to itself, it reverts to the multiplicity of inertia'.[11] The perennial action of entropy and concomitant destructive forces in the relationship of nature as producer and consumer of humanity and its habitat engender the universal tendency to dissolution from which they must be protected by disentropy or human work. Scarcity may of course prevent disentropy or work from being successful if there is an insufficiency, for instance, of building and refurbishing materials and of free energy; yet, while scarcity or at least its worst forms may one day be overcome, the action of entropy and natural destructive forces, such as microparasitism, will perforce remain to corrode the human species and its artificial environment.

Physical organisms, such as human beings, negotiate with their environment on different terms from inorganic objects. Not only must they combat the entropy afflicting their surroundings as products in part of their own imposition of order upon them, but they must also maintain a homeostasis of internal order by exchanging energy and matter with the environment as a whole via the medium of this artificial environment. They must also sustain a system of immunization against diseases and the effects of accidents by reproduction of antibodies and other recuperative agencies. Animal kind is required to ingest as much energy as it expends, to maintain its hydration, to repair its fatigue with sleep and to avoid detriment to itself, whether from accidents and exposure to the elements, from micro- and macroparasites and diseases or from incompatibility with its environment, its diet and its neighbours. In other words, it has to

---

10. J.P. Sartre, *Critique*, p. 169.
11. J.P. Sartre, *Critique*, p. 46.

provide itself with necessaries, food, drink, and shelter, to possess immunity or tolerance of diseases and parasites and to prove capable of withstanding predators, shocks and misfortunes and the depradations of time. Nevertheless, all living things are inescapably subject to the physiological clock of ageing and death so that even if successful in fending off the former types of destructive forces they cannot avoid being eventually destroyed. The replacement of extinct members of a society (or species) by new ones in biological reproduction becomes necessary to avoid the extinction of the society (or species) itself.

Life involves primarily a rebellion against entropy, preserving order amid resurgent disorder. This involves transforming stable systems into unstable systems to release free energy by the performance of work or the transference of free energy from another system. 'The whole of life and civilization as we know it depends on thermodynamic instability; the struggle for existence is a struggle for free energy available for work'.[12] This struggle for free energy, moreover, of necessity takes a social form for the human as for most other primate species. The more complex the environment humanity moulds and maintains for itself, the more sophisticated, as we shall see, must its structures of community become.

The replenishment, reproduction and protection of human organisms are prerequisites of social existence and the replenishment, reproduction and protection of social existence are prerequisites of organisms being truly human. Thus, the avoidance of forces destructive of a society and its members, which the fulfilment of these prerequisites makes possible, provides it with its primary tasks, if not of course, its only raison d'être. This requires in turn a wide range of material and cultural activities, such as provision of necessaries, medicine and military defence, reproduction and rearing of offspring and environmental protection, but also language and numeracy, knowledge of technology and the environment, public morality and mores and diverse means of cultural reproduction and education, all of which exist within the realm of necessity, as essential components without which a society and its members would be more or less assuredly destroyed. Their chances, in fact, depend upon the severity and urgency of the destructive forces in question; and these, as we shall see, in turn depend upon the specific *historical* geography and animal-cum-human demography of the society in the context of existing technology and its relations with neighbours and the outer world. The shifting demands placed by historical geography and demography upon their technological and other capacities to deal with them and the external constraints imposed by other societies, themselves bound to greater or lesser extent by their own environmental pressures, are forever altering the

12. *Encyclopaedia Britannica*, London 1955, Vol. 22, p. 86.

terms on which societies must negotiate their realm of necessity and the terms upon which they are then capable of autonomous creative activities in their realm of freedom.

The negativity of the ubiquitous destructive forces with which humanity contends 'constantly absorbs human action, lives on blood taken from man and finally lives in symbiosis with him', a symbiosis in which human societies may for a while survive, but in which successive generations of its members are fated to perish. This negativity forms the perennial counterpoint of human existence and the foil of its prized rationality. Homo sapiens, the rational species, whose intelligence enables it to choose through trial and error increasingly superior means to attain its ends, is persistently assailed by vampirish objects and agencies whose collective negativity can be designated as the predatory enemy of this rationality, the vampire of reason. This ubiquitous vampire is, however, reproduced not only by the perennial motion of matter and energy, but by homo sapiens itself as it strives to avoid its own destruction by wreaking it in turn upon other species, upon the environment which they share in common and upon its very own kind.

Societies can circumvent destructive forces by relaying them onto others through exaction of flesh, blood, and milk from animals and vegetables and of tribute, or surplus from other human societies, while denuding their environment of mineral and energy resources and even fertile soil. A rational and lucrative way for societies to cheat the vampire of reason of its prey is to incarnate it by preying upon other societies in turn, becoming themselves vampirish for others. 'Nothing – not even wild beasts or microbes – is as deadly for man as an intelligent, carnivorous and cruel species capable of understanding and outwitting human intelligence, whose aim is precisely the destruction of man. This species is of course our own, as each man apprehends it in every other in the context of scarcity.'[13] The context is however, as we have seen, far wider and more pertinacious than one of the contemporary and, in at least some forms, temporary contingency of scarcity itself; it is a context which includes wild beasts and microbes, indeed microparasites of all sorts, and the loss of energy involved in life itself in the struggle against entropy, disease and death. Societies in this sense resemble ant-hills, being perpetually vulnerable to ruination and decay at the hands of nature and each other unless timely preventative activity is undertaken.[14]

---

13. J.P. Sartre, *Critique*, p. 132.
14. This comparison with ant societies is not casual. As Darwin pointed out, they share many remarkable features of social existence with humanity, including domestication of animals or aphides, stratification into aristocrats and workers or slaves and intraspecies warfare. Charles Darwin, *The Origin of Species*, John Murray, London 1859, pp. 239–42 and 251–6.

Human beings must procure the necessities of life either by producing them themselves or obtaining them from others in trade and tribute. The origins of class society may often have lain in external subjection, as nomadic tribes imposed themselves on sedentary agricultural populations and societies. It has, nevertheless, been disputed whether such a conception is fact or the myth it clearly is in Plato's *Republic*.[15] Established class society involves the inheritance of class rights to tribute or property and the privileged class or classes obtaining the necessaries of life by extracting them from the underprivileged classes beneath. They will usually be in a position to procure more than is merely necessary to avoid their destruction, that is to say, luxuries and other privileges as well. Indeed such exploitation is perfectly rational from the point of view of the ruling classes themselves so long as it is compatible with the perpetuation of tribute or of their property regime. The ruthless exactions of the Roman propertied classes upon the slave and peasant masses of the empire, especially in the later years of the Principate and into the Dominate have inspired de Sainte Croix's already celebrated metaphor for its system of exploitation, 'the vampire-bat' of Rome.[16] The vampire of reason, therefore, comprises not only the original destructive forces of nature, but also the predation of humanity on other species and on their common environment and the interhuman predation involved in imperialism and class domination.

In the light of the turmoil of destruction which nature and human beings can wreak upon each other, it might be asked how either, or at least the latter, have succeeded in surviving at all. In fact of course the destructive forces at work in history are offset by even more powerful creative ones, both of nature and of life. Our species in particular possesses not only access to a bountiful planet, but recuperative powers and a rational intelligence which can pre-empt destruction, and indeed continues to achieve feats that would have astounded previous generations. Nevertheless, one form of its creativity has been an increasingly sophisticated capacity for devising means of destruction to the point where it is now able to destroy all life on this planet. Moreover, destructive forces are often inadvertently provoked in nature, as the emergence of new forms of pollution testifies today. Human powers of destruction avoidance are required to develop as rapidly as those of production to keep pace with destructive potentialities. It might well be asked why a generally creative outcome has in fact prevailed, why advanced civilizations have come into being which possess at least a chance of perpetu-

---

15. Plato, *The Republic*, tr. H.D.P. Lee, Penguin, Harmondsworth 1955, p. 161.
16. Geoffrey de Sainte Croix, *The Class Struggle in the Ancient Greek World*, Duckworth, London 1981, p. 503.

ating themselves and their culture. In the absence of any central global planning, it is possible to argue that the vampire of reason has to be continually cheated of its prey by the intermediary of a hidden rationality, of a ruse of reason itself. The human species as a whole may perform more rationally than any of its parts can on their own, due to a synergy inherent in social coexistence, much as capitalist economies can benefit from the operation of Adam Smith's hidden hand whereby individuals pursuing their selfish gains produce a general improvement for all.

This idea of a higher order of rationality in history not immediately apparent to human beings, which works, as it were, above their heads, is today viewed as the product of a theological conception of history. Yet, as the example of Smith's hidden hand shows, it can take a material form in the capitalist market-place; it was this instance that might first have suggested the idea to Hegel's mind.[17] It will be argued later that the notion of a higher form of rationality, once bereft of any commitment to the Logos which it possesses in Hegel, can be justified to a considerable, even an increasing degree, by material developments themselves. The price, however, is recognizing that it need not be immediately beneficent; indeed, as with Chinese deforestation leading to flooding and soil erosion, it can be highly damaging to at least an individual society. The logic of the argument for a more radical materialism than is to be found in Marxism returns one eventually to the need to recognize an aggregate, although indeterminate, finality in human activity, even if one to which individual actors remain blind. The very conception of matter in relation to ideas, which has been the subject of timeless historical debate, needs to be historicized itself. But before this can be attempted, it will be necessary to explore further the relationship between creative and destructive forces, whose tension underlies the dynamic of human history.

3. The Typology of Social Existence

It will assist our exposition to construct a table on which the various dimensions of social existence are charted. Its two sets of co-ordinates are

---

17. G. Lukács, *Der Junge Hegel: Europe Uber die Beziehungen von Dialektik und Oekonomie*, Europe Verlag, Zurich 1948. For a discussion of this work which brings out this point, see Jean Hippolyte, *Studies on Marx and Hegel*, tr. John O'Neill, Heinemann, London 1969, Ch. 4, particularly pp. 75–6. See also Robert C. Tucker, *Philosophy and Myth in Karl Marx*, University Press Cambridge 1961, pp. 66 f. Tucker argues later against Lukacs's claim that Smith was the main source for Hegel's philosophical system, pp. 123–4.

The notion of a sleepwalking emanation of economic rationality may well have been suggested to Smith by Mandeville's *The Fable of the Bees: Private Vices, Public Virtues*; poets, indeed, can be the 'unacknowledged legislators of mankind'.

provided by the outer terms of the interactions between creation and destruction and material and cultural levels. The two axes are given by their intermediary moments, the measures of preservation and the mode of mundane security. (See pp. 26–7.)

There are several aspects of the chart which need to be explored, although not all its items will be explained immediately. If the total and partial disasters of columns (A) and (B) have been successfully pre-empted by the activities of column (C), on the various social levels of column (D), then the realm of necessity encompassing them allows the creative achievements of column (E) to become possible. The modes of creation of column (D) encompass both the modes of preservation or pre-emption of column (C) and those of autonomous creation of column (E), since the means by which disasters are pre-empted can also be used in autonomous creation, indeed strongly influence its direction, as with the means of warfare, reproduction and knowledge. The forms of natural creation of column (D) on these different social levels are common to both the realm of necessity and the realm of freedom since nature's gifts can be used either for necessary or autonomous activities. Religion will be considered in chapter 8.

The table can be seen to be divided into four main quadrants, on either side of the mode of mundane security (5), which unifies them all:

Firstly   Parts (A) to (D) of 1 through to 5 comprise what may be called *the material sphere of necessity.*

Secondly   Parts (A) to (D) of 5 through to 10 comprise what may be termed *the cultural sphere of necessity.*

These two together comprise *The Realm of Necessity*, the two left-hand quadrants.

Thirdly   Parts (D) and (E) of 1 through to 5 comprise what may be called *the material sphere of freedom.*

Fourthly   Parts (D) and (E) of 5 through to 10 comprise what may be termed *the cultural sphere of freedom.*

These latter two together consist of *The Realm of Freedom*, the two right-hand quadrants.

The first and third quadrants, the material spheres of necessity and freedom, comprise the material social levels; the second and fourth are the cultural social levels. The traversal of the axes of idealism and materialism by those of creation and destruction is responsible for this quadripartite division. The modes of creation of column (D) conjoin the realms of

Dimensions of Social Existence

	FORMS OF DESTRUCTION		OPEN DIALECTIC BETWEEN	FORMS OF CREATION	
	(A) *Total Disasters*	(B) *Partial Disasters*	(C) *Preservation or the Pre-emption of Destruction*	(D) *Social Levels*	(E) *Autonomous Creation*
1.	i) Starvation, exposure ii) Disasters below	i) Physical entropy and undernourishment ii) Disasters below	i) Production and consumption of physical necessaries ii) The production of social necessaries, weaponry etc.	Mode of production and consumption	Production of luxuries and leisure
2.	Destruction by other societies	Defeat and subjugation by other societies	External defence and diplomacy	Mode of mundane security	External aggression and imperialism
3.	Pestilence, sterility, extinction of population	Disease and decline of population	Medicine, childbearing and child-rearing	Mode of reproduction	Demographic expansion and sexuality
4.	Natural disasters, nuclear or environmental holocaust	Pollution and deterioration of environment	Anti-pollution measures, public water works and infrastructure	Mode of environmental conservation	Parks, zoos, etc.
5.	Social disintegration (leading to above disasters)	Class conflict or social entropy (leading to above disasters)	Tribal organization, status, class society and the state, nationalism	Mode of mundane security	Autocracy, liberal democracy, socialism, revolutionary movements, etc.

MATERIAL

HISTORICAL

#				
6.	Ignorance (leading to above disasters)	Ignorance (leading to above disasters)	Technology, knowhow, foreknowledge	Mode of knowledge	Pure sciences and philosophy
7.	Lawlessness and anarchy (leading to above disasters)	Disorder, crime and corruption (leading to above disasters)	Law, morals and mores (e.g. traffic code)	Mode of morality	Moral and legal philosophy
8.	Absence of any communication (leading to above disasters)	Aphasia (leading to above disasters)	Language and other public sign systems (e.g. traffic signals)	Mode of communications	Literature and art
9.	Death of personality on physical death (and imaginary disasters to society and environment leading to above disasters)	Absence of sanctions for above modes (leading to above disasters)	Organized religion and sanctions for (1) to (8) and sometimes (10)	Mode of magical security	Religious reformations, mysticism, etc.
10.	Oblivion and extinction of culture (leading to above disasters)	Decline of culture (leading to above disasters)	Education and cultural preservation	Mode of cultural conservation	Renaissances, etc.

THE REALM OF NECESSITY

THE REALM OF FREEDOM

NATURE

CULTURAL

necessity and freedom on each social level, while the mode of mundane security (5) generally conjoins the material and cultural levels into one community or society. It is within the mode of mundane security that class and status relations are regulated, which will be discussed later.

The realm of freedom is defined here negatively as that sphere of a society's existence in which it is not obliged to inhabit the realm of necessity. The former is severely limited by the latter in ways which can only be relaxed by mollifying the necessary conditions of social existence, that is by a more successful forestalling of, or reparation from destruction, both of itself and its members. The negative freedom in question must not be confused with positive freedom; there is, usually, no agent or agency capable of determining the character of the realm of freedom. It remains the sphere in which social activity, however harsh, is not undertaken under the compulsion of avoiding destruction, although, as will be seen, other forms of compulsion can often, indeed usually do, characterize it.

The realms of freedom and necessity condition each other in an intimate and complex fashion. The realm of necessity, as its name implies, comprises the set of destructive forces capable of undermining social and individual existence and so the set of conditions which must be fulfilled for a society and for its members to exist at all (even if it allots the latter very different life-spans, as with slavery or feudalism). If this set of conditions is complete, then the satisfaction of its requirements suffices to ensure social (and, for some span, individual) existence. An additional requirement, however, might, it could be argued, consist in the very existence of free time for individuals. It is possible that no society would survive unless at least some sphere of individual autonomous creation, however humble it might be, remained. If true, the existence of individual realms of freedom is a necessary condition of social existence itself.

At this point a further pair of distinctions can be drawn, which help to clarify the relations between the respective realms. The realm of necessity harbours a province of freedom within itself and the realm of freedom a province of necessity: both provinces owe a double allegiance and therefore both realms deploy potential Trojan horses in each other's domains. The province of freedom in the realm of necessity consists of the alternatives open to a society in meeting the necessary requirements of its existence. Food must be eaten, but this can be within very different forms of cuisine. Dress must be worn, at least in some zones, yet a great variety of clothing and fashion can suffice for this purpose. Shelter must be provided, but buildings can vary widely in architectural style and even building materials within a locality, let alone the world. Defence and law and order must be supplied, but they can assume quite different forms. There are various alternative ways of doing things that must be done.

More formally, there is a range or set of non-trivially different and individually unnecessary but sufficient conditions of fulfilment, of each insufficient, but necessary, condition of social existence.[18] The set of such sets comprises the province of freedom in the realm of necessity.

In practice, this provincial freedom may be rather narrow, at least for a certain duration. Traffic codes can be easily replaced, but languages can be only with difficulty. Moreover, an industrialization or commercial urbanization may prove irreversible once the population surpasses the size which an agrarian or pastoral economy can sustain, at least without genocide; the depopulation measures of the Khmer Rouge in Cambodia were a necessary accompaniment of their programme of ruralization. Nevertheless, over time the realm of necessity may allow some scope for change and choice in the manner in which its exigencies are met; hence one reason for the local as well as global diversity of mores concerning basic requirements, such as cuisine, dress and domestic architecture and the great variety of languages, ethical and legal systems and other social institutions. These do not ensue only from the wide variations in the local dictates of the realm of necessity precisely since these are not univocal.

The existence of the province of freedom in the realm of necessity permits ideas to play a crucial role in influencing even the most apparently materialist affairs, such as the impulses behind economic development. At the same time, it indicates the limits on such ideas, a point that can be registered by considering a relevant example of Popper's. He argues that Lenin's socialist programme of the dictatorship of the proletariat and electric power was an idea that changed Russian economic life and its whole history.

> In a fight against tremendous odds, uncounted material sacrifices were made, in order to alter or rather to build up from nothing, the conditions of production. And the driving-power of this development was the enthusiasm for an *idea*. This example shows that in certain circumstances, ideas may revolutionize the economic conditions. Using Marx's terminology, we could say that he had underrated the power of the kingdom of freedom and its chances of conquering the kingdom of necessity.[19]

In fact, this example shows something rather different. As Popper's

---

18. These are instances of what can be called a 'usin' condition, that is an Unnecessary, but Sufficient condition of fulfilment of an Insufficient, but Necessary condition. A usin condition can be contrasted with what Mackie terms an inus condition, that is an Insufficient, but Non-redundant, component of an Unnecessary, but Sufficient condition, in *The Cement of the Universe*, Oxford University Press 1974, p. 62, where he expounds a theory of causation using the term.

19. Karl Popper, *The Open Society and its Enemies*, Routledge and Kegan Paul, London 1966, vol. II, p. 108.

own words indicate, Russia was gripped by enormous economic difficulties, to which some response was *necessary* if millions were not to perish. The choices of the early Bolsheviks were not made in the realm of freedom, but in the province of freedom in the realm of necessity. In fact Lenin opted, as is well known, for the **NEP** (New Economic Policy) in 1921 and Stalin later for collectivization and super-industrialization. These were choices among alternative ways of organizing the realm of necessity, Lenin opting for a partial restoration of capitalism to enable the economy to recover from the chaos of war communism and Stalin for wholesale collectivism and rapid equipment for defence to counter the threat from the advanced capitalist world.[20] It is of course arguable, although not certain, that the NEP was not so much an option as an urgent necessity and also, although even more uncertainly, for collectivism and super-industrialization; but it could hardly be denied that some significant *choice* remained in how they were to be carried out. Some margin of freedom, therefore, obtained in the realm of necessity.

The realm of freedom has contained in turn a recalcitrant redoubt of necessity, which it seeks, so far vainly, to conquer. While the realm of necessity comprises the set of necessary conditions of social (and so individual) existence, it need not include all those conditions necessary for the existence of a realm of freedom itself, and, more significantly, those necessary for the emergence and perpetuation of the often quite extravagant realms of freedom which have existed in history. For over and above those things which must be done for existence, there are further things which must be done to render autonomous freedom possible.[21]

Thus, the realm of freedom has for most historical societies been the privilege of ruling strata, their members requiring a surplus to sustain their comparatively free existence, whether by exploitation, tribute or trade. For instance, a necessary pair of conditions for the Roman Empire's rich and exuberant achievements in literature and the arts, luxuries and civic

---

20. It is being assumed, here, that, with the Bolshevik victory in the civil war in 1920, a full-scale capitalist restoration, without further foreign intervention, was inconceivable so that the range of choices in Russia's realm of necessity was confined to those open to the revolutionary state: that is, the province of freedom in the realm of necessity of Russian society was equivalent to that of the revolution itself.

It is also being assumed that the scope for *choice* in the realm of necessity coincided with the province of freedom in that realm, something likely to be roughly true in a consciously revolutionary epoch. In other times the freedom obtaining in the realm of necessity will merely be that of the range of variation feasible in meeting its requirements without incurring a concomitant destruction.

21. The province of necessity in the realm of freedom consists of the set of the sets of inus conditions of the realm of freedom, that is of the sets of insufficient, but necessary, components of the unnecessary, but sufficient, conditions of it, less any conditions of the realm of necessity. For inus conditions, see footnote 18.

architecture consisted of its panoply of imperial power and concomitantly extensive slave system, neither of which had been necessary for social existence under the frugal early Roman Republic. Geopolitics and economics, it will be argued later, provide essential preconditions of a flourishing realm of freedom, in particular for stratified or class societies.

The realms of necessity and freedom interact with each other in profound ways. A main set of problems to be resolved later on consists of how to estimate the extent and implications of this mutual influence and how to establish which among them is preponderant and, more important because less empirically obvious, why it is so. A preliminary assessment can help to determine the correct bearings and approach to such problems.

It is evident that the realms of necessity and freedom can confine or enlarge each other and redirect each other's course of development due, for example, to the interaction of the former with the latter's province of necessity. It is possible that features of a society, which begin as components of the province of necessity in the realm of freedom, where geopolitics and economics prevail, can become components of its realm of necessity itself. Thus, the emergence of capitalism and its class system, which were not at first indispensable to social life, were still a necessary condition of the prosperity of the urban population and even peasants, while underpinning the luxury consumption of the nobility. Yet by reason of the irreversible division of labour and scale of modern industry which capitalism introduced, populations grew to sizes which necessitated its ascendant sway and development. Here, the province of necessity in the realm of freedom encroached on the realm of necessity.

The direction can be reversed, however, by the realm of necessity encroaching on the province of necessity in the realm of freedom. Thus, for those countries with only little or a laggard development of capitalism, the modernization of their economics became a sine qua non of social independence, with immense consequences for the class structure: hence, Japan, for instance, escaped being colonized by the West at the price of abandoning feudalism for capitalism. The development of commerce and industry, which had been restricted in the Edo period, became a vital necessity after its encounter with the West in 1854 and during the Meiji restoration, as the contemporary fate of Chinese and other Asian societies showed. The contours of the province of necessity in the realm of freedom can alter, or be altered by, the realm of necessity, which is itself perennially shifting. This can then have consequences for good or ill on the other dimensions of social existence.

Conversely, the realms of necessity and freedom can influence each other through the manner in which the realm of freedom interacts with the province of freedom in the realm of necessity and so with that realm itself.

The former can take the initiative in their relationship. For instance, scientific ideas which begin as speculations of theoretical research can enlarge the alternatives of the province of freedom in the realm of necessity, even while adding new dangers to the realm of necessity as a whole. Thus, nuclear physics has come to alter drastically both the possibilities and problems confronting energy and military planners throughout the world. It is, indeed, as we shall see, by the often pervasive influence of the achievements of the realm of freedom upon the province of freedom in the realm of necessity that ideas and artifacts can play so powerful a role in history, even in the most mundane affairs.

Alternatively, it is often the case that the province of freedom in the realm of necessity takes the initiative and makes a decisive difference to the development of aspects of the realm of freedom. The problems and choices involved in necessary, practical activities can stimulate, as we shall see, theoretical innovations which can assume great import eventually for a society's whole development.

The realms of necessity and freedom, therefore, contend with the assistance of formidable allies in each other's camps, respectively their provinces of necessity and freedom.[22] It will be maintained later that the realm of freedom has been gaining ground upon the realm of necessity, although not without serious setbacks and remaining pitfalls. This position can be given a provisional clarification by comparing it to the positions of Hegel and Marx.

For Hegel, history is occupied only with the realm of freedom from the outset, there being no conception of a realm of necessity in his philosophy, whether one of destruction contention as here or one of material production, as for Marxism. Ultimately this oversight of Hegel's is due to his inability to conceive dialectical development except in an idealist and immanent form in which an antithetical moment issues from the thesis itself. He fails to consider the material, as well as idealist, possibilities of an open dialectic, in which a foreign destructive moment, whether from nature or other societies, threatens its first term or 'thesis' or in which a foreign complementary term is combined with the first term in a new synthesis. Hence, his anodyne notion of historical development as an unfolding of cultural freedom and reason and the inevitable resolution of conflicts within them in a higher form with all conflicts between freedom and necessity being strictly subordinate to, or an aspect of, the development of freedom itself.

---

22. It is for this reason that it will on occasion be useful to employ yet a further set of terms, that of the *domains* of necessity and freedom. The *domains* of necessity comprise both the *realm* of necessity and its ally, the *province* of necessity in the realm of freedom; while the *domains* of freedom comprise both the *realm* of freedom and its ally, the *province* of freedom in the realm of necessity.

Marx of course adopts a more realistic perspective than Hegel. He also, however, retains the conception of a generally closed dialectic, albeit in a materially productivist focus. The realm of necessity is confined to the sphere of production and reproduction of material life. For Marx the realm of freedom can only emerge after the realm of necessity has been more or less banished, that is in history proper; while in pre-history the realm of freedom is beyond very narrow limits illusory. This conception is at once more pessimistic and more optimistic than that developed here – more pessimistic with regard to pre-history in which little freedom can exist and more optimistic about a future in which necessity can be subjugated so as not to hamper a true realm of freedom.

The realm of necessity, which Marx confined to the need to supply means of consumption and reproduction of offspring, is in our sense far more extensive and likely to persist; it includes all those perennial activities essential for survival, such as medicine, military defence and environmental conservation on a material level, and knowledge, communications and public morality on a cultural level together with ways of preserving the community as an integrated whole.

It could be argued that military defence is only necessary so long as there is military aggression, while the latter in turn is due to economic factors. Thus, once a cornucopia of abundance is assured by widespread automation there will be not only an end to economic deprivation and basic scarcities, but also an end to war and the need for military defence – and so the realization of the Marxist realm of freedom. Even if this vision is eventually vindicated, there will still be other forms of destruction ignored by Marxism to be contended with, namely those listed above, excepting the economic and military ones, and perhaps new ones. Moreover, it is by no means clear that basic scarcities will vanish since new scarcities are created by productive development itself; also, certain items of consumption are naturally in limited supply, such as houses with enviable locations for reasons of their convenience or beauty. In addition, military aggression may prove to outlast conditions of economic deprivation. A realm of necessity in a wider sense than Marx's is likely to survive, while a realm of freedom in a wider sense than Marx thought possible – when the realm of necessity itself was itself still large – already has substantial scope.

A realm of freedom then, is already in perennial contention with a realm of necessity, both locally and globally.

When disaster actually strikes the immediate task becomes a recuperation of a society and its environment from its effects, as in the depths of the European Dark Ages or much of sub-Sahara Africa today; this itself requires a breathing-space in which further disaster can be forestalled. The dialectic between creation and destruction then assumes a melancholy aspect, with destruction and its pre-emption becoming the prevailing themes.

In one sense creation must always take precedence over destruction, since nothing can be destroyed unless it already exists, that is, has earlier been created. But while this remains an ontological fact, the history as opposed to the existence of a phenomenon will result from the interplay between its creation, its preservation and its actual or avoided destruction. The first priority for a society, once it exists, becomes its preservation or the pre-emption of forces threatening to destroy its existence; and (except in some cases of free activity warding off destruction spontaneously) only when this has been accomplished in the realm of necessity can societies concentrate upon creative activities and the avoidance of forces threatening them in the realm of freedom.

The latter form of avoidance, that is the protection of creative activities, takes place in the province of necessity in the realm of freedom; while the realm of necessity concerns itself with the preservation of existence. Success in the province of necessity presupposes success in the realm of necessity, while the reverse is not the case. Nevertheless, the means of pre-empting destructive forces for a society are likely to be the same in either the province or the realm of necessity, whether means of production, reproduction, warfare, knowledge or culture. Indeed, the very components of the realm of necessity may coincide with those of the realm of freedom and so with those which its province of necessity must defend. Food is necessary for life, but can still be made palatable, indeed delicious for gourmets and gluttons. Nature has rendered the most vital of human activities, sexual intercourse, capable of being the most pleasurable and meaningful. The rape of the Sabine women would have had a double significance for the Sabine men.

In practice, societies are obliged to be almost as wary of second-order destructive forces as first-order ones, assuming they are distinguishable. This is both on their own account and because of the minatory warning they convey of the imminence of yet more corrosive forces. Even seemingly innocuous disruptive forces can be harbingers of obnoxious ones and can only rarely be known for certain not to be. If allowed scope, destructive forces can become legion and lethal. Thus societies are obliged to defend not only their existence but also their historical achievements in the realm of freedom. The realm of freedom requires the protection of its own province of necessity, which, as we have seen, is dependent on the realm of necessity, a powerful constraint on its very freedom. Nevertheless, the realm of necessity can be altered in its path by developments in the realm of freedom itself, both within and between societies. It has yet to be made clear how the major relations between these respective realms are conducted.

4

The Realm of Necessity

The order of discussion of the main themes can now be outlined. The crucial framework is provided by the distinctions already drawn between the realms of necessity and freedom and their respective subdivisions. This approach has the advantage of placing the dialectic of creation contending with destruction in the forefront: the drawback, however, is that there is then an unavoidable disjunction in coverage of the different social levels, since they inhabit both realms.

It behoves one in theory, as in life, to concentrate first upon the realm of necessity. This chapter, therefore, will be concerned with discussion of the following: the role of disasters and natural creation and destruction within this realm; the rationale of life in society and the geoeconomic and geopolitical conditions of development and defence; the ensuing struggle for social existence; the priority of the material sphere of necessity over its cultural sphere; and the growing scale of the province of freedom within the realm of necessity. The fifth chapter considers the formative influence of the realm of necessity as a whole over that of freedom and then the significance of the intersection between the realms of necessity and freedom on different social levels. It will then be possible in the sixth chapter to examine the significance of the realm of freedom, discussing the role of economics, class and geopolitics in the vital province of necessity in the realm of freedom. The seventh chapter will then be able to assess the interaction of the different realms and provinces of necessity and freedom and of the various social levels which inhabit them.

A brief consideration of religion with its extraterrestrial concerns in the eighth chapter allows the black sheep of the family of social levels to be included, an essential prerequisite in many civilizations for any understanding of their unity and cohesion, otherwise epitomized by the state, the subject matter of the ninth chapter. The final chapter will provide a summary of the preceding argument.

1. The Roles of Natural Creation and Destruction in the Realm of Necessity

The perspective which has been so far outlined places an especial, indeed a controversial, emphasis upon the role of natural disasters and destruction in history in tension with creation. This needs further elucidation and justification.

There have been two chief ways of dismissing natural disasters and destruction and their effects as of only minor importance in economic and social life and so of little significance for any theory of history. Firstly, they have been regarded as primarily exogenous shocks or aberrations which disrupt the course of events for a while but can be safely ignored in more normal times. Secondly, they have been conceived as endogenous shocks, whose opportunity to occur stems from the societies on which they impinge: urban agglomerations, for instance, are vulnerable to plague, as is agriculture to the vagaries of weather, and mining and mechanization to resource depletion and pollution. They are seen either as occasional and thereby irrelevant or, however frequent, prolonged and pervasive in their effects, as primarily socially conditioned.

The latter position at least recognizes their importance, yet assumes the anthropocentric bias of recent social theory. The prime subject matter of enquiry can remain the structures of social existence in either case. This dispute can only be resolved by widening its scope of reference.

Disasters are merely the most sudden and dramatic of nature's destructive possibilities. The relentless pressure of entropy and the need to consume food and to protect life and its achieved conditions against human, animal and natural destruction require those apotropaic activities in the realm of necessity on which we have already dwelt. In the course of such preoccupations and of their autonomous creative endeavours societies can render themselves vulnerable to further destruction, as in agriculture to the vagaries of climate and geology, in industry to resource depletion and pollution and in urbanization to plagues and nomadic invasion. As Engels says,

> Let us not, however, flatter ourselves on account of our human victories over nature. For each such victory nature takes its revenge on us. Each victory, it is true, in the first place brings about the results we expected, but in the second and third places it has quite different, unforeseen effects which only too often cancel the first. The people who, in Mesopotamia, Greece, Asia Minor and

elsewhere, destroyed the forests to obtain cultivable land, never dreamed that by removing along with the forests the collecting centres and reservoirs of moisture they were laying the basis for the present forlorn state of those countries.[1]

Societies are obliged to counteract or pre-empt both first-order and second-order threats to their manner of life. These dangers, therefore, even when extraneous in origin, are internalized by a society, especially if they materialize. Those forces which culminate in disasters – such as droughts leading to famine, infestations to pestilence, and foreign invasion to conquest – are both extraneous afflictions and yet avoidable or remediable social evils. The devastations wrought by foreseeable disasters are a reflection on a society's organization for its failure to discharge its first set of duties, that of prophesying and preventing their occurrence; and its speed of recovery from them is a reflection on its second set of duties, that of reparation of their effects once they have happened.

These ambivalent and unpleasant obligations can be made clearer by further examination of the natural world which societies inhabit. The open dialectic between creation, preservation and destruction in human affairs to which we have been giving such emphasis, participates in a similar but more universal interplay within nature, that is physical, geological, geographical and biological nature.

The statement of this theme made in the outline of the previous chapter confined its purview to the general experimental science of physics and physiology. It also holds, however, for the historical sciences of nature and mankind.

It is evident that natural creation and triumphs and natural destruction and disasters played an enormously important role in the history of life on our planet long before the evolution of homo sapiens and indeed in that of the geology of the earth, both before and since the emergence of life itself. The common theme of the historical sciences of nature (and indeed it could be argued of the other sciences of nature, such as atomic physics and chemistry) has been one of the perpetual interaction between various forms of material creation and destruction.

In the case of historical cosmology, the point is so obvious that it does not need much emphasis: the creation and destruction of planetary systems, stars, asteroids, galaxies and the universe and of their constituent matter define the problematic of the discipline. In the case of historical geology, the recent acceptance of Wegener's long-spurned theory of

---

1. Frederick Engels, 'The Part Played by Labour in the Transition from Ape to Man', Marx and Engels, *Selected Works*, Moscow 1968, pp. 365–6.

continental drift is a pertinent instance. For in the 1960s the discoveries of plate tectonics suggested the crucial creative mechanism necessary to account for the movements of continents across the earth's crust. As Gould succinctly puts it, 'the earth's surface seems to be broken into fewer than ten major "plates", bounded on all sides by narrow zones of creation (oceanic ridges) and destruction (trenches). Continents are frozen into these plates, moving with them as the sea floor spreads away from zones of creation and oceanic ridges.'[2]

The development of the modern biological theory of life provides another example of the same theme. Before Darwin, the religious fundamentalists had explained life-forms in terms of divine creation, denying their evolution: Lamarck explained them as evolving in terms of the transmission of creatively acquired characters; while Cuvier explained them as the outcome of an original divine creation repeatedly thinned out by catastrophes without need of evolution (hence the imperfection of the geological record). Darwin's originality lay in emphasizing the role of preservation or survival as an intermediary between creation and destruction. He postulated that unequal destruction wrought by natural selection on random hereditary variations of species (which in neo-Darwinism become random genetic variations) would itself create an evolution of adaptations and species. Darwin in fact reduced the creative pole to a reflex of the all-powerful preservative medium, differential preservation or natural selection of random hereditary variants playing the creative role in evolution itself.[3] The theory of saltations or jumps which accelerate evolutionary change has recently qualified Darwin's gradualist approach in a way that emphasizes the creative role, not only of hereditary variation disciplined by natural selection, but also of major geological catastrophes, echoing Cuvier's preoccupation. Some biologists have even recently come to consider the possibility of an independent constructive force, that of paedomorphosis or the retention of the juvenile features of ancestors into adulthood, which comes about by means of an acceleration of sexual maturity (progenesis) or a slowdown in somatic development (neotony).[4]

Neo-Darwinian theory has had a curious asymmetrical relationship with Marxist theory, since, while the former stresses the destructive pole in a gradualist, non-catastrophic form, by which selective preservation of

---

2. Stephen Jay Gould, *Ever Since Darwin; Reflections in Natural History*, Penguin, Harmondsworth 1977, Ch. 20, 'The Validation of Continental Drift', p. 166.

3. The full title of Darwin's work is the *Origin of Species by means of Natural Selection or the Preservation of Favoured Races in the Struggle for Life*, John Murray, London 1859.

4. Stephen Jay Gould, *Ontogeny and Phylogeny*, Harvard University Press 1977. Mankind emerged as a result of neotony, retaining the juvenile features of its primate ancestors, not least their foetal rates of brain growth.

random hereditary creations occurs, the latter privileges the creative or productive pole from which destructive forces duly emerge. As we have seen, certain biologists question today whether natural selection as a discriminating principle of elimination of hereditary variants can bear the implicitly creative weight assigned to it in Darwin's theory. Likewise, it is possible to question whether known modes of production can explain the history of societies in isolation from the foreign destructive forces which they must negotiate, and the naturally creative endowment of their environments. It is arguable that just as a conception of independent creation and more comprehensive perspectives of destruction need to be integrated into the theory of evolution, so principles of natural and foreign creation and destruction need to be introduced to correct the anthropic, productivist bias of neo-Marxism. Moreover, fittingly enough, the set of destructive principles required possesses a strong affinity with the Darwinian principle of natural selection itself and the Cuverian emphasis upon catastrophes, even while being of course irreducible to them.[5]

It is not only historical biology but also historical geography and demography which signify the interaction of creative and destructive properties. Environments undergo both autonomous changes, such as climatic shifts or ice ages, and those that ensue from human intervention. But in the latter case a counter-finality can, and indeed often does, occur in which the intended aims are overlaid or subverted by unintended results; and these will be the outcome of local variations in historical geography. The perpetual processes of entropy are always at work as the creative potentialities of nature are dissipated by energetic fluxion, while rains, winds, tides or evaporation erode and reshape natural environments. By these means any human society is always being posed fresh challenges, yet also being offered new opportunities by nature. Indeed, it is not only geography but also animal and human demography which undergo such vicissitudes, in varying degree, from one environment to another. The macropredators of humanity have largely been tamed or become extinct, but its microparasites are variously at work altering local chances of human survival and influencing human demographic development. The great plagues of history have not, it is true, been the outcome of wholly autonomous activity by microparasites, whose opportunities for

---

5. For the relevance of destruction in human evolution; 'from the war of nature, from famine and death, the most exalted object that we are capable of conceiving, namely the production of the higher animals, directly results', the penultimate sentence of *Origin of Species*.

For the ambivalent attitude of Marx and Engels to Darwin and the relations between Marxism and Darwinism to date, see Yves Christen, *Le Grand Affrontement: Marx et Darwin*, Albin Michel, Paris 1981.

infesting human populations have rested on the type of activities and degrees of contact and concentration among them.[6] Their potency in changing history, therefore, cannot be accurately gauged without consideration of the economic and social levels to be discussed later. Geology, geography and human and animal demography undergo a restless and incessant motion whose historicity underlies and interacts with that of human societies.

The historical sciences of society, in other words, need to follow the example of the historical sciences of nature in recognizing the central significance of the open interplay between creation and destruction. The science of the human species or general anthropology is also obliged to consider the crucial importance of consciousness and ideas and of culture and structures of society in relation to material reality, hence its vaunted inability to emulate the methods of the natural sciences. But while the methods may not be helpful, the themes may well be, particularly in the form they assume in the neighbouring discipline of evolution theory. The old opposition between culture or society and material reality can be greatly illuminated once it is considered on every social level in terms of its creative and destructive moments, the destructive ones being primary to the extent that creation is undertaken to resist them; they are only subordinate once they have been mastered.

Our excursion into the galleries of the historical sciences of nature has been made not just to provide a reputable pedigree for the main theme, but to situate the subject matter of historical theory where it properly belongs, in a larger geographical, demographic and biological context. Societies inhabit an external world which is riven by a perpetual interplay between material creation and destruction, within which they are obliged to intervene as material realities themselves, due to entropy and the exposure to other forms of foreign creation and destruction. They have to harness the creative forces or amenable destructive forces of nature to achieve their own creative ends, not least the pre-emption of their disruption or outright destruction. The significance of the realm of ideas and freedom is that it allows the introduction of a quite new element, namely that of the pre-emption or reparation of destruction, measures of conscious preservation which mediate between natural creation and destruction, rendering their interplay dialectical. Only higher animals and humans can enter into a fully dialectical relationship with nature and with each other, in which conscious intervention plays a crucial role. These living creatures can transform the creative and destructive forces of the

---

6. William H. McNeill, *Plagues and Peoples in History*, Basil Blackwell, Oxford 1977, a work to which reference will be made again.

natural world which they experience in a conscious dialectic of challenge and response.[7]

The creative forces of nature are radically changed in the course of being put to use by man, as are by definition amenable destructive forces. Nevertheless, many destructive forces are not easily amenable, at least as yet. Death eventually ensues, even if the various activities of the material sphere of necessity, whether economic, reproductive or protective, forestall the destructive forces necessitating it. Death is for individuals 'the necessary end'. In the case of creative forces the raw material for even the most sophisticated human products derives either directly or indirectly from nature. The *fons et origo* of human creativity and invention consist of the panoply of creative properties in nature and of its recuperable destructive forces in all their variety and power; while insistent perennial stimuli to human creativity stem from the need to appease or withstand unamenable destructive forces by means of foodstuffs and medicaments, public works and weapons, offspring and childcare, lessons and signs, craft and cunning in a publicly responsible and reproducible social order.

2. The Rationale of Life in Society

The primary fact about human societies is not their economic plight alone but that they belong to a primate species. As a primate species, mankind is required to live in social groups, for nearly all primate activities necessary for survival presuppose a social framework. A human group, like any primate group, is obliged to provide itself with means of sustenance and habitation in nature and to reproduce its own kind; to defend itself against other animal species; and to protect its habitation and environment against the ravages of entropy and natural disasters, of other societies and of its own ecologically harmful activities, such as pollution.

In order to fulfil these basic pre-emptive or reparative requirements, the human species depends on collective knowledge of the disasters and the more insidious destructive forces threatening it and on the means to avoid them, as well as on a degree of altruism in social behaviour, such as is exhibited in care for the young, solidarity in combat and loyalty to the mores of the group. It also needs to possess means of communication to transmit information and instructions, much as other species do, to indicate the whereabouts of predators and prey, of food and pollen and of hazards and the way back home. In addition homo sapiens is not named

---

7. This is not to deny the possibility of a primitive dialectic of nature in which consciousness is absent, but merely to indicate the more advanced form dialectics can assume with the emergence of conscious mind.

in error to be wise. For it is the only species fully capable of bequeathing such acquired cultural characteristics not just by instinctive behaviour, but by instruction to its offspring; this mode of inheritance of acquired desirable features of experience or of cultural conservation has conferred great advantages in its struggle for survival.[8] Any human society may fail in one or other line of such activity, but it is then vulnerable to extinction, as any animal species is to natural selection in the wild.

It is for these reasons that human activities take place in societies. Indeed, as Malson points out, in the light of evidence on human heredity 'The search for "human nature" among "wild" children, has always proved fruitless precisely because human nature can appear only when human existence has entered the social context'.[9] Wolf children, those children reared by wolves after abandonment in the forests, resemble their lupine cousins in movement and behaviour and are only recognized as human beings in their physical appearance. The development and perpetuation of humanity has required the reproduction of its social forms of livelihood, not merely those of production, but those of destruction avoidance or reparation as well. Societies cannot be understood as being governed primarily by economic exigencies, as Marxism implies, but only as the outcome of a wide-ranging set of activities from language and education to defence and the provision of environmental protection and necessaries which assist in pre-empting or repairing outright destruction. Thus, the problem of why societies exist is not to be sought primarily in the exigencies of their modes of production qua Marxism, nor in the need to curb violence and mutual destruction qua Hobbes, but rather in the need to pre-empt or repair destruction by nature or human violence, in other words in the comprehensive set of requirements which must be met to assure human survival.

Indeed, it is not merely social existence itself, but the existence of a multiplicity of human societies in contact with each other that is necessary for human beings to realize their species-being. For a diversity of biological strains has been essential for fertile cross-breeding to take place and social existence to endure. Moreover, societies can greatly benefit from learning of new methods and artifacts in trade or other exchanges, while even warfare with others stimulates the development of tools and of

---

8. Darwin believed that the characteristics acquired through habit, thought, instruction and religious faith have been more important for the development of the 'highest part of man's nature' than the struggle for existence. *The Descent of Man and Selection in Relation to Sex*, John Murray, London 1922, see Ch. IV, 'The Moral Sense', pp. 148–94. He naturally explains the biological origins of these capacities themselves, however, by selection, albeit selection in relation to sex as well as nature.

9. Lucien Malson, *Wolf Children, Jean Itard, The Wild Boy of Avenyon*, Verso, London 1972, p. 12.

fertile competition between societies. The fate of isolated communities, such as that of the Yaghans of Tierra del Fuego, has been an unfortunate one, even if not so unfortunate as that of the wolf children. They have nearly all expired in the course of the twentieth century.

The stimulating effects of contacts with others are shown in the origins of early civilizations. Ancient Egyptian civilization 'took off' at the time when it borrowed certain ideas from Mesopotamia, the other great riverine civilization of the early West, namely its monumental methods of architecture, the cylinder seal and certain artistic themes as well as in all likelihood certain techniques of metallurgy, pottery and advanced hiero-glyphics.[10] Mesopotamian civilization itself was in contact with the Indus Valley civilization of Harappa and Mohenjo-Daro, as is indicated by seals found at Ur and other sites in Mesopotamia and at Bahrein, a vital link in their trade.[11]

While the requirements of human survival might well explain why it assumes a social form, this still leaves open two crucial questions: firstly, what gives individual societies their unity and enduring cohesion; and secondly, how is their historical dynamism to be explained? The principle of cohesion of a society may or may not coincide with its raison d'être or historical dynamic.

As regards the first of these two questions, social relations can become so diffused that it is unclear where one society begins and another ends. The very notion of a society itself can be impugned as ambiguous. For most epochs of history individuals have belonged to an economic group which provides them with their livelihood, say an agrarian village or district or nomadic tribe, while being ruled within a polity which is not coterminous with this economic group, let alone the type of economic group, say agrarian or pastoral. At the same time they may have subscribed to a religion, whose sway extended beyond either their economic grouping or polity. In Hindu India, for example, regions of self-subsisting villages were governed within a shifting medley of independent polities, even while all of them accepted the Hindu religion. It might well be asked at which level social cohesion obtained – at village level, at the level of the regional polity, or at that of Hindu India as a whole. The independence of different regions and towns within the loosely defined and overlapping sovereignties of medieval Christendom of the West provides another example of social ambiguity.

It can be argued that the boundaries of social existence are definable in different ways in different societies. In certain primitive tribes, which

---

10. John A. Wilson, *The Culture of Ancient Egypt*, University of Chicago Press 1954, pp. 37–42.
11. Roy C. Craven, *Indian Art*, Thames and Hudson, London 1976, p. 12.

possess no well-developed chieftainship or religious network of power, their common system of livelihood and above all kinship can give them a loose-knit cohesion, as with the cluster of fishing tribes of the Tierra del Fuego, the Yaghans, whose comparative isolation has earlier been mentioned. In the case of more civilized societies a set of overlapping forms of social life has been common, as in the already cited cases of Hindu India and medieval Christendom; the modern capitalist world provides another example, within which different nation-states maintain their political independence, despite belonging to a common economic system. Nevertheless, before the era of capitalism, the customary frame-works of social cohesion extending beyond the locality were the polity and religion. The main form of social cohesion could be either geopolitical and bureaucratic, as in the Chinese Empire and the Roman Republic and Empire, or religious, as in Hindu India.[12]

It will be argued later that it is by constituting themselves as modes of security that the political or religious levels can unify and define a social order. It is in providing security against destructive forces by either mundane or magical means that politics or religion can create social cohesion. Before considering how this can be so, however, the relationship of social life to nature needs to be further clarified. In the process of attempting an explanation of the long-term dynamic of social life, certain concepts, useful in defining its scope and limits, will be disclosed.

3. The Geoeconomics of Development

When early and, indeed, later civilized societies have achieved lasting economic viability or sometimes even growth, they have depended not just

---

12. Two outstanding works of historical sociology have recently appeared which inter alia expound and defend the thesis that the term 'society' is highly ambiguous, namely John Hall, *Powers and Liberties*, Basil Blackwell, Oxford 1985, and Michael Mann, *The Sources of Social Power, Vol. I, A History of Power from the Beginning to A.D. 1760*, Cambridge University Press 1986. They here draw upon the insights of Gellner in his extensive oeuvre, notably his work on the agro-literate polity and the Muslim world, *Nations and Nationalism*, Basil Blackwell, Oxford 1983, and *Muslim Society*, Cambridge University Press 1981. Indeed, both Hall and Mann flirt with the idea of abandoning the notion of society altogether, but in the absence of an alternative reluctantly resort to it. Their concentration on social power permits a most fruitful development of an 'organizational materialism' revealing the difficulties involved in mobilizing and deploying resources and labour across great distances in the pre-modern world. It has the disadvantage, however, of overlooking the fact that nature as well as societies possess power, depending on the character of different environments. The productive and destructive powers of nature need to be considered in developing an historical sociology as well as the social powers deriving from them. In their detailed historical analyses Hall and Mann are, indeed, sensitive to nature's volatile pressures; but like their predecessors, including Marx and his followers, they have not integrated the volatility of nature into their theoretical frameworks.

on the stimuli of intercultural contacts and competition, but also on those involved in inhabiting a fruitful, yet challenging, physical environment.

The nature which societies inhabit is profoundly historical in character, changing both by reason of the independent vicissitudes of its creative and destructive properties and by responding to the social activity of man. Societies, thereby, participate in a historical nature, which they have often striven to transform in beneficial ways.

This transformation has so far been locally differentiated by the historical geography and demography within which a society exists. It inhabits historical nature in common with other societies, and within nature it inhabits its own historical environment or what can be called its own historical materiality, that is, a historical geography, demography and technology, which its own activities perpetually refurbish and ornament, repair and maintain. The historical materiality of a society in the context of historical nature and other historical societies determines of which forms of creation it is capable and with which forms of destruction it must contend.

The material basis of any society's predicament is neither its productive forces, nor its pre-emptive and reparative forces, let alone its means of violence, but rather its historical materiality as a whole, inclusive of its historical geography and demography, from whose bounty the afore-mentioned forces are made and with whose creative and destructive properties they must perforce negotiate.

The fundamental problems of survival for any society arise from its geoeconomic relationship to its environment – and, in most cases, also to trading partners – and from its geopolitical relationship to other societies, as mediated by its environment, the exceptions being quite isolated communities. Economic activity is primarily conditioned by the physical environment and by foreign partners in trade and secondarily by the institutions which comprise the property system or the mode of production in a Marxist sense. Indeed, in the long run the former relationship largely explains the latter.

This is shown firstly by the severe limits imposed in the long term by the historical geology and atmosphere of our planet upon economic activity. Only certain areas are inhabitable, most of the polar regions, the Alpine and Himalayan peaks and the high seas being inhospitable to human habitation. The extent and location of habitable territory on the earth's surface has varied in the history of our species, partly for autono-mous geological and climatic reasons and partly because humanity has striven to enlarge the habitable terrain by land reclamation. The spread and perhaps even invention of agriculture would have been impossible without the retreat of the glaciers from northern Europe and Siberia at the end of the last mini ice age. Human civilizations have emerged in an inter-

glacial period, which began some 12,000 years ago and may be terminated quite abruptly at any time, since the average duration of interglacial
periods in the present long ice age, so far some 40,000,000 years old,
through which our planet is now passing, is only 10,000 years. Another
period of glaciation, which would alter economic and social conditions
profoundly across the globe, is already overdue. Clearly the arrival of
glaciers on the Thames, the Vistula, the Volga and the North American
plains would shatter the complacency of those who conceive the
relationship of economic activity to economic structures to be primary,
whether Marxists or non-Marxist economists, and force a realization that
the relationship of economic activity to its material environment is more
fundamental, although certainly requiring an appropriate economic
system if it is to prove a fruitful one.[13] The development of the forces of
production and reproduction and of pre-emption of and reparation from
natural destruction (of such forces) has to be governed by the opportunities and dangers posed by the historical environment. When new
opportunities and dangers arise, then the development of these forces is
required to correspond to them.

This might be admitted to be true in general. Nevertheless, it could be
said that ice ages or global warmings are sufficiently rare for the basic
Marxist proposition concerning the social primacy of the relationship of
the development of the productive forces to the relations of production to
obtain on the whole. The fact that human history has enjoyed a dispen-
sation for several millennia from ice ages and undue global warming, it
might be argued, does not belie the claim that the Marxist form of basic
relationship has explained actual human history to date.

Yet even with the qualification that such a primacy thesis holds only for
the past and not necessarily for the future, it still remains inadequate. For
the history of human societies reveals that historical geography and
demography have played and continue to play decisive roles in economic
development. This is shown by the profound delimitation by historical
geography and animal-cum-microparasitic and human demography of the
lines of economic activity in which a community engages, whether
predominantly pastoral, agrarian, extractive, commercial or industrial –
albeit in the light of existing technology, which develops to exploit the
former's possibilities and to avert or reduce their dangers and disasters.

One of the most sensitive and illuminating evocations of this theme has
been made by Braudel in his chef d'oeuvre on the Mediterranean world of

---

13. The more immediate danger might well of course be that of a planetary warming
due to the greenhouse effect; itself the outcome of pollution. The global consequences,
however, could be as disastrous as those of a new ice age.

the late sixteenth century.[14] For Braudel, historical geography and demography provide the underlying conditions moulding the character and development of societies in the long run. Braudel points out that the conquest of the plains, where most of the Mediterranean society has thrived, involved a long and arduous struggle against natural obstacles and destructive forces, namely: the sometimes disastrous flooding in winter, which is the Mediterranean rainy season, requiring dams and channels; the fever-ridden swamps and marshes which tended, and still tend, to form wherever in the flats the waters cannot run smoothly to the sea, necessitating expanded settlement at high human cost before the malarial mosquitoes could be kept at bay; and the soil erosion due to deforestation involving an abandonment of terrain before unforeseen and therefore unhindered destruction. The canals, ditches, dams, drainage works and pumps employed in contending with water, whether in floods or stagnation, often proved unavailing; many setbacks were suffered and areas of settlement abandoned. A development of pre-emptive and reparative forces of this type, then, was as vital as that of the forces of production, the hand- and watermills, ploughs and implements which loom so large in modern conceptions of medieval machinery.

Braudel of course confines himself to the Mediterranean scene. The argument commonly adduced against geographical explanations of economic activity points out that the locus of its advance has so widely shifted in history from Mesopotamia and Egypt to Rome, Italy, the Low Countries, England, the United States and Japan.[15]

This fact is by no means incompatible with a geographical explanation once it is remembered that the relevant factor is always the *historical* geography and demography, both human and animal-cum-microparasitic, in relation to the prevailing technology of a society which delimits its prospects for economic development. The river basins of India, China, Mesopotamia and Egypt were the most feasible sites for early civilizations with their rudimentary agrarian techniques and their dependence on natural forms of irrigation and transport. Nevertheless, they involved continual setbacks since river flooding and fever-ridden marshes and swamps were even more difficult to tame than in the later Mediterranean societies.[16] The centre of Mesopotamian civilization perforce shifted

---

14. Fernand Braudel, *The Mediterranean and the Mediterranean World in the Age of Philip II*, 2nd edn 1966, tr. Sian Reynolds, Fontana/Collins, London 1972.

15. For instance P.A. Samuelson, *Economics*, 12th ed., McGraw-Hill, New York 1985.

16. John A. Wilson, *The Culture of Ancient Egypt*. See the opening two chapters, entitled 'The Black Land, Geographic Factors of Egypt, and 'Out of the Mud, The Long Prehistoric Struggle'. After noting the tribulations which the fickleness of inundation of the Nile could lay upon Ancient Egypt, famine and starvation being not unknown, Wilson says of its response to this challenge, 'In Toynbee's terms of an environmental challenge and a

northwards from Sumer in the delta to Akkad and from Akkad to Babylon as salting of the soil due to evaporation damaged the fertility of down-stream fields and as the upstream city (in warfare) could cut the canals and water supply of those downstream. Harappan civilization fell victim to environmental deterioration from geological causes long before its conquest by the Aryans in c. 1500 B.C.[17]

Europe and northeast Asia possessed the potential for a more extensive development once deforestation opened up their river-crossed temperate heartlands to cultivation and settlement, although such development was more of a sustained success in northern Europe than in southern Europe and China for primarily geographical reasons. In northern Europe the mountains were not so high and the rivers not so intractable in winter as in southern Europe, while the low-lying terrain and clay soils facilitated, after the invention of the mouldboard plough, a less catastrophic expansion of cultivation into the forests. Northern Europe possessed an ideal topography of rivers, extensive coastline and access to the high seas and oceanic trade, in particular in the British Isles, which in an epoch of water-borne transport gave it inestimable geoeconomic advantages in addition to those above and to its well-known abundance of coal and mineral resources. Hence the siting of the Industrial Revolution in England. The introduction of the railways, the canals and the steamships then gave land masses, above all the United States, the great opportunity to organize and develop their enormous resources and territory, over-coming the great handicap of slow mobility which mainly water-borne forms of transport had previously imposed upon them.

Meanwhile, China, the other great civilization promising to break through to modernity, was constrained by a host of geoeconomic problems. Southern China, with its semi-tropical climate, was restricted by high levels of disease for centuries, like India. In the north the Yellow River was always liable to flood the surrounding plains due to its accumu-

---

human response, these were problems to be met progressively. The full potentiality of climate, water and soil was a challenge which demanded long centuries of back-bending toil to drain the jungle marshes and reclaim the land nearest the River, then centuries of weary labour to carry the River water against the greedy desert by canals and catch basins. Thereby the ancient won great richness of crops and these, in turn, set new challenges', p. 11.

Recent research has corrected this view of events somewhat, see Michael A. Hoffman, *Egypt Before the Pharaohs*, Ark, London 1979, Parts III, IV and VI.

17. 'During the later Harappan period a tectonic shift slowly took place along the coast of the Indus Delta. A steady upthrust of the earth extended the shores and changed and blocked the river's flow. This created wide, long-lasting floods that varied with the seasons, and with a steady accumulation of silt Mohenjo-Daro slowly became a city in a marshy lake. Each year the city-dwellers were forced to raise their structures higher and higher. Gradually their culture declined and finally was eclipsed by the new aggressive barbarians from the North.' Roy Craven, *Indian Art*, p. 25.

lation of sediment and rising bed levels. This was accentuated by deforestation, which loosened the upland loess and congested the river's many tributaries, leading to the terrible floods that periodically devastated north Chinese agriculture with its reliance upon the rice-growing wetlands. The most disastrous of these inundations was probably that of 1194, which was due to the Yellow River finding a new route to the sea. This not only devastated much of the richest agrarian land in north China but also destroyed the canal system over a wide area, with a grave impact on the iron and steel industries of Honan and Hopie, which never really recovered. Nature turning nasty, then, was a major factor in destroying the incipient industrial revolution of China in late Sung and Chi'n times, which had brought Chinese iron production, using coke as fuel in blast furnaces, to levels two-thirds higher than those of England in 1788.[18] The relationship of an economy to its environment is thus fundamental to understanding its dynamic.[19]

This argument is of course too spare even in its own geoeconomic terms; Malthusian population growth, consuming agrarian productivity advances, for instance, became a major problem in the second half of this millennium. Mention should also be made of the refusal to continue China's highly promising naval expansionism in the early fifteenth century; the Ming court shifted the capital to Peking in the far north in 1421. Soon afterwards preoccupations with pressures from the nomads ended the overseas expeditions of Cheng-Ho, the great eunuch admiral of Chinese naval history. Japanese and Malay pirates began to dominate the

---

18. William H. McNeill, *The Pursuit of Power*, Basil Blackwell, Oxford 1983, p. 25–33, where McNeill discusses the subject and the literature upon it.

19. The argument here places emphasis upon the creative forces favouring as well as the destructive forces impeding civilized advance; by contrast to Toynbee for whom the challenge of destructive obstacles alone suffices to provoke the rise of early civilizations as a response. The favourable environments of great river basins are dismissed as explanatory variables on the grounds that they were neither sufficient, since the Colorado and other great river basins did not spawn civilizations, nor necessary since Minoan civilization emerged in Crete, while the river basins of the Nile, Tigris, Euphrates and the Yellow River were in fact harsh and inhospitable to human life before civilization commenced. *A Study of History*, Oxford University Press 2nd ed., 1935, Vol. I, pp. 253–71. However, Toynbee ignores the major role of easy water-borne transport which in conjunction with natural irrigation, once the delta swamps were cleared, gave the river-basin civilizations' inestimable advantages. It is true that they were obviously insufficient by themselves and not strictly necessary, since Crete is an island. But a river basin environment, just as appropriate technology etc., can be regarded as one of the inus conditions of early advance, that is an insufficient, but necessary component of an unnecessary but sufficient condition of it, as was the Mediterranean and its climate for Crete and the Aegean and its climate for the Greek cities at a later date. For empirical objections to Toynbee's view on this matter, see the articles by Huntingdon, Grey and Spate in M.F. Ashley Montagu, ed., *Toynbee and History*, Sargent, Boston 1956 and E.T. Gargan, ed., *The Intent of Toynbee's History*, Loyola University Press, Chicago 1961.

China Sea and even to make incursions into inland waters. This, however, debouches on to geopolitical considerations, which, as we shall shortly see, have also to be assessed in accounting for differential economic development.

While historical geology can be decisive over millennia and historical geography and demography over centuries in deflecting economic development, it might be questioned whether they alter much in the short term and, therefore, whether they are relevant to short-range analysis. It might be disputed whether environmental factors occupy the foreground of economic development, except in the 'abnormal' cases of natural disaster and the 'normal' ones of seasonal variations. Few would deny that historical geography and demography play a crucial role in economic life; the histories of civilizations and epochs customarily commence with a survey of the relevant geographical and demographic endowments, as does Braudel. Yet, geography and demography are considered even by Braudel as forming the backdrop of social life in the 'longue durée' against which more immediate forces, such as technical advances, investment levels, fluctuations in the demand and supply of inputs and political or social upheavals, including wars and revolutions, interact to determine short-term economic change.

It will be argued that this is not incorrect; it is merely incomplete unless it recognizes the intimate manner in which these variables can interact, not only with each other, but with the 'constants' and vicissitudes of historical geography and its concomitant demography.

The appeal of the argument that geographical and demographic factors are comparatively constant and therefore irrelevant to a short-term or even a longer-term analysis of history is attested by the wide range of thinkers espousing it, from sociologists and Marxist theorists to empirical historians and even geographers and demographers themselves. Talcott Parsons, for instance, regards it as one of the presuppositions of Marxist or any other social theory.[20] Parsons is not here misrepresenting Marxist thought on the subject, as is shown by the fact that even such an inveterate champion of materialism as Timpanaro accepts this perspective: 'If, therefore we are studying even a very long period of human history to examine the transformations of society, we may legitimately pass over the physical and biological level, inasmuch as relative to that period it is a constant.'[21]

---

20. Talcott Parsons, *The Structure of Social Action*, The Free Press of Glencoe, Macmillan, New York 1949, p. 490.

21. Sebastiano Timpanaro, *On Materialism*, Verso, London 1975, pp. 43–4. Timpanaro quotes Leopardi to this effect, 'Nature is ever green, or rather goes/By such, long paths/That she seems still', 'La Ginestra', lines 292–4.

Such an argument is vitiated on two grounds. Firstly, it is quite false to suppose that geography, let alone demography, are constants. Geography of course is inherently variable over space as all would agree. It is also indisputable that it possesses certain features which are comparatively constant over long periods of time measured in terms of human history, namely mountain ranges, ravines and coastlines, although even these undergo perpetual, if slow, change under erosion or deposition by the elements. In the case of climatic features and the characteristics of soil, water supply and vegetation, change, and sometimes dramatic change, is the order of the day. The ice ages have already been mentioned as longer-run macrodeterminants of undeniable importance. Within a matter of a century or even decades, however, rainfall patterns can alter and rivers change course, with devastating consequences for whole regions of the globe, as much of Africa is discovering to its cost today. The floods and natural disasters of Ancient China were instrumental, as we have seen, in aborting its highly promising economic development in Sung times. The very absence of such events in western and especially northwestern Europe in recent centuries made possible the Industrial Revolution. The fact that China experienced adverse environmental developments as deforestation took place, while northwestern Europe did not, is explicable largely, if not exclusively, in terms of the inherent possibilities of their respective geographies, as has been argued above.

Quite apart from the powerful influence of geographical shifts on economic development, of which further instances will be cited below, the logic of the anti-geography argument is flawed in its depreciation of constant features of ecological processes. It needs to be recognized that even in those epochs when demography and non-climatic geography undergo changes so slowly or regularly as to render them imperceptible, they both can, nevertheless, have profound effects on immediate behaviour. A change can be induced by a constant accumulative change, not just by a fickle change, as with the boiling and evaporation of water by the constant application of heat.[22] Constant regular rainfall can induce floods and swamps and the persistent silting of a river can lead to the salination of land which then at a critical stage precipitates famine, as with Harappan civilization mentioned earlier.

Moreover, a geographical constant in conjunction with an economic variable, such as investment, can induce profoundly different results on the varying fortunes of different zones depending on the *spatial* variations of the *temporal* geographical constant. Thus, the spread of new means of

22. See G.A. Cohen, *Karl Marx's Theory of History: A Defence*, Oxford University Press 1978, p. 154.

transport can alter the significance of perdurable features of topography, such as the extent of land masses and the location of coastlines. The advent of railways, steamships and motor vehicles, for example, reversed in a short period long-established economic relations between different zones of the world. Land-based transport was exceedingly prohibitive of trade before the railway and motor engine, confining economic development to areas accessible by sea or river until the nineteenth century, when North and South America and Russia could begin to mobilize their immense resources for internal colonization and expansion on a major scale. The main loser in this process has been Britain. The colossal historical advantages of Britain's compact, insular geography, criss-crossed with rivers and streams, and its position in the most advanced temperate zone of the world, encouraged a global naval-based commercial development and industrial revolution in the seventeenth, eighteenth and nineteenth centuries; it depended also of course on other peculiar assets, whose possession, however, notably in the case of Protestantism and solid nation-statehood, owed a great deal to the insular impregnability which Britain came to enjoy in war.

Whether 'variable' or 'constant', therefore, geographical factors can have a decisive impact on economic development. To render this proposition telling in the present, mention may be made here of the ongoing crisis of the world economy, in which at least two distinct types of system have been affected, namely capitalism and socialism. The roles of oil depletion and now substitution and of population and labour trends are clearly fundamental aspects of the crisis. Furthermore, much of the Third World today is gripped by the anxiety arising from fickle and inclement conditions of historical geography and demography, that is by forces of destruction. Sub-Saharan Africa is undergoing rapid population growth due to improved medical practices at the same time as contending with grave problems of desertification and deforestation, partly induced by the demographic expansion itself, and with drought and consequent famine. This is happening in countries with quite different economic and social systems – Ethiopia, Mozambique, Kenya, Chad and Uganda among many others – while being compounded of course by further intractable problems, not least the depressive effect on the production of food and the expansive effect on that of cash crops of controlled food prices for the urban poor. The impact of pollution and resource depletion is aggravating the economic crisis of the industrialized world, both in the capitalist and the socialist camps. A provisional case then has been proposed that the open geoeconomic relationship of an economy to the destructive and creative forces of its environment and to its neighbours or trading partners within a wider environment is more fundamental in determining its character and fate than the internal relationship of its relations and forces of production, which is obliged to respond to the exigencies of the former.

The existence of a basic, open relationship of this type has not been entirely ignored by Marxism. Lange in his *Political Economy* points out that the most fundamental relationship for any society is that between the development of its productive forces and nature.[23] The other two relationships of Marxism, he adds, derive from it, namely that between the development of the productive forces and the relations of production, which alter to conform to the former, and that between the relations of production or economic base and the political, legal and ideological superstructures, which alter to conform to the economic base.

Lange's thesis advances discussion onto a more materialist plane but remains insufficient as it stands: 'nature' is conceived as a passive and largely constant (or only slowly or seasonally changing) context for human activity, not as an actively destructive and creative foundation of all life, capable of an abrupt and dramatic or of a gradual and yet decisive deterioration or improvement within the life-spans of societies and even individuals. The previous discussion has at least established that in the longer and medium run geography needs to be conceived as historical in character, a historicity which is accentuated by human reactions themselves. Historical geography of course also varies widely from one place to another, as does human and animal demography, generally delimiting possibilities for economic development.

Lange, however, does not conceive that the primary relationship of the development of the productive forces to nature is economic in character, being the concern of physiology, agronomy, engineering and other sciences and technologies. This is consonant with Marx's own exclusion of the productive forces from membership of the economic base of society, which, as Cohen has argued, consists for him only of the relations of production or economic structure.[24]

---

23. Oscar Lange, *Political Economy*, Vol. 1, Warsaw 1963, pp. 40–42. The Russian geographer Dulov has examined the general economic significance of this relationship in a perceptive article on Russian economic history, A.V. Dulov, 'The Physical Environment and the Development of the Productive Forces of Russia in the 18th Century and the First Half of the 19th Century', Soviet Geography, Dec. 1980, Vol. XXI, No. 10, pp. 651–70. See his bibliography for further works in the Russian geographical school exploring the same theme in other contexts. Marxism in the East has a tradition of geographical enquiry that is lacking in the West, the main exponent of which is G.V. Plekhanov, *The Development of the Monist Conception of History*, Moscow 1956. The nearest approach to a radically materialist outlook in Western Marxism is made by Sartre in *The Critique of Dialectical Reason*, Verso, London 1978. Sartre's concepts of the 'practico-inert' and 'worked-on matter', however, lack any reference to geographical or demographic differentiation. Moreover, they are historical for him merely in so far as they experience and themselves react to human activity.

24. G.A. Cohen, *Karl Marx's Theory of History*, pp. 28–31.

'An economy', however, in usual parlance also refers to what is owned and developed within the economic structure, namely the forces or factors of production, and to the process of production, its output, and the consumption and consumption patterns of the society. It would be anomalous to exclude North Sea oil rigs and reserves from the economies of the UK and Norway, for instance, whose performance is so much affected by them, while including the multinational corporate structure within which they are possessed and exploited. Lange's primary relationship, suitably qualified to allow for environmental historicity, of which the development of oil extraction in offshore waters is a notable instance, is not only the concern of engineering and other sciences, but is also geoeconomic in character. The availability and feasibility of development of land, resources and labour is influenced by geography and demography; hence also are their prices and use. Thus, the relation of historical geography and demography to development of the productive forces is of enormous economic significance and may justly be deemed geoeconomic in character.

It is possible to argue that the development of the productive forces is not merely strongly conditioned by historical geography and demography, but actually consists of a development of the physical environment, at least for the most part. As Cohen says,

> The development of the productive forces is expressed in the transformation of nature, and socio-economic structures are the forms in which this development proceeds, its 'forms of development'. The external development of the productive forces – as opposed to the development of labour-power – is the imposition of a *new* geography, a new material environment.[25]

If the internal development of the productive forces, that is the development of labour-power, is defined as a property of historical biology, as its earlier manifestations, such as the invention of hunting tools and clothing, certainly were, then the development of the productive forces can be seen as a development of nature, not just for the most part, but entirely.

Cohen's position is compatible with two quite different interpretations of the relationship of the productive forces to nature. Either the productive forces can be defined as inclusive of geography and demography and some of the cosmos, since even sunlight contributes greatly to production; or historical geography and demography can be defined as inclusive of the productive forces, which in turn are exclusive of much geography and demography. The latter interpretation is preferable on several counts. Nature can destroy as well as create, so that creative properties or objects

---

25. G.A. Cohen, *Karl Marx's Theory of History*, pp. 96–7.

are merely one set of natural properties or objects. Moreover, the productive forces are merely a sub-set of this set of creative properties or objects, namely those which contribute to the production of economic goods and services and are capable of being owned and developed, or more strictly those that are actually owned and developed.[26] Only such features as soil and labour-power, as energy resources, fields and shipping, but not the sun, the earth's crust, its atmosphere and oceans, qualify, therefore, as productive forces in the economic sense. However important in production the latter may be, they are not economic in the sense of being capable of being owned, sold and developed; they lack value in exchange. Access to them, such as is given by sites of production, is a productive property in the economic sense and is constantly exchanged and developed. It is more plausible, then to define the productive forces independently of historical geography and demography; the development of the productive forces, indeed, with the help of pre-emptive and reparative forces continually encroaches further on geography and demography, changing their historical form.

It is possible, therefore, to define an economy as does Marxism, in terms of its mode of production or more inclusively of its productive forces as well. 'An economy', however, in the usage which is employed in this work, refers also to the relationship of the productive forces to the physical environment. More extensively, a geoeconomy consists of a society's mode of physical livelihood, that is its mode of living within a particular, historical environment, consisting in the first place of some mode of subsistence, hunting, pastoralism, slash-and-burn or settled agriculture, extraction, commerce or industry. The mode of (physical) livelihood is wider than Smith's mode of subsistence or the provision of necessities, the key concept of his 'four stages' theory of human development.[27] The mode of livelihood reflects the historical environment, as it has been changed by human activity and its own autonomous movement; and comprises not only the strictly economic activities of providing necessaries and luxuries, but also the travail of contention with destructive forces of nature, as in caring for the environment, and the enjoyment of its creative forces, as in athletics and hunting the chase, sexuality, bathing and climbing: that is, as Webster's dictionary defines 'livelihood', the

---

26. The ability to be owned and the capability for development are persuasively chosen as criteria of the definition of productive forces by Cohen, pp. 34–5. To them may be added that a productive force needs indeed to be productive, not pre-emptive of or reparative from destruction, nor of course destructive, as with weapons (which can also be pre-emptive of or reparative from destruction).

27. Adam Smith, *The Wealth of Nations, Book III*; see Ronald L. Meek, *Smith, Marx and After*, Chapman and Hall, New York 1977, pp. 15–16 and Ch. 2, 'Turgot, Smith and "Four Stages" Theory'.

'means of support or subsistence' and 'the quality or state of being lively'.[28]

The mode of livelihood, therefore, extends into the realm of freedom in more ways than one. The concept of a mode of livelihood is in fact similar, although not equivalent, to Ibn Khaldun's notion of a way of life. For Ibn Khaldun, *umran badawi*, desert habits, and *umran hadari*, urban habits, are instances of ways of living in their entirety, the fundamental aspect of which is economic activity. As Ibn Khaldun points out,

> Both Bedouin (*umran badawi*) and sedentary people (*umran hadari*) are natural groups. Differences of conditions among people are the result of different ways in which they make their living. Social organization enables them to co-operate to that end and to start them with the simple necessities of life, before they get to conveniences and luxuries. Some people adopt agriculture, the cultivation of vegetables and grains ... Others adopt animal husbandry. Those who live by agriculture or animal husbandry cannot avoid the call of the desert ... Their social organization and co-operation for the needs of life and civilization, such as food, shelter and warmth, do not take them beyond the bare subsistence level, because of their inability to provide for anything beyond these things. Subsequent improvements of their conditions and acquisition of more wealth and comfort than they need cause them to rest and take it easy. Then they co-operate for things beyond the bare necessities. They use more food and clothes, and take pride in them. They build houses and lay out towns and cities for protection ... Here, now, we have sedentary people.[29]

It is of interest that Ibn Khaldun distinguishes between those activities undertaken for necessity and those for freedom, while even those undertaken unnecessarily in the towns have to be defended. By including both, 'the mode of livelihood' is a wider concept than that of Smith's 'mode of subsistence'. It is not as wide as Ibn Khaldun's notion of way of life (*umran*), since this encompasses all forms of civilization, inclusive of warfare.

The mode of livelihood, indeed, consists of a delimited range of physical activities, the mode of subsistence and provision of luxuries (for Marx the material mode of production), the mode of demographic reproduction and the mode of environmental habitation and enjoyment. It excludes as *umran* does not, warfare, security and the cultural levels of social existence, while it is compatible with several different property

---

28. *Webster's New Collegiate Dictionary*, Merriam, London 1974, p. 673.

29. Ibn Khaldun, *The Muqaddimah* tr. Franz Rosenthal, 1958, vol. I, pp. 249–50, quoted by Yves Lacoste, *Ibn Khaldun*, Verso, London 1984, p. 94. Lacoste provides a magisterial account and explanation of Ibn Khaldun's ideas.

regimes, or social modes of production in Marxist terms. Feudalism and settled Islamic society, for example, coexisted for a long time as different social orders with incompatible property regimes or social modes of production in the Marxist sense, but a common mode of agrarian livelihood, differentiated by their demographies and environments and spurred by their respective creeds.

The tools and implements at the disposal of a mode of livelihood are not just forces of production. As has already been argued above, it is not only productive forces, but also pre-emptive and reparative forces which are needed to conduct human relations with nature. Dams and dykes, ramparts and walls, ditches and trenches, pesticides and rodenticides, veterinary science and medicine are necessary to fend off the adverse elements and predators of mankind and its domestic animals and plants. Improvement of pre-emptive and reparative as well as that of productive forces is crucial to geoeconomic and so, a fortiori, economic development, the more so in some cases than in others depending on the historical geography and demography in question. The success of the Dutch economy over the centuries has been cited as the clearest instance of this, since it was based literally on its reclamation and protection from the sea of most of its agricultural area by dams and dykes, water channels and pumps, ditches and drainage systems. Yet, as we have seen, the efforts of the Dutch have not been unique in European and world history in their triumph over environmental problems, even though they are remarkable for their longevity and latitude. The further problems which any environmental achievement such as theirs involves – the erosion of the dykes by the ceaseless motions of the sea, the risks of salination of the irrigation supply and of the soil, the recurrence of inundations which cannot entirely be avoided – all emerge, in the first instance, within the relationship of the society to its habitat and only secondarily within that of the society to its mode of production or of the latter to its productive forces. The fundamental background for any economy, therefore, consists of the geoeconomic one of the wider mode of livelihood, whose development of productive, pre-emptive and reparative forces in its historical geography and demography governs the prospects for economic development. Geoeconomics, therefore, concerns not only what is normally considered economic, the issues of production and consumption, but also those of demography and the geographical environment.

There is a fourth dimension of the material sphere of necessity which has yet to be explored, that of geopolitics and defence in warfare. The destructive forces threatening a society can emanate not just from nature but also from other societies. Most societies need to protect themselves against human as well as animal and natural agents of their destruction.

4. Geopolitics and the Mode of Security

The necessity of defence

Warfare can be analysed in several different ways. It is of course instructive to enquire into the causes and consequences of warfare for different societies. An equally illuminating enquiry, however, is to examine the reasons and repercussions of the absence or prevention of warfare. For while wars have often dominated whole historical epochs, their impact on social organization and structure has not been confined to their immediate consequences; it has involved a lasting obligation on all those under threat of engagement to undertake diplomatic as well as military preparations against such an eventuality. Such precautions can thus prevent the occurrence of warfare and yet remain profoundly relevant to understanding the structure as well as the history of their societies.

Just as modes of production and reproduction are needed in the first place to avoid the disasters of famine and depopulation, which, if the modes are efficient, may never happen, so the mode of security is required in the first place to ensure freedom from attack, or in the case of attack, from defeat or subjugation by alien powers, which again, if efficient, may never happen. It is not only actual events which can be decisive in history, such as disasters and conquests, but also certain non-events, namely events prevented in the realm of necessity. The duties of avoiding disasters and defeat are imposed by the exigencies of this realm, but do not exclude the possibility that production, reproduction, diplomacy and warfare can also assume an expansive direction in the realm of freedom. In the case of warfare, indeed, the situation is complicated by the further possibility that attack can sometimes offer the best form of defence. The need for external security is as basic a requirement of social existence, given the multiplicity and proximity of states, as are production of necessaries, environmental maintenance and reproduction of the population.

This point can be illustrated by asking a question that reveals the crucial significance of force in social coexistence, namely, why do states possess the borders they in fact do? Clearly, a fear for security can involve not just a fear of destruction or subjugation, but also, and indeed more immediately, a fear of encroachment. States are generally afraid of loss of territory to others, among other reasons because this can be a prelude, if not discouraged, to outright subjugation of the population. The frontiers demarcating states have of course often shifted in history and sometimes have been diffused in a complex hierarchy of sovereignties and jurisdiction, as with early feudalism. The immediate causes of such shifts have usually lain either in warfare, or, in the peculiar cases of feudalism, in dynastic alliances as well. Yet, as Cohen points out, while warfare and its outcome have to a large extent determined where the borders between countries appear on the map of Europe ... no-one who wants these borders explained will be content with an answer which terminates in a citation of the relative military strengths at various times of contending armies. He will want to know why the strong were strong and why the weak were weak.[30]

Marxism has an economic answer to this question or at least to the question why borders exist at all – that the nation-states of Europe are the consequences of the rise of capitalism – while, as we shall see, geopolitics suggests other answers to both questions. What is relevant to note here is that what are at stake in military conflicts are, among other things, the very boundaries of social existence itself. The security of any society from military encroachment or destruction remains a prime requirement of its realm of necessity, as fundamental as production of necessaries, or any other form of destruction contention.

One objection which could be raised against this proposition is that it unwarrantably presumes that society is the term to which popular allegiance is owed rather than class. If economic development and class struggle are the prime motors of historical change, as Marxism insists, then there is no reason for members of a society to owe it any fidelity unless they belong to its ruling orders. Subordinate classes may evince a strong loyalty to the social order and, therefore, endorse its defence, but in doing so they are victims of ruling-class mystification and are really acting against their own interests. Hence loyalty to the state is more of an aberration to be accounted for in terms of class relations than a persistent and independent mainspring of history.

In those cases, where an enemy is aiming to occupy a foreign country in order to exploit its economic resources and the labour of its people, then, it could be argued, there is a strong reason for its ruling strata and officers to restrain the troops under their command from harming the landscape or agriculture and from committing outrages against the occupied population. All that the latter have to fear is the substitution of one ruling class for another; and this might even lighten, not worsen, their exploitation and improve their prospects. Feudal serfs, for example, could sometimes find their lot improved by new masters, as was the case for the Balkan peasantry, whose landlords were removed and whose rents and labour services were alleviated at first under Turkish rule in the Middle Ages.[31]

---

30. G.A. Cohen, *Karl Marx's Theory of History* p. 148.

31. Fernand Braudel, *The Mediterranean and the Mediterranean World in the Age of Philip II*, Fontana, London 1975, Vol. II, p. 663. Nevertheless, there appears to have been no great welcome by the peasants for their liberators; Braudel in the second edition qualified his earlier claim that the invasion was not opposed, citing D. Anguelov, *(Bulgarian) Historical Review*, to the effect that 'Bulgarian resistance to the Turks was stronger than I have suggested'.

This interpretation of nationalism and other manifestations of cross-class solidarity as superstructural phenomena is profoundly misconceived. There are numerous pressing reasons why it is in the interest of the members of a civilized society to defend it against outside assaults. Societies are not merely systems of exploitation for the benefit of their ruling classes in their domains of freedom, but are also complexes of institutions needed to protect their members from natural and human destruction. War can prove disruptive of a society's vital activities, both material and cultural activities, and of life itself.

Even if the masses can on occasion benefit from foreign invasions, resistance to them can be quite rational and pertinacious. For the population of countries or areas under attack usually have evident reasons to fear the worst from conquering troops, and even in the best of instances to fear accidental loss of life, limb or property for themselves personally or their relatives in the course of the conflict. Wars, even in the twentieth century, have not been conducted in a manner that conforms to the interests of their privileged instigators in minimizing damage and despoliation, death and disease, in order to faciliate later economic development and exploitation.

Once an army is on the march, it needs to feed and supply itself and this has commonly been done by living off the land and by requisitions from the towns. The larger an army sent into the field, the better, other things being equal, the chances of victory; but also the greater the problems involved in victualling and equipping it. It is scarcely surprising if before the days of modern logistics states concentrated upon providing weapons and essential military supplies, while leaving the troops to fend for themselves in the matter of food and luxuries, a form of enterprise which they were only too ready to practise.

The increased resort to mercenaries from the thirteenth century onwards in Europe worsened the impact of warfare upon civilian life. For mercenary soldiers were even more likely to be rapacious than troops under traditional feudal levy, which were mustered for brief, for example, forty-day, campaigns. They were more similar to the notoriously destructive mercenaries employed by Rome. Medieval mercenaries embarked on a military career with the express purpose of enriching themselves by plunder and booty, particularly the roaming bands of the later Middle Ages and the early modern period which lived on the land as they went by. As foreigners, they were likely to feel less compunction towards civilians than the local soldier in defence of his land. As the size of armies mounted in the sixteenth century, their pay was often if not usually in serious arrears since states were nearly all in financial straits. The sack of Antwerp, for instance, in 1585, which was contrary to the interests of the Spanish crown, was due to its failure to pay its own troops adequately.

The sack of Rome in 1527 by imperial troops showed that even religious scruples were unavailing against soldierly rapine and greed.

The destruction and pillage involved in the Thirty Years' War from marauding mercenaries became notorious and probably exceeded the well-known havoc of the Hundred Years' War when armies were smaller. The *landsknechte* of the time tormented the German civilian population, which shrank from 21 million to 13 million in the 1618–48 period.[32] The population of animal livestock probably contracted even more sharply. The setback to economic as well as demographic advance was incalculable, and helps to explain why Germany, which was in the van of European prosperity in the sixteenth century, lagged far behind in the next hundred years.

The immediate effects of warfare on civilian life were by no means confined to slaughter and plunder but included losses of life due to the viruses which armies harboured and disseminated. Trade, whether by land or sea, was also a major carrier of many diseases, although the long periods elapsing between ports in the days of sail could allow time for infections to die out. The concentration and movement of people, whether in merchant caravans and ships or on a larger scale in armies, brought about a confluence of disease pools among world populations; this occurred notably in the first centuries of the Christian era, contributing gravely to the crisis of the Roman Empire in the third century, and during the closure of the ecumene in the late medieval and early modern periods.

The deaths occasioned by epidemics among alien peoples in the wake of wars and conquest greatly exceeded those incurred on the battlefields. The most notorious pestilence in history, the Black Death of 1346-53 in Europe, together with its recurrences thereafter, reduced populations by one third or more by the mid fifteenth century. The plague was brought to the Crimea and Europe by Mongol armies in 1346; McNeill postulates that the plague bacillus, *Pasteurella pestis*, spread across the Eurasian continent because of the Mongol Empire and its disruption of traditional prophylactic measures against it.[33] Another striking instance of warfare instigating the spread of disease, again an east–west transmission, took place with the Spanish conquest of Mexico and Peru, which introduced the American Indians to old world contagions, such as influenza, typhus and smallpox, with particularly devastating effects. The population of Mexico, some 25–30 million on the eve of conquest, plunged to some 3 million by 1568 and about 1 million by 1620.[34] Similar depopulation

---

32. *The Times Concise Atlas of World History*, Times Books, London 1982, p. 76.
33. William H. McNeill, *Plagues and Peoples*, Ch. 4, 'The Impact of the Mongol Empire on the Shifting Disease Balances, 1200–1500', pp. 149–98.
34. Ibid., pp. 203–4.

occurred among the Incas and other Amerindians, whose complete lack of immunity made the disaster unique in scope among large populations in history. Plague stalked in the rear of armies in ancient medieval and early modern times: it was not until the late nineteenth century that advances in public hygiene and medicine, in particular in inoculation, made armies and civilian populations safer from the scourge of pestilence.

It is hardly surprising, therefore, if the instinctive reaction of the peasant and burgher to the prospect of armed foreigners was one of alarm and dread. Fear of the alien, in particular the alien soldier, had a quite rational basis which helps to explain the frequent manifestations of xenophobia and particularism that were characteristic of the pre-modern world. The encroachments of advanced people upon backward ones, especially those of a different racial composition, have always aggravated fears of the alien, whether as intruders or as subjects. The victims of fascist, Nazi or Western aggression in this century need no reminders of the cruelty which racialism can impart to conquerors, reaching a ferocity, by reason of technical sophistication, that bears comparison with any horrors in history. The Mongols, for instance, in the thirteenth century, killed at least one million in the northern provinces of China, following their policy of slaughtering all the inhabitants of a town that showed the least resistance. Nazi genocide exterminated three-quarters of European Jewry, while millions of Slavs, gypsies and others died in their concentration camps and labour gangs. Korea and Indochina were each visited with more tons of bombs than Germany and its allies throughout the Second World War – in Indochina's case, some seven times more – as well as napalm, chemical and bacteriological means of destruction.[35] The nuclear arms race now puts the populations of whole continents under the menace of annihilation from afar. Distrust and fear of lethal foreign power, the more threatening because of its scientific precision and impersonality, is well founded for most of the advanced world's population.

In fact, foreign invaders have been disliked or hated not just because of the material destruction they have wrought or brought in their train, but because of the affront to the culture of a people or civilization which foreign occupation characteristically involves. The desecration of Hindu temples and shrines by Moslems in northern India was not merely a material matter: it struck at the heart of Hindu civilization. The Tibetans, not without reason, have always been fearful of foreign invaders because

---

35. For Korea, see Jon Halliday, 'The North Korean Phenomenon', *New Left Review*, No. 127, May–June, 1981, p. 29 and references given; for Indo-china, Ronald Aronson, *The Dialectics of Disaster, A Preface to Hope*, Verso, London 1983, p. 100 and references given.

of the disruption to their ancient religion and way of life that they threatened. A tribe, people or civilization seeks security for its culture as well as
for its own physical existence. An indigenous government, even if highly
oppressive, may on these counts be deemed superior to any foreign rule.
Life and limb itself have been risked again and again in history to defend
autochthonous regimes against invaders. As Byron has his Greek song say
of Polycrates of Samos, 'A tyrant: but our masters then/Were still at least
our countrymen'.[36]

Fear of loss of independence can be strong enough to motivate
defending states to carry out 'scorched-earth' policies, denuding their own
landscapes of livestock, food supplies and means of transport in order to
deny them to the enemy. These policies may not always have been
popular, but they would have been unlikely to have been effective without
mass co-operation. Rome with its peasant militia carried out scorched-
earth tactics to defeat Hannibal, just as both Tsarist Russia and the Soviet
Union did against Napoleon and Hitler. In Spain, the masses participated
fervently in scorched-earth tactics against the French in the Peninsular
War. These experiences have penetrated into popular memories in the
countries in question. Fear of the need to adopt such tactics gives a further
reason for mass distrust of the alien.

Thus, history has given many reasons why populations should rally to
defence of their locality against aggressors. Wars of liberation are rare in
history and can only be attended with success under unusual circumstances, such as the popular hatred for an *ancien régime* that provided
temporary support for Napoleonic troops in Italy and Germany. Appre-
hension at the prospect of invasion is far more common; and defence
against outside aggression is accepted as a sine qua non of civilized
existence.

The burden of the present reply to the Marxist position on nationalist
or collective forms of solidarity which transcend class distinctions rests on
the proposition that foreign destruction avoidance has priority over
creative endeavours so long as the threat of destruction itself is real. That
destruction from outside can cause a massive regression in history was
acknowledged by Marx, even while he deemed it inappositely as only bad
luck: 'Mere chances, such as irruptions of barbaric peoples, even ordinary
wars, are sufficient to cause a country with advanced productive forces
and needs to have to start right over again from the beginning.'[37] This
proposition entails that defence against aggression can often be needed to
protect productive achievement and by implication also human lives. The
incursions of barbaric peoples, particularly of the Mongols, and of modern

36. Lord Byron, *Don Juan*, Book III, Ch. LXXXVI, verse 11.
37. K. Marx and F. Engels, *The German Ideology*, Moscow 1964, p. 69.

equivalents, such as the Nazis, have left behind folk memories in their various eras of history of destruction and devastation against which vigilance is essential, ordinary wars bringing reminders of this fact.

The aftermath of the decline of Rome, for example, ushered in the Dark Ages; and this has entered popular memory as a caution against disorder and anarchy, one which for the masses themselves was not without a rational justification since they suffered much from the violence of the time. The pre-emption of foreign invasion by defensive capability has accompanied most stages of civilized life and appeals to provide defences are not necessarily a mere mystification, even if, as with invocations of famine and economic disaster to justify perpetuation of a property regime, they are susceptible to ideological misuse by interested parties.

The basis of the mode of security

However ambivalent the immediate and underlying causes of military conflicts to be considered later, their course and outcome are generally decided, according to Marxism, by economic considerations. For Marxism has always maintained that the underlying determinant of a society's military prowess and of the factors immediately conditioning it resides in the strength and dynamic of its economy, of which military success becomes but the capstone. The mode of production can thereby determine the mode of security and type of belligerence of a state. This, it might be argued, is why Holland and England, the early bourgeois states, prevailed over their absolutist rivals, Spain and France; and why the USSR defeated Nazi Germany, where Tsarist Russia had lost to the French and British in the Crimea, to Japan and then to imperial Germany.

It will be argued here, by contrast, that this perspective greatly over-simplifies the true picture. It is more plausible to maintain that a country's military prowess is immediately decided by the condition of its mode of security, which cannot be explained in turn in any simple way by reference to its mode of production. Societies can possess a strong mode of security with a backward mode of production, or a flourishing economy with a vulnerable mode of security. Nevertheless, it will be argued that material factors, albeit of a less 'economic' kind, indeed the very geoeconomic factors of the mode of livelihood considered above, have, until quite recently been crucial in determining the character and quality of a society's mode of security.

The mode of security consists in its external aspects of the organization of defence and diplomacy, that is of armed forces and logistics and of embassies and foreign offices. They can of course also be organized for attack, as with Nazi Germany's rearmament drive. Nevertheless, as Clausewitz argued, defence demands priority over offence in any rational state, unless circumstances dictate that attack is the only method of defence. Defence capabilities prevent destruction, without assurance of which any attack can prove disastrous, as it was for Nazi Germany.[38] Offensive capabilities are, indeed, intimately conditioned by defensive ones. Security from defeat, therefore, remains the first military duty of any society.

The tools and weapons employed by the armed forces can prove adequate or inadequate to this task, determining the suitability or otherwise of the mode of security. Their degree of adequacy in turn will depend on the character of the terrain and the dispositions of the population, some societies requiring naval forces and others military ones; by and large, the development of the means of violence needs to be related to historical geography and demography as well as to the mode of security. As regards the former proposition Marx suggests a good analogy.

> Those social relations into which the producers enter with one another, the conditions under which they exchange their activities and participate in the whole act of production, will naturally vary according to the character of the means of production.
> With the invention of warfare, firearms, the whole internal organization of the army necessarily changed; the relationship within which individuals can constitute an army and act as an army were transformed and the relations of different armies to one another also changed.[39]

The development of the means of security, such as weaponry, therefore, has a decisive impact on a society's defence and diplomacy and can in turn influence its whole character and history.[40]

The geopolitical base of the mode of security consists not only of a society's terrain and means of violence, but also of the geoeconomic endowment of its means of livelihood: the resources and equipment employed in its economy, the management of its environment and its population size. Hence, the rationality of the mercantilist state's patronage of civilian industry, commerce and agriculture, which underpins logistics and the arms industry.

The mode of security and the mode of production, fashioned by the

---

38. Schacht cautioned Hitler that Germany did not possess the resources to engage in a world war without serious risk of defeat.

39. Karl Marx, *Wage Labour and Capital*, 1849, in *Marx and Engels Selected Works*, Vol. I, Moscow 1969, pp. 89–90.

40. The morale and assertiveness of a society's armed forces can be profoundly influenced by its religion, its customs and the type of polity. This very fact requires them to conform to some degree to the military exigencies of the mode of security if a society is not to perish, of which more later.

mode of livelihood, can combine to form the structural complex governing a society's evolution for whole periods of history, although not necessarily for all. The mode of livelihood and the mode of security in its geopolitical base fashion the character of its realm of necessity and so demand prior consideration. The mode of livelihood and the property system, its concomitant 'mode of production', have come to prevail, as will be seen later, in the realm of freedom, albeit with warfare often playing a prominent auxiliary role. The relationship of the mode of livelihood to that of security has not yet been explored in sufficient depth.

Modes of security are heavily conditioned by historical geography and demography, some societies being far better situated to prevail in warfare due to their geographical and demographic advantages, such as insular location off a continental land area, as with Britain and Japan, or mountainous remoteness as with Switzerland, Korea and Afghanistan, or vastness and cold, as with Russia. Such an advantage is neither sufficient to ensure victory, since each of these countries has been defeated, nor necessary, since states which lack it have triumphed. Nevertheless, possession of a historical geography favoured by existing military technology has often been a necessary component of a sufficient condition, or inus condition, of victory. Effective equipment, organization and morale are also vital inus conditions.[41] But favourable geographical conditions, unlike these human ones, are more difficult to squander and are less likely to be superseded. In the long run, if taken advantage of, they can give certain states a decisive superiority over their rivals.

Thus, the successes of Holland over Spanish absolutism in the late sixteenth century and seventeenth century and of England over France in the late seventeenth and eighteenth centuries were the outcome, not just of the advance of their modes of production, important as they undoubtedly were or at least became, but also of their favourable endowment of historical geography, to which in addition their economic advance was itself partly, if not largely due. They benefited from a fortunate constellation of geopolitical and geoeconomic conditions, religious vitality and then post-revolutionary élan, that combined to give them military success, precocity in capitalist development and a bourgeois nationalism.

In the case of the Low Countries, the southern provinces which became the Spanish Netherlands were economically more advanced in the mid sixteenth century than the northern ones, which became Holland, Antwerp being the commercial capital of northern Europe. But while the terrain in the south is still today, as it was then, viable campaigning country, even in the Ardennes, the Dutch territory was already a maze of

---

41. An inus condition, it may be recalled, is an insufficient but necessary component of an unnecessary but sufficient condition of something, see p. 29 fn. 18.

dykes, canals and rivers, which could be made impregnable against field armies by the construction of suitably spaced fortifications and by the guerrilla tactics of the Sea Beggars. As Geyl says,

> in the trial of strength between Spain, based on the perimeter of the Nether-lands – from Grevelingen (Gravelines) over Nivelles, Leuven (Louvain), Maastricht, and Roermund to Groningen – and the revolt, based on the mari-time provinces of Holland and Zeeland, the geographical configuration of the country, in particular the inestimable strategic importance of the great rivers was to be the determining factor.[42]

Intractable and inaccessible territory was the unusual inus condition of the victory of the Dutch Calvinists, lacking to their coreligionists in the south or naturally to the Huguenots in Paris at the St Bartholomew's Massacre of 1572 or in La Rochelle in 1629. The religious separation of the Dutch provinces preceded their economic advance over the southern provinces, which only became pronounced with the closing of the Scheldt in 1585 and, thus, the eclipse of Antwerp by Amsterdam. Their respective religions and geopolitical fates explain their divergent economic performance and so their divergent social character: Holland became the spearhead of bourgeois advance throughout Europe, while the Spanish Netherlands languished under absolutist reaction.

In the case of England, its insularity and compact size gave it a great advantage in its contest first with the Dutch and then the French. The Dutch could scarcely prevail in the long term against so much larger an opponent, which enjoyed undistracted access to the oceans and remained free from occupation. Once the English navies were organized under the Commonwealth on a rationalized basis by the commercial imperialism of a bourgeois state, then the advantage of Dutch priority in this regard was doomed; hence English victory in the Anglo–Dutch wars of the latter half of the seventeenth century. In the long duel with France, which extended from 1689 to 1815, the British at first enjoyed the benefit of a rationalized bourgeois order against an absolutist regime. But as the final phase in the Napoleonic period was to show, its crucial advantage lay in its insularity. Even when the French state became bourgeois and fielded the most redoubtable armies in Europe, giving it command of the resources of a continent, it was unable to prevail against a rival whose geopolitical power was based on an insular invincibility in an epoch of naval gunnery

---

42. Pieter Geyl, *The Revolt of the Netherlands (1559–1609)*, Williams and Morgate, London 1932, p. 179; a classic account of the effects of geography on historical development.

and on a geoeconomic strength nurtured by its single-minded naval imperialism.

Indeed, the quite different outcomes of the English revolution under the Protectorate from the French under the empire reflect the opportunities of a compact, medium-sized insular state. England, once Ireland was subordinated and Scotland incorporated into Great Britain, and once its navy dominated the seas, was possessed of an invincible mode of security. It was consequently able to concentrate upon naval and commercial expansionism leading to a worldwide empire, while France remained preoccupied by localized military adventures, as it had been under the Bourbons, to the detriment of its imperial career beyond Europe. The fate of the French armies in Egypt and at Acre in 1798–99, cut off by Nelson, and the debacle of the French settlements in the West Indies in the 1800s echoed the mishaps of the War of Austrian Succession and the Seven Years' War and witnessed the revenge of geography on Napoleon's Alexandrian ambitions of world conquest. Confined to continental proportions, his pedestrian imperialism marched his armies to ruin in the Spanish and Russian wastes, where they were unable to live off the land, as they had in Italy and Germany, and were confronted with a popular resistance as intractable as the terrain and geography.

The singularity of the British state was the precondition of the continued existence of the European state system. A balance of power was maintained in Europe by the English or British policy of opposing any power aiming to dominate it, whether Spain, France or Germany. The frontiers of individual states have been partly decided by the resultant warfare, as with the independence of the Low Countries from Spanish, French or German control and of Portugal from Spain, and have been ratified at key treaties – Utrecht, Paris, Vienna, Versailles and latterly Yalta and Potsdam – in which the dominant extracontinental powers of the time (either Britain, Russia or the United States, the latter two by force of circumstance) have ensured that Europe remains disunited.

The mode of security then, plays a crucial role in its natural environment in delimiting possibilities for social development, even for economically advanced societies. The potency of the geographical and demographic dimensions of geopolitical capability are shown even more clearly by those cases where an economically less advanced country resists conquest by a more advanced one, as with Tsarist Russia against Napoleon's France or, more recently, Vietnam against the United States. In each instance, geographical circumstances told heavily against the foreign intruders: the jungle density in the lowlands of the subtropics offered the North Vietnamese the possibility of the 'Ho Chi Minh Trail', an advantage lacking to the North Koreans, whom the American army under Ridgeway were able to contain along the 38th parallel by a demarcation zone across the isthmus.[43]

The most striking instance in history of backward peoples proving more redoubtable in warfare than advanced ones was given by the invasions of the Roman Empire by barbarian tribes. Those living close to the Empire, along its vulnerable northeastern frontier from the Rhine to the Danube, had undergone a measure of assimilation to its social structure, adopting the villa economy and even slave plantations but still falling short of full Romanization. Barbarian mercenaries supplied much of the Roman army's troops, even in positions of high command. The Visigoths had already become agrarian when, as mercenary federates, they were settled in Lower Moesia in the 370s, just as the Ostrogoths and the Burgundians had also done. It was the impact of the Huns in that decade upon these border tribes that compelled the former, followed later by the latter, to migrate westwards and breach the Roman defensive system.[44] They were thus well placed to make the fateful march on Rome in 410. The Huns were pastoralists, themselves ejected from their own pasture-lands by the Juan-Juan or Avars, also pastoralists. Thus, the most backward tribes, the pastoralists, forced the less backward agrarian tribes into the Roman Empire, itself of course more advanced than either, with fatal consequences.

The defensive abilities of a society are heavily assisted by a favourable historical geography and demography and those possessing such a geo-political base for a strong mode of security can enjoy a quite different type of development from less fortunate lands. Thus the mountain regions of Europe have experienced an independence of social life which has been the envy of the neighbouring lowlanders. The sturdy husbandmen-farmers of the Swiss Cantons, for instance, despite economic backwardness escaped the servile dependence of the peasants in the surrounding plains in the Middle Ages. They retained their 'mountain freedom', within an indomitable mode of security, because of their capacity to resist feudal, in particular Austrian, attempts at domination, as with their slaughter of Austrian knights by pike and halbert (or axe) in the defiles at Morgarten in 1315.[45] It was Swiss pikemen and halberdiers who obliterated the Burgundian cavalry in 1476 and 1477, effectively wiping Burgundy as an independent polity off the map of Europe. The Swiss, the Albanians, the Welsh and the other mountain peoples of Europe provided it with its most formidable mercenaries for centuries, bred in a spirit of independence and

---

43. Vietnam has always been vulnerable to assault from the northeast, whence Chinese conquerors came over the centuries. But this route was not open to the Americans.

44. E.A. Thompson, *The Visigoths in the Age of Uffila*, Oxford 1966, pp. 25–7.

45. Michael Howard, *War in European History*, Oxford University Press, 1972, p. 15. Swiss infantry phalanxes prevailed again over the Austrians in the open fields at Laupen in 1339 and Sempach in 1386.

proficiency at arms; the Welsh crossbow and the Swiss pike being their major contributions to the advance of military technology.[46]

The internal dimension of the mode of security

The mode of security consists not only of the defensive dimensions of warfare and diplomacy, but also of the maintenance of internal law and order by prevention of internecine strife and destruction. The very survival of life itself and the protection of limb, person and property from arbitrary damage requires a rule of law, which comprises the internal arm of the mode of security. In most epochs of history murder and rape, intimidation and theft have taken petty forms, needing local enforcers and courts of justice to be kept in check. The more dangerous forms of internecine strife for social existence as a whole have usually come from ruling-class dissensions, such as during the intermediate period of anarchy and economic depression, c. 2200–2000 B.C. which brought the Old Kingdom of Egypt into 'feudal' disarray, or the more genuine feudal anarchy and destruction of the English Wars of the Roses or the French Wars of Religion in early modern times. Internal disorder of this sort can stem from external defeat, as in the English case; while its persistence for any length of time can render a society vulnerable not just to defeat, but to outright occupation, as with Mughal India at the time of Persian and then British and French encroachments on the subcontinent. The maintenance of internal order is a prerequisite of external security.

The creation of the rule of law occupied long periods of history. Such an achievement has been much easier in some societies than others due to the very nature of the terrain in question. Weber's famous definition of the state as the power that 'successfully upholds a claim to the monopoly of the legitimate use of physical force in the enforcement of the order within a given territory' has attracted attention more for its insistence on the role

---

46. The Welsh crossbow was by no means the first in history, the Romans and Franks in the West and the Chinese in the East employing crossbows. The Welsh crossbow, however, was remarkable for its range and force. Wales, which is strictly only a hilly, not a mountainous, country, was of course soon absorbed into Great Britain. However, the Swiss were not the only mountain-bred mavericks in Europe. Braudel has pointed out that the mountainous regions of the Mediterranean zone have always exhibited a marked idiosyncrasy of tempo and type of development. 'The feudal system as a political, economic and social system and as an instrument of justice failed to catch in its toils most of the mountain regions and those it did reach it only partially influenced. The resistance of the Corsican and Sardinian mountains to lowland influence has often been noted', Fernand Braudel *The Mediterranean* Vol. I, Ch. I, 'The Peninsulas; Mountains, Plateaux and Plains', and its section on mountain freedom, pp. 38–41; see also Emmanuel Le Roy Ladurie, *Montaillou: Cathars and Catholics in a French Village*, Penguin, Harmondsworth, 1980, for a vivid account of the religious separatism of the shepherds of the Pyrenees.

of violence than on its spatial reference.[47] No easy correlation obtains between size and compactness on the one hand and security on the other, since the location and vulnerability to outside assaults of a society can heavily influence the outcome. Thus Russia, despite its vastness, has succeeded under outside pressures in welding itself into a secure unity; whereas mountainous Afghanistan, due to its very freedom until recently from successful invasion, has been characterized by anarchic and lawless social life. Despite their common insular character off continental land-masses, England was unified early on while Japan long remained prone to anarchy. Yet, geography in its historical character has been a condition of anarchy in some states and of a strong rule of law in others; England's lending itself to an early unification under peril from abroad, while Russia's making it quite imperative and Japan's and Afghanistan's not.

Class struggles, such as peasant or slave uprisings and revolutionary movements, represent a special case of internal dissension, which has been influenced to some degree by historical geography. They may aim to destroy the social order in question, but not social order itself; on the contrary their aim is usually to establish a new and allegedly better basis for such order. Where their claims are justified then their success can be regarded as pre-emptive of social decline or outright disintegration, as with France in 1789 and China in 1949, in the latter case the Long March being greatly assisted by the country's hilly geography. As Marx said, 'in order that they may not be deprived of the result attained and forfeit the fruits of civilization, they are obliged from the moment when their mode of intercourse no longer corresponds to the productive forces acquired to change all their traditional social forms'.[48]

The maintenance of security, then, internally and externally, is a prime requisite of social cohesion and existence.

The security mainspring of aggression

A fact of great significance in history has been that security has often been attained by external aggression and imperialism. This is not to deny that external expansionism can be strongly motivated by economic consider-ations in the realm of freedom, but merely to point out that security can also provide a mainspring of aggression. There are several types of reason why a state may begin a war, which are by no means exclusive of each other. They fall into two broad categories: first, that concerning economic

---

47. Max Weber, *The Theory of Social and Economic Development*, Free Press, New York 1966, p. 154.

48. Marx to Annenkov, 23 December 1846, *Selected Correspondence*, Moscow 1975, p. 31.

gains; and secondly, that concerning security, either external or internal. Warfare stems in general either from the dynamic of the mode of production or the dynamic of the mode of security. Thus, states may become aggressive from considerations of imperialism and acquisition, whether of slaves and land in antiquity, of serfs and estates under feudalism or of colonies or commercial 'spheres of influence' under capitalism; these are to be considered below in the context of the realm of freedom in which they occur. Alternatively, states may be motivated, even in their aggression, by the needs of survival in their mode of security.

Thucydides's explanation of the Peloponnesian War is pertinent here: 'What made war inevitable was the growth of Athenian power and the fear that this caused in Sparta'.[49] Similarly, the First World War was immediately caused by German fear of growing Russian power and the British and French fear of Germany. Attack came to be seen as the best form of defence. In the case of Athens and Russia or Germany, the growth of their real or prospective geopolitical might was the manifestation of an ascendant economic strength favoured by population growth and a new historical geography due to technological and transport development (naval transport with Athens and railway transport with Russia and Germany – hence a geoeconomic strength). Moreover, their geoeconomic and geopolitical expansionism threatened to continue apace at the expense of their competitors. The causes of the Peloponnesian War and the First World War remain, therefore, explicable generally in geoeconomic terms and locally in geopolitical terms, as the outcome of security needs. The economic origins of warfare in general can be mediated by fear on the part of potential adversaries for their very survival, that is by geopolitical motives in which their mode of security leads them to assume the offensive. This local determination by the geopolitical cannot be ignored, since for any given state it can become decisive of its history for the duration of an epoch.

Moreover, once engaged in hostilities, any state has reason to fear for its survival even if it began them for reasons of acquisitiveness, since the fortunes of war can always turn against it. Warfare cannot be reduced, as is the practice of Marxism, to being only a pursuit of economic aims by other means, even if a state aggressive from economic expansionism may hope that this will remain so. Warfare becomes the concern of the realm of necessity as well as that of freedom.

Another reason for a state to start a war can be to exact vengeance on those who previously defeated it. A severe peace treaty can nourish an ardent desire for revenge among the vanquished, as the Versailles Treaty

---

49. Thucydides, *The History of the Peloponnesian War*, I, 23, Oxford University Press 1943, p. 46.

notoriously did with the Germans. The chances of such a resentment leading to war clearly depend on the relations of force obtaining between the erstwhile adversaries. Where one side is completely crushed in perpetuity this renders a war of revenge impractical; but where, as with Germany after 1919, a country possesses a considerable economic potential and geopolitical resilience, then a régime favouring war can exploit wellsprings of hatred and desire for vengeance to further its own expansionist designs. The desire for reparation of past wrongs can, in these cases, nurture plans to inflict humiliation and destruction upon the ancient enemy. A vengeful imperialism of this kind can also find ample nourishment from ongoing economic hardship and the prospects for enrichement and aggrandisement which future victories hold out. Belligerence in any circumstances is likely to be multifarious in its origins.

External aims are not, indeed, the only security reasons for embarking on warfare. Again and again in history, states and societies have launched into military adventures to pre-empt internal strains from disrupting them. This has sometimes involved pre-emption of class struggle, as with imperial Germany, which was motivated to prevent German Social Democracy's rise to office, as well as by fear of Russia. More often it has been an outcome of internecine ruling-class conflict, as with feudalism, or non-class conflict, as with the tribal societies of Arabia and the Maghreb. Feudal society might be held to exhibit this characteristic by reason of its structure. Yet this structure can be seen as one possible solution to the problem of maintaining a balance between internal and external security; the reason why it emerged when and where it did, then, can only be understood by exploring the destructive forces that it contained and regulated. These will be considered later.

It is not only defence, then, but also offence, which can serve the interests of the mode of security. Some economically backward peoples can excel due to the social cohesion resulting from belligerence in exploiting geopolitical advantages, stemming from their mode of livelihood. The most notable example of an environmental asset providing a backward people with an inestimable advantage in warfare and so social advance is given by the herds and mounts of nomads, both those of Central Asia, particularly the Mongols, and those of Arabia and North Africa. It must be remembered that nomadic peoples were in turmoil in their own habitats so that conquest of sedentary societies offered not only booty but security, at least temporarily. Nomads showed themselves outstanding warriors capable of defeating and occupying far more advanced agrarian civilizations. Their mode of livelihood was of course of great military advantage to them, since they were expert riders and hunters by horse or camel and perforce possessed enormous endurance and courage: the deployment of these qualities against settled communities and tribes again and again had devastating effects in history.

In the Maghreb the cycle of conquest and disintegration took on a specific form, which was subjected to perceptive scrutiny by Ibn Khaldun.[50] His whole analysis rests upon the crucial concept of *asabiya*, which Rosenthal translates as 'group feeling'. As Lacoste points out, this is too general since not all forms of social solidarity are conveyed by the term.[51] *Asabiya* in fact refers to a group cohesion, based on a warlike spirit with a strong leadership which governs the fortunes of the tribe. Military aggression is a sine qua non of tribal cohesion and success.

Asabiya is an instance of the concept of the mode of security invoked here, with reference to tribal nomads. It denotes the strength of protection by a tribe of itself and its members, and, as Ibn Khaldun points out, is enhanced by military aggressiveness: 'Group feeling produces the ability to defend oneself, to protect oneself and to press one's claims.'[52] It is assisted by common descent: 'the hamlets of the Bedouins are defended against outside enemies by a tribal militia composed of the noble youths of the tribe who are known for their courage. Their defence and protection are only successful if they are a close-knit group of common descent.'[53] *Asabiya* is bred by *umran badawi*, desert habits, or *umran jabali*, mountain habits, and it is undone by *umran hadawi*, urban civilization.[54] Hence the dialectic of tribal conquest, and occupation, for several generations, of settled urban civilizations, giving way to fresh tribal conquest. *Umran badawi* and *umran hadari* encompass moral, political and other dimensions beyond the merely physical conception of 'the mode of livelihood' invoked above. Nevertheless, just as *asabiya* is an instance of a mode of security, so *umran badawi* and *umran jabali* resemble instances of a mode of livelihood.

It is not only tribal nomads of the Maghreb whose mode of security benefited from a warlike spirit and external aggression, but also the nomads of the Eurasian steppe. In the case of both types of nomads, they had one source of insecurity which they could do only a limited amount to remove by protective measures, namely the defence of their flocks; animals in herds tend to disperse unless shepherded and even then some go astray. A perennial attrition of nomadic herds, then, took place, which could be made good by seizing others' animals. Warfare to replenish flocks, therefore, had a security aim, even while it could of course offer the chance, not just to maintain, but also to enlarge herd size. This provides

---

50. Ibn Khaldun, *The Muqaddimah*.

51. Yves Lacoste, *Ibn Khaldun*, pp. 100–108.

52. Ibn Khaldun, *The Muqaddimah*, p. 289.

53. Ibid., pp. 262–3.

54. Lacoste's excellent account ignores *umran jabali*, mountain habits, as a source of *asayiba*, which was in some cases of considerable importance in later Arab history.

another reason why warfare was endemic to nomad pastoralists.[55]

In the Eurasian steppe, as in Arabia, caravan trade offered alluring bait; but this would tend to fall off if depredations became too frequent. The provision of protective services for the caravans by some nomads against other nomads gave them a further reason to launch wars. The conditions of nomad existence in the steppe were so volatile – whether due to climatic changes affecting pasturelands, the natural attrition of herds or the arrival of caravans or outsiders – that warfare was endemic to the way of life, necessitating pre-emptive belligerence by all. The highly differentiated nomad societies that resulted could only be kept together by perpetual struggle: and most had only a brief life. As Crone remarks:

> It was thus possible to found a state in the steppe; but the caravan trade notwithstanding, it was scarcely possible to *maintain* it there. Hence such states had no option but to conquer, and from the Hsiung-nu in the third century B.C. to the Manchus in the seventeenth century A.D., northern China was the seat of a long succession of barbarian states bent on the absorption of their rivals along the wall on the one hand, and the annexation of the fertile lands behind it on the other.[56]

Aggression, therefore, can be the outcome of the need to ensure internal, as well as external security. A dialectic of perennial attack and defence can be sustained with its own internal momentum. Great advances in civilization have coincided with imperial orders capable of breaking out of such a negative development, as with the Pax Romana, the Pax Britannica or the Pax Americana, albeit at the cost of intensifying warfare on the periphery or outside. The progress in each case involved an imposition of an international mode of security within their pale, backed up in the latter two cases by productive systems capable of providing growth in economic wherewithal without warfare.

5. The Struggle for Social Existence

Societies, indeed, are subject to a struggle for social existence with nature and other societies, similar to the group form of the natural struggle for existence of animal species in the wild. Their mode of livelihood and their mode of security are both in peril, being required to withstand natural and human destructive forces, much as animal groups are in their capacities to

---

55. Michael Meeker, *Literature and Violence in North Arabia*, Cambridge University Press, 1979, pp. 7–9.
56. Patricia Crone, *Slaves on Horses*, Cambridge University Press, 1980, p. 20.

gather food, to shelter themselves against the elements and to resist
predators and microparasites. The comparison being made here is with
group natural selection in the wild, not with individual natural selection.[57]

It is crucial to emphasize at this point that the human struggle for social
existence involves only a selection of social structures, not of biological
characteristics, while group selection among animals has been invoked to
explain the latter as well. Animal group selection does involve, according
to its main advocate, Wynne Edwards, a selection of social, as well as
biological, structures: 'it is necessary to postulate that social organizations
are capable of progressive evolution and perfection as entities in their own
right.' In the case of human societies their development has not of course
been invariably either evolutionary or progressive, let alone tending
towards perfection, but, nevertheless, it undergoes the pressures of
selection in historical nature.

Human social existence can transcend individual natural selection of
human biology as co-operation between different group members
enhances the survival prospects of all. It is the capacity for rational and
conscious co-operation and indeed the related capacity for moral conduct
and altruism which distinguished human beings from animals, as Darwin
pointed out in *The Descent of Man*, where he explains the biological
evolution of our species in terms of sexual selection, the one form of
individual selection still active for it.[58] The absence of moral capacities in
the animal world is what makes modern biologists sceptical about the
widespread existence of group selection in the wild; most apparently
altruistic animal behaviour can be interpreted as selfish and genuine
altruists among animals would not survive to bequeath their genes to
offspring as often as non-altruists. Individual selection thus tends to
eliminate the possibility for group selection. But the human ability to co-
operate rationally and to behave altruistically under moral restraints
permits group selection to develop among human societies, even while
individual selection survives in sexual selection and often in mollified or
symbolic forms as status competition or the like.[59]

---

57. The theory of group selection has been advocated by V.C. Wynne Edwards, *Animal
Dispersion in Relation to Social Behaviour*, Oliver and Boyd, Edinburgh, 1962, as well as by
Darwin himself, who introduced it as an ancillary hypothesis to rescue his main argument
from the objection that animal societies, such as those of ants and bees, are characterized by
instincts and caste forms of sterility anomalous for the theory of individual selection, *Origin
of Species*, Chs VIII and IX.
58. Charles Darwin, *The Descent of Man*, See especially Ch. IV, 'Moral Sense',
pp. 148–94.
59. The idea that societies are subject to group selection as a result of moral and other
supersession of the individual struggle for survival, was put forward by Carr Saunders, who
maintained in 1922 that 'those groups practising the most advantageous customs will have
an advantage in the constant struggle between adjacent groups over those that practice less

The theory being proposed, then, is that characteristically human development has involved a transition from natural selection of individually inherited traits of biology to that of social structures of groups under the impact of the human capacity to co-operate and to behave altruistically. Co-operation and altruism have been decisive in permitting modes of livelihood and security to develop and thrive. Hunter-gathering or pastoralism among tribal groups would have been impossible without them, as would have solid formation in battle. Modes of livelihood and of security, therefore, are characteristically human institutions, whose only close parallels in the animal world are among the ant and bee societies that have so beguiled naturalists with their ingenious methods of subsistence and warfare (although our primate cousins have also possessed rudimentary forms of social life).

The operation of the struggle for social existence can be seen in an

---

advantageous customs'. Quoted by W.G. Runciman on p. 1 of 'On the tendency of human societies to form varieties', *London Review of Books*, 5 June, 1986, pp. 16–18. Runciman objects to the circularity of the reasoning, a charge reminiscent of the accusation of circularity often made against the notion of the 'survival of the fittest' – Spencer's celebrated phrase of natural selection – on the grounds that the fitness in question is merely the fitness to survive, 'the survival of the fittest to survive' being an obvious tautology. However, the neo-Darwinian theory of natural selection can be rescued from this accusation both by specifying independent criteria of fitness or concomitant principles of variation at work, such as those of genetic inheritance, and by pointing out that the non-tautologous and so falsifiable character of the theory is shown by the fact that if other theories, such as Lamark's thesis of the inheritance of acquired characters or that of orthogenesis (the determination by internal structures of the life-spans and development of species), are true then neo-Darwinism would be false. Similarly, the non-tautologous and non-circular character of the theory of social selection or of the struggle for social existence can be shown if independent criteria of fitness for social survival can be identified. These are, in the version put forward here, the capacities of the mode of livelihood and the mode of security to forfend destruction at the hands respectively of nature and of other societies (or of internal fractures). Carr Saunders suggested the maximization of income per head, which, as Runciman points out, is empirically false (thereby, however, belying his own charge of circularity). The existence of alternative theories of history to this one, establishing its falsifiability, is not of course wanting.

A change of circularity might still be pressed by claiming that 'destruction avoidance' and 'survival' remain virtually synonymous terms. This is not, however, the case. The destruction avoidance activities of the modes of livelihood and security do not consist only of those promoting *survival*. They also include those providing *security*, security both of survival in the realm of necessity and of creative achievements in the realm of freedom. The pursuit of security over and above survival as well as other creative endeavours shape social development in the general struggle for social existence.

The struggle for social existence, indeed, unfolds in the domains of necessity, which consist of both the realm of necessity and the province of necessity in the realm of freedom. What is at stake in this struggle is not only the survival and security of a society and its members in the realm of necessity, but also those of a specific form of social organization and property regime, such as of a particular feudal or capitalist order, extending into the province of necessity in the realm of freedom. A theory postulating that the struggle for social existence in the domains of necessity has a primacy in explaining social life and history is, therefore, not circular and tautological.

exemplary form in the transition from hunter-gathering to settled agriculture. Hunter-gathering spread over Europe as the ice age receded 20–10,000 years ago: for steppe and tundra, which had prevailed in the Pleistocene epoch, gave way to forests capable of supporting not just hunters of big game, but also gatherers of plant foods, waterfowl and small game.[60] The new mode of livelihood, then, responded to the new historical geography of the time.

The wide fluctuations in the species on which the postglacial societies survived gave hunter-gathering a considerable instability, from which agriculture could provide escape. But the right types of plants and species for agriculture and animal husbandry were often lacking in the northern forests. Hunter-gatherers specializing in certain species could become vulnerable to resource exhaustion or disappearance; and a diversification into new plants and animals occurred with the development of versatile, all-purpose tools, the microliths, permitting flexible hunter-gatherers to augment the output of specialized forms of hunting. Northern and eastern parts of Europe, where hunter-gathering was most advanced, resisted the spread of agriculture for millennia after its proliferation in southern regions over 5,000 years ago; the incentive for switching was small so long as hunter-gathering was successful.

However, resource depletion and climatic changes eventually provoked the adoption of agriculture in the redoubts of hunter-gathering. As Zvelebil says,

> the essence of the complex foraging economy was the balance between the few species that were intensively exploited by means of specialized technology and the larger group of prey exploited on a 'chance encounter' basis using multi-purpose tools. As long as the delicate balance was maintained, the complex foragers were able to reduce risks and maintain productivity. The disappearance of a single intensively exploited resource, however, could destroy the balance and throw a foraging community into crisis ... in Denmark, the vanished resource was the oyster, in Southern Finland, the seal, in north-western Russia, the water chestnut along with wild cattle and the wild pig. Farming appears to have been taken up in all three regions as a stopgap intended to overcome the crisis caused by resource failure.[61]

Here, the mode of livelihood changed at the behest of nature, albeit often after nature had been over-exploited.

As Zvelebil also says,

---

60. Marek Zvelebil, 'Postglacial Foraging in the Forests of Europe, Scientific American, May 1986, Vol. 254, No. 5, p. 86.
61. Ibid., pp. 92–7.

the integrity of foraging economies may also have been disrupted by competition with groups that practiced agriculture. In the frontier zone foraging and
farming communities must have competed for a variety of resources; among
the most significant of them was territory. The end of the Pitted Ware culture
provides an example of how loss of territory could bring with it dire consequences for hunter-and-gatherers. In about 2600 B.C. Pitted Ware bands
occupied the interior of middle Sweden along with the coastal areas and the
islands between Sweden and Finland. That broad territory supplied a variety of
terrestrial game together with the seals on which the Pitted Ware groups
specialized. By 2300 B.C. farming had been introduced in the Swedish interior.
As a result Pitted Ware communities were restricted to the coast, and their
dependence on seals increased greatly. As a result of the destruction of their
balanced economy, Pitted Ware groups were poorly equipped to cope with the
fluctuations in the seal population that accompanied a change in climate
between 2000 and 1800 B.C. The foraging economy disappeared, and the
people of the Pitted Ware Culture were probably absorbed by the farming
population of the interior.[62]

Zvelebil is here implicitly invoking the struggle for social existence in full,
both with nature and other societies, to account for the switch from one
mode of livelihood to another. Natural group selection ordained the
adoption of agriculture for individual societies, although its inception of
course was more a matter of independent inspiration. Indeed, a switch
from one to another mode of security doubtless accompanied the change
in livelihood, even if the historical evidence is too scanty to record this.

Some degree of individual competition could well have remained in the
hunter-foraging societies and in early agricultural ones. Nevertheless, the
operation of the struggle for social existence tended to mollify the rigours
of this form of competition, except in sexual selection and in transmuted,
symbolic forms, such as competition for status. Zvelebil goes on to make
this latter point as well and to implicate its possible development in the
eclipse of hunter-gathering.

Another form of competition may also have had a role in the transition to
agriculture: competition within a foraging society. As I have described above,
in the late Mesolithic period there seems to have been an increase in social
differentiation and in striving for status, much of it directed towards objects
serving as value tokens. In the frontier zone where farming and hunting
communities interacted, foragers would have become aware of objects that
were exotic to them and on which they may have put great value. For example
in the third millennium B.C. trade among a chain of farming communities might
have brought well-fired pottery or polished axes north from central Europe to
southern Scandinavia. Foragers there might have seen such goods and coveted

62. Ibid., pp. 92–7.

them as symbols of status. To get them, the foragers would have had to intensify their search for the kind of goods they could offer in return, such as beaver pelts. Quite soon, however, the foragers would deplete the stock of beaver or reach the point where further intensification of hunting became uneconomic. In such cases they might well have turned to farming's greater productive capacity as a means for satisfying the desire for acquisition.[63]

These cases of course represent only some among several possible routes to agriculture, which, as Zvelebil points out, could have been multifarious. While its spread in the north was mainly regulated by the dictates of the struggle for social existence and of individual rivalry for social status, Zvelebil does mention, however, that agriculture could have spread initially because of cultural imitation or migration.

An objection which could be raised against the idea of a struggle for social existence is that societies are not in fact only related to each other by antagonism in a life and death struggle, but also by mutually beneficial contacts, such as trade and cultural influences, which can have profound repercussions on them. This of course is true; but it does not preclude the fact that societies are forced to engage in a struggle with nature and other societies. Trade and the exchange of ideas can improve the chances of a society's survival in this struggle, as with the imitation of agrarian production methods mentioned above. They can also promote their social and cultural development generally, as with the opening up to the West of Japan in the last hundred years.

The objection, indeed, reflects the fact that any society inhabits both a realm of necessity and a realm of freedom. The struggle for social existence dominates the domains of necessity; while other forms of intersocial relations can influence or even transform the domains of freedom. Moreover, these latter intersocial relations can still have a profound effect upon a society's chances in the struggle for social existence in the long run, as their impact on the society's realm of freedom can influence the province of freedom in the realm of necessity and so the realm of necessity itself. Thus, a society which adopted agriculture from imitation, rather than duress, could later be capable of survival under different conditions when it would have expired had its mode of livelihood remained, as with the Pitted Ware people, based upon hunter-gathering.

The mutual influence possible between the struggle for social existence and freely begotten intersocial relations are complex and various. It is not necessary to consider them all here. But one point can be made, that societies are only governed primarily by the struggle for social existence in so far as their realms of necessity dominate their realms of freedom. When the reverse is the case, then a development undertaken in the realm of freedom can come to govern the society's whole course and character,

---

63. Ibid., p. 93.

notably with the emergence of capitalism as a luxury in Tudor and post-Tudor England, concerned, indeed, at least at first with the provision of luxuries for the better-off. The mode of livelihood here changed not primarily due to the struggle for social existence but because of autonomous development in Renaissance and Reformation Europe, mediated through the English state and civil society.[64]

In societies governed by their realms of necessity, however, modes of livelihood and security change at the behest of the struggle for social existence, that is, to permit enhanced development of the productive and destruction-contending forces and the means of violence in order to facilitate survival. This may sometimes have required the mode of livelihood to be transformed for new security reasons, as when Japan industrialized to resist Western imperialism or when lowland peoples migrated to the mountains to escape subjection. Alternatively, this may have involved modes of security being transformed to protect new modes of livelihood and social life, as with the emergence of class society and states at the time of the transition to agriculture. As has often been said, wars alone cannot account for early statehood and class society, since they had taken place from time immemorial without producing that result. Rather they may sometimes have been the catalyst for the process in societies already undergoing a shift to agriculture and thus a more advanced division of labour. Agriculture requires storage for the output of the harvest which then becomes vulnerable to outside attack, and so necessitates either fortified villages and towns for the farmers or a network of defence of the countryside based upon warrior aristocrats and their fortifications.[65] The transition to agriculture, therefore, required a trans-

---

64. Rostow has attempted to explain industrialization as the response of nations to military pressures. W.W. Rostow, *Politics and the Stages of Growth*, Cambridge University Press 1971. The obvious difficulty with this view is to account for the first industrialization itself. Rostow ascribes the English Industrial Revolution to the break with Rome and clash with Spain in the sixteenth century, the Anglo-Dutch wars of the seventeenth century and the long Anglo-French rivalry for colonial empire in the eighteenth and nineteenth centuries (pp. 63–5). While these events were of course very important in stimulating economic growth, it is by no means evident that they all stemmed from reactive nationalism, the Reformation having a certain autonomy for instance and the drive towards empire being primarily aggressive and acquisitive in character, not defensive. What made the English Industrial Revolution so remarkable was its unpremeditated and spontaneous emergence.

65. Arthur Ferrill, *The Origins of War*, Thames and Hudson, London 1985, p. 29. Ferrill actually argues that walls and fortifications, such as at Jericho, may well have been built for security reasons before crops were raised on a significant scale; archaeological evidence is too scanty to justify the assumption, so often made, that agrarian wealth financed the first town walls and fortifications. Yet, this point about chronology does not itself exclude the possibility that walls and forts were kept because of the shift to agriculture as a functional necessity. Jericho was an important centre of the trade in salt, itself in increasing demand because of the rise of agriculture and animal husbandry. Walls were required to protect this trade.

formation of the modes of security and hence production, the latter point to be enlarged on later.

Generally, therefore, the struggle for social existence can lead a society either to change its mode of livelihood to match new security needs or to change its mode of security to match new needs of livelihood. Yet, while for individual societies there is no necessary reason for either change in the mode of livelihood to have causal priority over change in the mode of security, or vice-versa, nevertheless it is arguable that modes of livelihood themselves do globally have such priority over modes of security. For modes of security are primarily, although not only, concerned with requirements in the realm of necessity, those of forfending external or internal disruption or destruction of society. Thus they become usually, although not invariably, reactive to outside events rather than instigating them; modes of livelihood, however, can to a great extent transcend the realm of necessity by initiating activities in the realm of freedom which are superfluous to survival yet possess profound implications. Agriculture, commerce and industry, to take the most momentous, emerged spontaneously at first as creative endeavours with an autonomous momentum. Yet they rapidly became necessities for rival societies as their relations with the pioneers changed (so making them in turn necessities for these pioneers). For they commonly have involved new tools, materials and capacities for making weapons and waging wars, as with the chariot warriors of the Bronze Age, the armoured infantrymen of the Iron Age and the stirruped cavalry of the nomads and their early civilized rivals.

The most notable example of new weapons and military science emerging in the wake of a new mode of livelihood has of course come with modern industrialization, the permanent military revolution of the last two centuries depending closely on new productive advances. Japan and others were obliged to industrialize if they were to escape subjection at the hands of the early industrializers. Thus, while for Japan itself its mode of livelihood changed at the behest of its mode of security, this was in turn only necessary because of the global spread of a new mode of livelihood, industry. A similar example for other societies millennia before, is the spread of agriculture to northern Europe from the south. Once a new mode of livelihood has become established, then others may require it for security reasons to lessen the risk of subjection.

New modes of livelihood, then, seize the initiative and instigate security and other problems in their wake. They have persisted, moreover, for millennia over vast regions of the planet, giving their names to whole epochs: the Stone, Bronze and Iron Ages, the coming of agriculture and the Industrial Revolution. Thus, while it is true that for individual societies their modes of security might have precedence in explaining their course and character over modes of livelihood, this is not true for modes of livelihood as a whole or the zones of societies they occupy which expand, develop and decline or are eclipsed not for security reasons but because of their comparative potential for benefiting from contacts with nature and, in the case of commerce, with other societies. The raison d'être and dynamic of modes of livelihood resides in their relationship to nature, as they evolve increasingly sophisticated ways of dealing with it – hunter-gathering, extraction, pastoralism, agriculture, industry. On the other hand, those of modes of security lie in exploiting the possibilities created by new means of violence, issuing from the mode of livelihood, and in localized contention with problems, often ephemeral ones, of human destruction (excepting the nuclear epoch in which we actually live, precisely because of the universal destructive power of nuclear weapons, capable of ruining and even terminating human habitation within nature). Religion, however, can effect certain strange reversals here and this will be explored later.

While the relationship of early property systems to modes of livelihood and security has been mentioned briefly in discussing the onset of agriculture and class society, this still leaves open the question of how more generally such systems relate to them. A property regime or social mode of production, indeed, need not merely reflect the dictates of livelihood and productive development, but also security needs, a subject to which we must now return.

6. The Security Basis for Class

Class can be explained mainly in economic terms, as with Marxism. For the latter, class structure reflects the mode of production or property regime, which allots individuals their class roles. It remains to be asked, however, how modes of production themselves are to be explained. It has often been argued that they reflect different levels and types of development of the productive forces. Yet the latter are developed in a wider geoeconomic context of the mode of livelihood, which includes all forms of living with nature, those necessary to contend with its destructive, as well as to exploit its creative powers, and in the context of security problems.

There are six main types of mode of livelihood, based on six main modes of subsistence: hunter-gathering, pastoralism, agriculture, extraction, commerce and industry.[66] Hunter-gathering and pastoralism are

---

66. The mode of livelihood, it may be recalled, is wider than the mode of subsistence in the Smithian sense, since it includes not just productive activities, but also demographic reproduction and environment management.

usually undertaken in tribal forms. But the other four types of livelihood and subsistence can be compatible with a wide variety of social orders and corresponding modes of production. It is arguable that, with the partial exception of capitalism, these modes of production themselves are selected, not just on economic, but also on security grounds. The mode of livelihood rules out certain modes of production: thus, industry is incompatible beyond a certain, limited period with feudalism or slavery, and agriculture cannot progress beyond a primitive slash-and-burn cultivation with nomadic indifference to landownership. While the mode of livelihood delimits the mode of production, it does not, however, determine it. The determination of which mode of production obtains among the possibilities open within the mode of livelihood rests, it can be argued, with the mode of security. The most viable possibility from a military point of view usually prevails. The mode of security is under compulsion of threatened defeat to correspond to the level and type of development of the means of violence, which in turn, however, reflect the mode of livelihood. The mode of livelihood, it might be argued, then, ultimately determines class, both directly by delimiting possible modes of production and indirectly by delimiting possible modes of security; the winner among the latter selects which among possible modes of production in fact obtains.

The argument so far can be opposed on several grounds, not least because it ignores those cases mentioned above where the mode of livelihood itself is changed for security reasons, as with Japan's and others' industrialization or with flight to life in the mountains to escape subjection in the plains. Yet, as we have seen, there are modes of livelihood across whole regions of the world which do not arise and decline for these reasons, but autonomously at the hands of technological development, which then profoundly influence modes of security, as with Japan's and others' industrialization. While locally variable, modes of livelihood in fact remain globally dominant in relation to modes of security, whose essential weaponry and martial spirit they can foster.

The local determination of modes of production by modes of security, while not invariable, has frequently obtained. The Balkan peasantry, for instance, escaped serfdom with the Turkish conquest of the late Middle Ages, falling prey eventually, after a considerable easing of their situation, to a sharp oppression. Their fate under feudalism would have been quite different. Yet this was scarcely decided by the level of the productive forces obtaining in the Balkan peninsula at the time, which was not markedly more backward than that of neighbouring feudal peasantries; it was rather the outcome of superior Turkish military capacities.

It is notable in this regard that among settled populations those that inhabited remote upland regions or were mounted and accustomed to weapons escaped subjection. There was a successful resistance to nomad conquest among the herdsmen of the Maghreb, who were either nomadic or semi-nomadic themselves (raising crops and stock). For, as Lacoste says, 'the herdsmen always had a mount, which, given the military techniques of the day, meant that he was either actually or potentially a warrior'.[67] This permitted the tribal structures of the region to persist since warlords could not extend their authority beyond certain limits. As Bloch says, 'Where every free man remained a warrior, liable to be constantly called to service and distinguished from the pick of the fighting-men by nothing essential in his equipment, the peasant had no difficulty in avoiding subjection',[68] an argument which applies to the Swiss, the Albanians and other mountainous warrior peasantries of Europe. Class structure here succeeds and reflects exigencies of security, not vice-versa.

Mountain folk and medieval nomads are not the only instances in history of a geoeconomic basis for military prowess and thus class domination or resistance to it. The extent of ownership of effective weapons and military skills in the context of a society's natural habitat has long been a decisive factor in its evolution. The early civilizations of the river basins and the Middle East were buffeted or overthrown by nomadic barbarians towards the middle of the second millennium B.C.: these barbarians possessed superior means of warfare in bronze chariots, giving them the three cardinal advantages of mobility, firepower and armour; Hsia China fell before the Shang; the Indus Valley civilization succumbed to the Aryans; Ancient Egypt was occupied by the Hyksos, and Mesopotamian civilization by the Kassites.[69] The enormous expense of bronze chariots, manned by a few skilled warriors, made aristocratic rule inevitable, in which alien agrarian populations were kept in uneasy subjection.

The Iron Age of the twelfth to tenth century B.C. introduced improvements in agriculture and urban crafts, but a notable social impact came with its military applications. The invention of iron weapons and armour was first exploited by non-barbarian invaders, who toppled the chariot empires, the Medes and Persians in Iran, the Phrygians and Dorians in the Aegean area and the Philistines, Hebrews and Aramaeans in Syria and Palestine. These tribes were originally organized on a rudely egalitarian basis since every man could be a warrior. The use of cavalry, however, led

---

67. Yves Lacoste, *Ibn Khaldun*, p. 23.
68. Marc Bloch, *Feudal Society*, tr. L.A. Maryon, London 1961, p. 248.
69. William H. McNeill, *A World History*, Oxford University Press, 1979, pp. 49–52. It has, however, been disputed whether chariots played such a decisive role in the Hyksos invasion of Egypt, indeed whether there was a Hyksos invasion at all, instead of merely a takeover by local militia, recruited or hired from Palestine. See Alan R. Schulman, 'Chariots, Chariotry and the Hyksos', *Journal of the Society for the Study of Egyptian Antiquities*, Vol. 10, 1980, pp. 105–53.

to some degree of social differentiations. As knowledge in the use of iron weapons spread, subject populations in turn were able to rebel against their new masters. By 650 B.C. a great change in Greek military tactics took place, the deep iron-clad infantry phalanx proving invincible against chariots and cavalry, at least on hilly terrain. Numbers once again counted on the battlefield. The more democratic epochs of Athens and Sparta were based upon this development, and later in Athens also upon mass participation in naval warfare. The farmer-infantrymen and the urban-poor oarsmen of Athens provided the base of its democratic polity.[70] The ownership of and familiarity with means of violence are crucial in social organization, although admittedly themselves in the long run generally explicable by wider historical forces, in particular by the mode of livelihood.

The relation between class and the mode of security is an intricate one. Modes of security offer protection in return for service to individuals on different terms, depending on conditions of status. Indeed, status is mainly defined by a person's position in the mode of security, just as class is by that in the mode of production.[71] Status can sometimes have a decisive effect on class position, as under the chariot empires and with the independent landholdings of the Athenian and early Roman peasantries, while class can condition status, as with the gradations of wealth and status in the US today. Class and status have been intimately interdependent in most periods of history, and can even fuse, as under early European feudalism. This will be examined later.

This analysis of class and security implies that for long epochs of history the decisive arbiter of social organization and class structure within the limits set by the mode of livelihood was war. The struggle for social existence has entailed that those societies with the most effective

---

70. William H. McNeill, *A World History*, pp. 54–6, 93–6. Also argued in Ellen Meiksins Wood, *Peasant-Citizen and Slave*, Verso, London 1989.

71. In the ancient world, for example, the obligations of the state to the citizen or non-citizen and vice-versa, defined status, which played a vital part in shaping not just social consciousness but social roles: 'Legislation municipal and imperial did indeed mark off the city dweller from the peasant, town councillors or Roman senators from plebians, honestiores from humiliores (gradations of the peasantry) and so on, in dozens of over-lapping categories. The very number of these, however, seems to have worked against the formation of class feeling; and besides, they were defined by purposes of state, thereby accustoming people to think of the state as the tyrant – quite correctly, since rank as town councillor, shipowner, landowner or whatever, determined what burdens of public service one had to support'. Ramsay Macmullen, *Enemies of the Roman Order*, Harvard University Press, Cambridge 1975, p. 198. For a perceptive analysis of this complex of problems, considering Weber as well, as Marx, see Brent D. Shaw, 'The Anatomy of the Vampire-bat', *Economy and Society*, Vol. 13, 1984, pp. 208–49.

The status of certain groups – priests, nuns and mystics – it will be argued, was and is defined within the mode of magical security.

modes of security prevailed in military conflict and imposed their social pattern on the vanquished. One problem with this approach is that it is difficult to see how it can account for the class and other developments of societies which generally did not engage in war, such as Ancient Egypt under the Old and Middle Kingdoms. While feudal societies were explicitly based on the principle of perpetual internecine conflict, albeit tempered by religious and bourgeois exhortations for peace, social evolution in other times has been less clearly influenced by the demands of war.

However, decisive social changes have usually taken place in crises of a systemic kind; and these crises have generally been marked either by grave environmental setbacks or by outbreaks of civil war, as with the First Intermediate Period in Ancient Egypt intervening between the Old and Middle Kingdoms or the centuries of the 'Warring States' Period' of Ancient China which led up to the First Emperor of Ch'in and his unification of China in the late third century B.C. These periods have been characterized as 'feudal' epochs by historians; this designation, while not strictly accurate, nevertheless conveys the turbulent aspect of the times in which new institutions took root and grew. The significance of the environmental calamities and the civil strife of the third century in Roman history and of the early seventeenth in Ming China are other examples of the formative power of ecological pressure and civil war.

The struggle for social existence, therefore, can be internalized in the crucial epochs of history, as societies contend with the destructive forces of nature and of internecine conflict, which are often accompanied by external disturbances as well. A theory of history emphasizing the struggle in which societies are engaged with nature as well as internal strains and external enemies can be sufficiently general to hope to account for social development in its most significant phases.

7. The Marxist Reply

While the foregoing arguments may have some validity, it is possible for a Marxist to reply firstly that the mode of livelihood being invoked is basically an economic level of society: status and then class structure may reflect defensive and, indeed, offensive dispositions, but these in turn reflect economics. All the instances given so far could be said to confirm that the economic circumstances of different populations are precisely what make some successful warriors, capable of escaping subjection or even of imposing it on others, and some exploited peasants or subdued merchants. Secondly, when the levels of economic development and civilization of an occupied society are higher than those of its conquerors, the newcomers normally adapt to them as a new ruling class or stratum. When others possess the same levels, as with feudal principalities, little structural change ensues. The mode of production and hence putatively the social order in either case remain the same in structure. The Manchu invasion of China did not lead to the pastoralization of the Chinese, nor even a major change in their patterns of property ownership, but rather to the sedentarization of the Manchu in the south as landlords, bankers and bureaucrats or their Sinicization as traders, warriors and warlords.

To take the second point first, it is of course true that occupation by others does not necessarily lead to the dismantling of the structures of society. In the case of more advanced peoples, it may well do so as they introduce their own methods and ideas, as did the Romans in northern Europe and the Spaniards in the Americas. This is compatible with, even if it does not entail, the view that economic determination is primary since advance can be defined here in economic terms. In the case of more backward conquerors, several possibilities obtain. The advanced social order may succumb because of internal strains as well as external pressures, as with Rome in the fifth century or the Indus Valley civilization two millennia before, although the strains may often have largely arisen within the mode of security from the difficulty of sustaining military readiness and upkeep, which, it can be argued, was the case for Rome. Alternatively, the more advanced peoples may be vanquished and yet their social order survive, the conquerors adapting to it as a new ruling class: only the personnel in the higher echelons, not the social roles themselves, are changed in these instances. The successive invaders of China and India were domesticated in this way, while Chinese and Indian society remained structurally unaltered for centuries, the one based upon the mandarin-cum-warlord-cum-landlord-peasant class system in a unified state and the other upon caste and religious sanctions in a shifting medley of polities. The Manchu, and to a lesser degree the Mongols in China and the Mughals in India, adapted to their new-found realms, not vice-versa. It was only the more advanced Europeans who irretrievably transformed Chinese and Indian Society.

This does not, however, entail that the invasions made little difference or that the social orders in question were not determined by military as well as economic imperatives. For it is possible to argue that they were already pre-adapted to occupation by the time of the more famous invasions in their history, their modes of security having evolved to absorb foreign rule on their terms. It would take us too far afield to sustain this proposition here; it expresses of course a not unusual position, the mandarinate and the caste system having often been interpreted as shock absorbers to neutralize occupying forces. The mandarinate, for example, embodied Confucian values which resisted its transformation into an instrument of new policies and forms of rule. As Crone says when comparing Moslem conquerors with the barbarian invaders of China, 'it was their good fortune that whereas the Chinese bureaucracy was the backbone of Chinese civilization, those of the Byzantines and the Sasanids were mere instruments of government'.[72] In the case of Indian society, the caste system was incomparably suitable to domesticate invaders as new castes. The mode of security here was not so much involved in a preemption of foreign destruction as in a reparation or mollification of it, given the impossibility of prolonged adequate defence. It nevertheless remained profoundly marked by external conditions and tended to involve a preternatural estrangement of the mass of the population from their rulers, since they were aliens as well as oppressors.

After the initial turmoil, the various invaders of China and India tended to adapt to existing techniques of production, yet to reinforce and rigidify their modes of security, and so their property systems and modes of production. This did not exclude novelties in policies and institutions, but they appeared in a customary framework refurbished for the convenience of the new rulers. The Mongols were somewhat exceptional, being highly destructive in lives and property in northern China which they at first attempted to turn into pasture, before occupying the more civilized south. Disease and depopulation took their toll even there and economic depression ensued. They abolished the mandarinate and moved the capital to Peking in the north in order to shorten lines of communication with the steppe. They thereby reinvigorated the northern orientation of the Chinese mode of security, so evident in the completion of the Great Wall by the First Emperor of Ch'in in the late third century B.C. and in its maintenance and defence by successive dynasties thereafter. In this spirit, the security-motivated prohibition by the Ming dynasty of shipbuilding and oceanic expansion in the 1430s, the prohibition of foreign trade between 1371 and 1567 and the predatory exactions of the Mongol and Ming rulers, precisely as traditional landlords and tax officers, reinforced the existing subjection and alienation of the peasantry and rigidified structures of society.[73] Chinese industry failed to make the further advances which its precocity before the Mongols had promised.[74] A similar isolationism and

---

72. Patricia Crone, *Slaves on Horses*, p. 29.

73. For the ill effects of Ming security policies on economic development see R. Huang, *Taxation and Governmental Finance in Sixteenth-Century Ming China*, Cambridge University Press 1974, for instance: 'As the Ming administrators saw it, to promote those advanced sectors of economy would only widen the economic imbalance, which in turn would threaten the empire's political unity. It was far more desirable to keep all the provinces on the same footing, albeit at the level of the more backward sectors of the economy', p. 2.

74. This epoch saw the well-known retrogression of the iron and steel industries that had flourished under the Sung. See W.H. McNeill, *The Pursuit of Power*, Ch. 2, pp. 25–33.

traditionalism, it is true, characterized Japanese history under the Tokugawa, but without the demographic setback suffered by China under Mongol rule from over 100 million to 65–80 million. Moreover, Japanese isolation came only after the crucial opening to the West in the sixteenth century, which permitted Japan to continue a fruitful exchange with the Portuguese and then the Dutch through the port of Nagasaki and to persist in technological and urban advance to its ultimate benefit in the nineteenth century.

It is notable in fact that those oriental countries which had already undergone occupation by foreign conquerors, such as Moslem Turkey, Persia and India and Manchu China, were unable to rally their populations against the incursions of the West since they lacked the necessary popular mandate: those experiencing an autonomous development under an indigenous ruling class of leadership, such as Japan and Afghanistan, were better equipped to withstand Western encroachment successfully. Underlying factors of terrain and position were also helpful here, just as they had been in keeping these latter countries free from conquest in the first place. Invasions by backward peoples, then, can leave profound marks on a society's history and so its long-term structural character and course.

Elsewhere in the world, there have been many instances of invasions by more backward, rather than barbarian societies or by merely *different* societies making a considerable *difference* to the country of occupation, instances which Marxists themselves sometimes mention. The culture and mode of security of the conquerors could be so distinctive and exclusive as to resist adaptation to defeated civilizations. The jealous god of the Jihad, for example, demanded the spread of Moslem civilization in a defeated area.[75]

To take the case of the Turkish occupation of the Balkans in the aftermath of the Battle of Kossovo in 1389 whose 'liberating' removal of the landlords, as has already been mentioned, improved the lot of the peasants. Anderson says that

> although the great mass of the rural population benefited materially from the initial impact of the Turkish conquest, because it led to a decline in the volume of surplus extracted from the immediate producers in the countryside, the other side of the same historical process was an interruption of any indigenous social development towards a more advanced feudal order, a regression to pre-feudal

---

75. Islamic conquerors could be tolerant of Judaism and Christianity, from which their own faith was derivative, but they were usually implacable to Hinduism and other 'idolatrous' religions outside the Judaeo-Christian tradition, Akbar's heterodoxy in India being a temporary exception. The destruction of Hindu temples and civilization is well known. Mirad C. Chaudhuri, *Hinduism*, Chatto and Windus, London 1979, pp. 125–9.

patriarchical forms and a long stagnation in the whole historical evolution of the Balkan peninsula.[76]

This implies that external intervention can alter the society of a whole zone deeply and lastingly, even when the conquerors are no more economically advanced than the subject populations and do not oppress them savagely. The external determination of social existence can, therefore, be quite decisive.

Let us return to the other objection which a Marxist could make to the geopolitical argument being put forward: that, if the various dimensions of the mode of livelihood in its geoeconomic setting condition military capabilities and so social history and structure, this is because economic factors are primary among them. Even if this were true, the argument involves explaining social development in at least certain cases by economic factors only via the mediation of military factors. Moreover, the mode of livelihood in fact is by no means dominated by economic forces alone. Habitation within the environment ensures that the mode of livelihood reflects more than just an economic rationale of life. Those activities undertaken in the realm of freedom such as sport, amusements and physical play can lead to inadvertent inventions, capable of development into military technology, such as the Roman crossbow or the Chinese gunpowder used for elixirs.[77] The renowned physical prowess of mountaineers and nomads stems from their whole mode of intercourse with nature, their free as well as their necessary physical activities. Indeed, 'mountain freedom' comprises the lively arts of material culture, not just impregnability to outside attack, which can then nurture the martial arts.

Even if the economic activities of the mode of livelihood can be admitted to possess more perennial urgency and so explanatory power, they are not equivalent to economic life in the Marxist sense. To explain the various fates of groups of societies in terms of the peculiarities of their modes of livelihood is, translated into Marxist terms, to be invoking the

---

76. Perry Anderson, *Lineages*, p. 514.

77. The Romans developed the crossbow for hunting birds, the Franks and later the Welsh perfecting it in the West for military purposes. Lynn White Jr, 'The Crusades and the technological thrust of the West', *Technology and Society in the Middle East*, ed. V.J. Parry and M.E. Yapp, Oxford University Press 1975, p. 101. Crossbows had developed in China by the fourth century B.C. Gunpowder was invented in China around the ninth century A.D., three hundred years before its appearance in Europe, and was first considered important for its possible use in alchemy, in particular in attaining an elixir of immortality. See Robert K.G. Temple, *China; Land of Discovery*, Patrick Stephens, London 1986, pp. 218–29. Temple's work is a condensation of Joseph Needham's many-volumed magnum opus, *Science and Civilization in China*, Cambridge University Press. Needham himself introduces and endorses Temple's book, which includes material from Needham's forthcoming volumes.

quality, not just the *level*, of their productive forces, and more fully of their pre-emptive and reparative forces as well. It is the quality of the forces of production and destruction contention with nature and their technical mode of operation that directly influences military and so social developments in these cases, not the relations of production.

Furthermore, the very dependence of military strength on the mode of livelihood is not incompatible with, but on the contrary helps to explain, why an individual society may adopt or abandon a mode of livelihood and property regime due to the pressures of security. Those fleeing to the hills to escape subjection in the plains have altered their whole mode of livelihood in the process. Similarly, Japan adopted industrialization and abandoned feudalism in order to maintain its geopolitical inviolability. For the individual society, this phase of its history is explicable primarily by its mode of security. Nevertheless, for regions of the world, the modes of livelihood established within them or spreading to them, largely account for the types of security system and modes of production of which they are capable; the Iron Age or the Industrial Revolution, for instance, inspired new military technology, and so forms of battle and state power, and new civilian technology made possible new modes of production. Modes of livelihood, then, govern the development of groups of societies over the long run, militating strongly in favour of certain modes of production and security.

These positions depart from the Marxist canon to a considerable degree; they are more compatible with the outlook of Scottish Enlightment sociology than with that of Marx. Smith explained the nature of society, its politics, institutions and customs by its mode of subsistence, equivalent to the Marxist material mode of production, not the property regime.[78] On this interpretation, military capabilities and their social implications are to be explained not by the social mode of production, say slavery or feudalism, which on the contrary are their immediate outcome, but by what ultimately accounts for them both, the forces of production and destruction contention in their natural setting, that is, to geoeconomic factors. This viewpoint is strengthened if it withholds any claim to explain all social forms in history and in particular those of urban life and of capitalist economies once they have gone beyond the stage of primitive accumulation by plunder, enclosures of peasant plots and other violent forms of dispossession of pre-capitalist classes. These points can only be addressed properly, however, when the realm of freedom and its geo-

---

78. See Ronald L. Meek, *Smith, Marx and After*. pp. 18–32. The material mode of production is equivalent to the techniques or method whereby production is undertaken and hence to Smith's mode of subsistence, whereas the social mode of production consists of the property regime or relations of ownership within which the method of production or subsistence occurs.

political and economic preconditions are brought into the picture.

An interim conclusion is that military factors can play a decisive role in social differentiation into classes; and that these factors cannot be always attributed in individual instances, as Marxist insistence on their 'super-structural' character might imply, to the type of economic structure or mode of production a society possesses. This is because, at least in pre-capitalist societies, military factors characterize the mode of security, and this in turn reflects the mode of livelihood, or the means of production and pre-emption or reparation of destruction in their natural setting. The development of the productive, pre-emptive and reparative forces in contention with the destructive forces of nature fosters the development of the mode of security's means of violence; and the latter in turn, conditions the distribution of property in land and moveables and the structure of social classes in the countryside. Thus, nomadic pastoralism answered to natural needs in certain environments and facilitated military prowess and means of security and so nomadic domination of sedentary peasants and mobile merchants, whose lack of proficiency in warfare led them into subjection or subservience, albeit a subjection or subservience answering in its division and character of labour to the demands of their own sub-sistence in their natural setting. The development of the means of violence becomes the crucial precipitant or inus condition of the rural class structure, while both are in general accounted for by that of the productive and destruction-contending forces in relation to their natural environs. Geoeconomics, not economics, and geopolitics, not politics, comprise the decisive social levels.

Nevertheless, it has been argued, for any given society security needs can lead to a change of livelihood and so of property regime, even if in general expansive modes of livelihood account over time for the types of security systems and property regimes of which various regions of the world are capable.

The main preoccupation of this chapter so far has been to explore the fundamental reasons why the avoidance or reparation of destruction has such a powerful sway over social life. The means of contention with destruction that have been considered have been geoeconomic or geo-political and hence primarily physical in character. This theme is well summarized by Braudel when he writes of

the vulnerability of the gardens – whether in the plains or the oases – in that they had constantly to be recreated and protected against their tireless enemies: in the case of Mesopotamia, the sand, the silting up of the canals, the bursting of the dykes, as well as the near-primitive nomads from the neighbouring steppe, from whom, as if from locusts, the gardens had to be defended.[79]

---

79. Fernand Braudel, *The Mediterranean*, Vol. I, p. 186.

It is as well to remember that Mohammed launched a new religion from oasis gardens such as these, Mecca and Medina, which was to leave its own mark on history.[80] The role of religious forces, when they can transform the structure of societies and their organization of the material sphere of necessity, as was the case with Islam, requires further consideration; their wider significance, extending into the realm of freedom, will be assessed in a later chapter. It is now possible to explore the complex relations between the material and cultural spheres of necessity, even if in only cursory terms.

8. The Primacy of the Material Sphere of Necessity over the Cultural Sphere of Necessity

The cultural sphere of necessity comprises the set of cultural activities, such as speech, and institutions, such as language, without which a society would be destroyed.

Once it is accepted that the cultural sphere of necessity exists, then it might seem anomalous to suggest that it is less powerful than its material equivalent in explaining historical development. For among the necessary conditions of a phenomenon, it is self-contradictory to assert that one is more necessary than another. However, while the cultural sphere of necessity may well be as indispensable, once it exists, as the material sphere of necessity, the former's existence and development can largely be explained by their utility for the latter, while the reverse is generally not true.

It is material disasters which both the material and cultural spheres of necessity are primarily concerned to avert. The cultural disasters of ignorance, anomie, aphasia and oblivion are dangerous to a social group because they lead to the material disasters of starvation, disease, conquest, rapine and death; while the reverse is generally not the case. Material disasters can easily lead to cultural disasters, but this is not the primary reason for them to be avoided.

The cultural sphere of necessity developed initially to provide means of pre-empting destruction on the material plane, much as animal species have developed warning signals, hunting calls and homing instincts. Those areas of knowledge, morality, language and education, which are culturally indispensable for human social existence, are defined by their

---

80. While Medina was situated in a flourishing oasis, Mecca, in a barren countryside, owed its pre-eminence by the sixth century to its position as a haram, or shrine enclave, and as a centre for the caravan trade. See F.M. Donner, *The Early Islamic Conquests*, Princeton University Press 1981, pp. 14–15.

relation to the imperatives of the material sphere of necessity. Knowledge of material disasters and of the circumstances in which they are likely to occur is crucial, if the foregoing argument is correct, to the constitution of societies; but such knowledge is itself of course the outcome, by experience, hearsay and extrapolation, of past and present material disasters. Ideas, mores, signs and instructions are more flexible than material realities and the costs of changing the former are considerably less to any social group than altering the latter, where this is actually possible, as in the case of conquest. For instance, the Vikings who conquered Normandy adopted the language, manners, religion and arts of the Franks to their great advantage. In the realm of necessity, humans need to communicate, to abide by moral rules and to educate offspring in certain ethics and cognitive ideas in order to enable their communities to defend and reproduce themselves. It is only in the sphere of freedom that they can engage in physical activity as a diversion, that they can speculate and play, that they can superfluously create and can gratuitously destroy, that they can live in order to be free.

It might be contended by Marxists that, even if the realm of necessity encompasses more than one level, nevertheless, the economic level occupies a privileged position within it. Economic activity requires more persistent and unsparing effort and absorbs more time than any other activity that has been mentioned. Reproductive and cultural activities, such as language learning and initiation into cognitive and ethical notions, occur spontaneously without much effort. Moreover, economic activity is a precondition of most of them, providing the social necessaries without which they cannot be conducted, whether houses, schools, temples, books or other implements of use.

This argument has its beguiling points. Economic activity is doubtless more consuming of energy and time than other activities, earning a certain priority in that regard. Nevertheless, there is an evident lacuna in its logic. There is no point in expending a great amount of effort upon an activity, whether economic or any other, if its fruits are then expropriated by others. In many epochs of history a distinct possibility could lurk of hostile alien peoples seizing the husbanded grain or the accumulated wealth of a community. A swift military engagement could lead to the confiscation of the output of many months, decades or even centuries. Geopolitical defence was then as indispensable as economic activity precisely because of the many hours invested in performing the latter.

The additional argument, moreover, that economic activity is privileged as a prerequisite of other levels by reason of it providing social necessaries loses its force once it is recognized that all the activities of the realm of necessity are necessarily prerequisites of each other. The language, ethical mores and knowledge of a society, together with its reproductive powers, are preconditions or 'social necessaries' for economic activity itself and for each other.[81]

Geopolitical and geoeconomic activities are, nevertheless, usually distinguished among them by their capacity to bring about social *change*. For they possess a privileged relationship to those features of historical nature or a society's historical materiality and open external situation, whose volatility and pervasive urgency often demand that society give them their first attention. The biological requirements of reproduction and speech formation and the cultural ones of knowledge, communication, education and ethical mores necessary for social life to persist do not usually undergo such rapid changes; and if they do, they do so under the pressure of geopolitical and economic developments, as was the case with the Jesuit state in Paraguay.[82]

The rise of Islam offers another instructive example of this generalization. The merchants of the Arabian caravan trade had possessed iron weapons with which to defend themselves against nomad marauders. But after the adoption of the North Arabian saddle the camel-breeding nomads came to dominate the caravan trade with their greater height and force in a skirmish, new advantages of camel cavalry. This led to the trade's swift decline, particularly as incense for Roman pagan rites, the staple commodity, was in much smaller demand after the rise of Christianity.[83] Mecca, as the vital trading town in the Hejaz, itself controlled the traffic between the southern agrarian kingdoms and the north. The Quraysh, who were settled in Mecca, succeeded in establishing a hegemony over their tribal neighbours in order to co-operate with the caravan trade and so encourage its revival, by offering it protective services.[84] Elements of instability, however, remained so long as the tribes

---

81. There is one clear historical confirmation of this. The Jesuits of Paraguay owed allegiance to the Papacy and papally legitimated Spanish monarchs of the Americas: hence, their compliance when they were banned from the Spanish Empire in 1767. The removal of some 300 Jesuits from their 100,000 strong missions in Paraguay deprived the Indians of political leadership, religious spirit, knowledge and education, leading to the swift disintegration of their otherwise economically successful and militarily redoubtable state.

82. The slaveholders in the neighbouring Iberian domains had been repulsed from their slave raids on the Garani Indian labour-force of the Jesuit missions, yet succeeded in discrediting them with the help of rival religious orders in the eyes of the Spanish crown. Hence the fatal decision to expel them in 1767.

83. Watt has ascribed the rise of Islam to the disruptive effect of a spreading commercial activity for the clannic system of Arabia. The trade between the former and the north, however, was in decline due to the collapse of the incense trade, henceforward relying on spices. See Richard W. Bulliet, *The Camel and the Wheel*, Harvard University Press 1975, pp. 87–110. This very decline, as we shall see, was the real precipitant of the new faith; M. Watt, *Muhammed: prophet and statesman*, Oxford University Press 1981. For effective criticism of Watt's claims, see M. Cook, *Muhammed*, Oxford University Press 1983.

84. Richard W. Bulliett, *The Camel and the Wheel*, pp. 87–110. The nomad tribes comprised a minority of the peninsula's population, most tribes, such as the Quraysh, being settled.

were united only by a prudential interest in mutual co-operation, since, as in the 'prisoners' dilemma' of games theory, one partner in a consortium or one car in the traffic can break the rules to its own advantage whatever degree of compliance with them is shown by others. Arabia needed a creed which could intimidate and unify its tribes better than their pagan polytheism could possibly do.

Islam was unusually well suited to respond to the exigencies of the Arabian tribes' modes of security, enabling them, for a while, to be unified into one, with the settled tribes achieving ascendancy over the nomads. The peculiar form Islam assumed was greatly influenced by the political and religious intrusions on Arabia from the outer world. Byzantium and Persia were both exerting military pressures on the region, and both were possessed of monotheistic creeds. Christian and Jewish commercial and religious activities were highly visible in Arabia itself; and an elaboration of an indigenous monotheistic system, indebted, like Christianity, to Judaism, had the advantages of countering the charge of pagan idolatry and backwardness so often levelled by Christians and Jews against the tribesmen of the peninsula, while yet providing it with a distinctive cultural identity of its own.[85] Moreover, Islam's emphasis upon the one god and the afterlife, transition to which remains assured for those falling in battle, provided a mode of magical security for both individuals and tribes within an Arabian mode of mundane security, albeit one which proved to be only tenuous. The decisive conversion of the Quraysh of Mecca, who had originally spurned it, was due to the fact that its superiority to pagan polytheism was proved in battle at Badr in 624 and, after the setback of Uhud in 625, in its astounding recovery from defeat.[86]

Once Islam had united Arabia, prevention of further disorder was guaranteed for several generations by jihad, holy war. This gave an outlet to the restive, perhaps growing, population of peacetime, above all the troublesome nomads of the desert, thus pre-empting sources of conflict at home; expansion also offered economic benefits of booty, tribute and,

---

85. See John Hall, *Liberties and Powers: the Causes and Consequences of the Rise of the West*, Basil Blackwell, Oxford 1985, pp. 86–7 for an illuminating discussion of this complex of questions. Also Michael Meeker, *Literature and Violence*, pp. 7–11, who places Islam in its Arabian context.

86. Maxime Rodinson, *Mohammed*, tr. Anne Carter, Allen Lane, London 1971, Chs 5 and 6, 'The Prophet in Arms' and 'Birth of a State'. Mohammed also favoured the Quraysh, of which he was after all a member, and other settled tribes over the nomads. Indeed, originally, he made settlement a condition of being a Moslem, only relaxing it on terms which maintained nomads in subjection to the Moslem state and its settled elite. See F.M. Donner, *Early Islamic Conquests*, pp. 79–83 and pp. 263–7. The infantrymen, with their swords and bows, who undertook the bulk of the fighting during the early conquests of Egypt, Iran, Syria and Iraq, were mainly from the settled areas of Arabia (p. 223).

important for the Quraysh, control of the Syrian trade.[87] The Moslem conquests of the Fertile Crescent, Egypt, Iran and Spain were the result, involving an exportation and adaptation to settled agrarian conditions of the mode of security, which had regulated tribal warfare and then exploit- ation of the caravan trade in the first place and now permitted their super- session in emigration. As Crone says, comparing Mongol with Moslem conquest:

> Where a Mongol statesman could accumulate earthly power, the Arab prophet tapped divine authority; and where the Mongol conquests were an explosion caused by the *disintegration* of a tribal society, the Arab explosion by contrast was caused by its *fusion*. Once invented, the idea was applied again and again by impoverished tribes in Arabia and North Africa who re-enacted the Prophet's career in areas which had previously seen only monotonous raids and revolts.[88]

Religion, then, can come to inhabit and help regulate the realm of necessity once it succeeds in magically organizing a new mode of security.

Subsequent developments in Arabia are not without interest. The very success of Islam abroad, ironically, led Arabia to become a backwater, neglected and increasingly misunderstood by the caliphates in Damascus and Baghdad. Its nomadic tribes were able to replenish their numbers after the depletions of emigration within a few generations, when newcomers became less in need in the conquered lands. Within a century, Arabia was once more rent by outbreaks of tribal strife; and the sway of the caliphate was far more secure in the Fertile Crescent. Indeed, Near Eastern politics reverted to its pre-Islamic pattern with 'a powerful state or states centred in the Fertile Crescent and Egypt, supported especially by the rich taxes to be drawn from those regions, relying on standing armies made up of settled soldiers native to those regions – and struggling with variable success to extend its control over, or at least to keep at bay, the nomadic warriors of the Arabian peninsula, who remained generally outside its firm grasp'.[89]

---

87. This is essentially the conclusion of F.M. Donner, *Early Islamic Conquests*, pp. 267–71, except that he disputes whether population increase played a role, citing complaints of manpower shortages for the army.

The explanation for Islam's career put forward here is not evoking a single need to which the explanandum as a response is attributed, a common fallacy of functionalism. There were, indeed, other creeds contending to convert Arabia. The explanation consists rather of indicating how Islam could respond to several requirements of the Quraysh and other Arabian tribes, military, commercial and demographic as well as cultural ones, and hence succeed over any rival.

88. P. Crone, *Slaves on Horses*, p. 25.

89. F.M. Donner, *Early Islamic Conquests*, pp. 277–8.

This anomalous outcome seemingly endorses the Marxist view that forms of state respond to the requirements of the mode of production and the manner whereby the surplus is extracted from the working masses. For the restless, nomadic and semi-nomadic elements in Arabian society rendered regular exactions impractical compared with those from the peasant populations of the Fertile Crescent and Egypt upon whose backs a strong state could be built. However, the very difficulty in regulating and taxing nomads or those under their protection, and hence the backwardness of class relations and the fragility of the Arabian polity, were due to the nomads' retention of their own mobile modes of livelihood and security within the larger forms of state. In other words, the Islamic solution to the problem of unifying the Arabian peninsula eventually foundered on ultimately demographic and military grounds, that is, because of the replenishment of nomad numbers and vitality after the first waves of emigration, and the nomads' retention of arms and abodes of refuge and surprise attack within their desert way of life. It was only in the agricultural societies of the conquered lands that the Islamic system of settled security and property could be lastingly implanted with its peculiar combination of a state monopoly of land and private property in the towns, hence the concern of Islamic rulers to settle or subjugate nomads in their domains.

The modes of livelihood and security, then, inhabit powerful dimensions of a society's realm of necessity, generally governing the secular course of its other institutions and activities. What is required to satisfy the need to eat, to take shelter and to provide self-protection changes with every fluctuation in the soil and climate and every shift in the dispositions of neighbours. Human intercourse with its physical and human environment, whether mainly creative with economic life or mainly pre-emptive of destruction with geopolitical life, transforms the immediate conditions of social existence in a manner that usually insists upon being given prior attention by societies. Geopolitics and geoeconomics occupy a privileged position within the realm of necessity, even if religion can come to ratify them, a condominium that extends into the realm of freedom.

9. The Extension of the Province of Freedom in the Realm of Necessity

The realm of necessity contains its own province of freedom, the scope that exists for its exigencies to be met in a variety of different ways. There is reason to suppose that this scope for choice and change in meeting basic requirements has increased in the course of history. The very advance in productive powers to which Marxism ascribes such importance has made possible not only the satisfaction of basic, economic needs more easily and so the diminution of the realm of necessity at the hands of the realm of freedom, but also a greater variety in the ways in which such basic needs can be met. Agriculture can now assume a wide range of forms, not just the cultivation of a few locally available crops, but that of many unknown in earlier times or in certain neighbourhoods. The 'green revolution' of recent years in the Third World has allowed farmers to diversify into new crops and strains and to adopt new fertilizers and nutrients for their soil.

It is not only a growth in productive powers which has altered the scope for improving chances of survival, but also that in pre-emptive and reparative powers. Indeed better crop protection against rodents and microparasites is one instance of this, albeit protection mainly of production. But the forestalling of forces destructive of humans them-selves, notably by advance in medicine and public sanitation, has con-tinued apace, as have methods of environmental conservation or land reclamation.

Yet both those types of preservation have provoked a counter-finality of response as rodents and microparasites have built up resistance to the poisons which earlier kept them in check, and as lower infant mortality rates and improved health in later life have worsened overpopulation. The result in each case, nevertheless, has been the emergence of higher-level problems than obtained before. A definite progress in curtailing destruc-tion has widened the gamut of choices available to Third World countries in ensuring survival.

Their demographic growth has remained recalcitrant to collective attempts to control it. An unintended impact of greater affluence has of course been the lower family size of the advanced countries, which is now, without having been planned, curbing or reversing the expansive population trends of the postwar world in both Western and Eastern Europe and non-Islamic Russia. The chances for population control in the Third World probably depend heavily on their prospects for economic development.

There is a further extension of the province of freedom in the realm of necessity which has long characterized human history. And that is the perennial improvement in means of violence at the disposal of the mode of security. Improved means of surveillance and control of domestic populations and improved means of warfare have created wider scope for dictatorial regimes and arms races between different states. These developments are of course ambivalent: they have widened the scope for states to protect social order against internal subversion and to protect themselves or rather the leaders in an arms race against their rivals. They raise, therefore, issues which can only be discussed in a broader frame-work, some of which will be broached later.

The decisive role in this complex and contrary development of powers of survival has been played by the dissemination of new ideas across countries and climes about how the realm of necessity can be mollified and regulated. The role of ideas here acquires a new aspect, transforming material prospects worldwide. The discovery of viruses and of inoculation by Pasteur and that of nuclear energy by modern physics has unleashed new forces, either pre-emptive or perpetrative of destruction. The age-old diseases of mankind have receded, even while new possibilities of human self-destruction have materialised.[90] Yet the advances of science, medicine and technology have not taken place in a vacuum, but have themselves been made possible by the finance and resources available for expenditure upon them released by economic growth in the already developed world. It would be premature to infer that a growing importance of ideas is incompatible with insistence on the decisive significance of economic development in the modern world, a question to which further attention will soon be given.

The province of freedom in the realm of necessity, then, has been enlarged in many ways, even if the comparative importance of the main instigators of this process has not yet been identified.

---

90. See William H. McNeill, *Plagues and Peoples*, the final chapter, 'The Ecological Impact of Medical Science and Organisation since 1700', pp. 235–9, for the triumphs of modern medicine. The spread of AIDS, however, indicates how fragile they are.

5

Social Realms and Levels

1. The Influence of the Realm of Necessity as a Whole over the Realm of Freedom

It is possible to argue that the realm of necessity as a whole exerts a formative influence over the realm of freedom. There are three main reasons which can be adduced in favour of this thesis.

Firstly, we can adapt an argument of Cohen's concerning the primacy of the economic base in relation to the superstructures.[1] This thesis, however, is different from that put forward here. The realm of necessity needs to be substituted for the economic base and the realm of freedom for the 'superstructures', the economic level lying partly in the one realm and partly in the other, while by no means exhausting either, as do the levels composing the 'superstructures'. The fact that certain conditions must obtain for the realm of freedom to be possible at all indicates one clear limitation upon the scope of this freedom; it cannot involve activities which seriously harm these basic conditions. Societies are not free to engage in activities which destroy economic life or impair military, reproductive or certain cultural capabilities except at their peril. Nor are they likely to pursue activities, even if they are not at least immediately fatal, when there are grounds for believing them to be harmful to the interests of independent survival. For those which stubbornly engage in malefic pursuits risk being eclipsed in competition with neighbours or destroyed

---

1. G.A. Cohen, 'Restricted and Inclusive Historical Materialism', *Marx en Perspective*, textes reunis par Bernard Chavance, Ecole des Hautes Etudes en Sciences Sociales, Paris 1983, pp. 53–76, where Cohen suggests that one restriction on the superstructures imposed by the economic base is that the former cannot involve harmful effects on the latter; hence one form of primacy the latter enjoys.

by natural events (facts, however, which do not necessarily deter them, either from ignorance or folly), while those which do abide by this proscription, changing their ways if and when necessary, have a better chance of avoiding such fates. Societies are obliged to be aversive of evil with regard to their survival in the realm of necessity and at least unharmful in this regard in the realm of freedom.

Nearly all societies (or species) in history which contravened one or both of these crucial rules have perished. It is not surprising, therefore, that the survivors generally are immensely cautious about renouncing their responsibilities in these respects. The innovative epochs of history evince many instances of societies engaging in unwittingly self-destructive activities, such as the heedless deforestation of ancient Mediterranean civilizations, the freewheeling belligerence of Nazism and the religious extravagances of Meso-American civilizations, most notably those of the Aztecs. They share one common characteristic today: they are extinct. The growing contacts between societies and the volatile pressures of natural existence have tended to eliminate those with dangerous idiosyncracies and to impose an increasing conformity of less erroneous beliefs and of less irrational forms of organized activity on the survivors.

These constraints may still leave a society with a wide range of alternatives in the realm of freedom since there are many errors and irrationalities that can be committed in avoiding those of one's predecessors. Nevertheless, a tendency towards validity in relation to beliefs and rationality with regard to activities must have prevailed or there would have been no advance in the sway and power of societies and civilizations.

It is also probable that among the alternatives open to any society there will be a tendency for those which are not only non-harmful but are positively helpful to its preservation to come to the fore. Creative ideas and projects which assist a society's chances of survival in the realm of necessity tend to be fostered by the powerful interests which inhabit that realm. It is not only societies, but also institutions and cultural movements within them, which are obliged to reproduce themselves; and the latter require allies in order to perform the task, than which none will have a better claim to be heard than those representing the interests of the realm of necessity. Thus the economic, military and cultural authorities necessary for survival will favour the inception and retention of those materially and culturally creative institutions and movements which in turn favour them.

Thirdly, the means of autonomous creation will often be the same as those of averting destruction, especially in the material sphere of freedom. Thus, an economic surplus, particularly in primitive societies, can more easily assume the form of a superfluity of those goods, the production of a minimum of which is essential for a balanced diet, such as meat and honey and fruit and vegetables, than the creation of new goods; although of course higher forms of luxury are likely to require a certain versatility. Similarly, armies which are necessary for defence can also be employed in offensive operations, indeed may only be known to be reliable in the former, if they are sometimes shown to be effective in the latter. Education into the components of necessary knowledge and communications can provoke and prefigure the emergence of new speculative ideas and of literature and art. In these ways, the realm of necessity exerts a directly formative influence over that of freedom.

Conversely, the realm of freedom exerts its own formative influence on the realm of necessity. Elements of the autonomous realm of freedom, as we have already remarked, are continually becoming importunate candidates for inclusion into the province of freedom in the realm of necessity and more directly into the realm of necessity itself. Means of transport and communication at first as ideas and then as real options for an economy, can become indispensable in the present to withstand foreign competitive pressures. Weapons which one side in an arms race adopts as an aggressive extravagance become obligatory means of deterrence for the other. Scientific theories, which were recently only speculative, such as relativity and quantum physics, can become essential items in the arsenal of survival. A rational anticipation of such developments justifies the vigilance and curiosity of the modern state about the potential of economic, military and scientific novelties.

The realm of necessity, therefore, casts a long, if not baleful, shadow on the realm of freedom, increasingly predisposing it towards those activities which are at least conceived as unharmful and as positively encouraging to the interests of survival and security, whether of social existence as such or of its achieved levels of creative activity. The element of credulity involved has left scope for variation in history, but, as we have seen, the selective filter of struggle, both with nature and other societies, has increasingly eliminated those societies which prove unable or unwilling to conform to its requirements, leaving the less misguided in belief and less irrational in organization to survive. Nevertheless, the realm of freedom can throw its own backward spell upon the realm of necessity in an interaction whose decisive moment has yet to be established.

2. The Concert of Social Levels

It is normally assumed in Marxist or, indeed, any philosophy of history, such as the Hegelian one, that there is one level of society which is predominant in determining its whole course and character, subject to constraints from the other levels. For Marx this level is economic and for

Hegel it is spiritual. In either case, there is just one level which is decisive. It is by no means self-evident, however, that this unitarian bias is justified. A dyadic or even a triadic complex of ultimate determination is also conceivable, indeed, we shall argue, typical of actual societies.

It could of course be disputed whether any ultimate determination need exist at all. Functionalist anthropology, for instance, dispenses with the need for it and so with the need for historical explanation. If all levels are of equal significance due to their functional role in social reproduction, then there is no reason why any level should prevail over others in explaining development, except for chance exogenous shocks. For a historical theory, however, it is desirable, if novelties are not merely to be ascribed to chance, to distinguish an inequality of social levels in their mutual interaction to account for change. Yet this can be compatible with more than one level assuming a decisive importance in the whole. It will be argued that there is at least one in the realm of necessity and another in the realm of freedom which combine to determine the structure, if not the history, of any society. Nevertheless, the realms of necessity and freedom will themselves be of unequal significance, depending on whether society is ensnared by destruction or its imminent threat or whether it possesses the security to embark upon creative endeavours of a more autonomous kind.

The positions here outlined have failed to specify the sense in which such terms as 'predominate' and 'ultimately determinant' are being used. An admonition of Marx's is helpful at this point: it is necessary to avoid the error of the 'English, who have a tendency to look upon the earliest appearance of a thing as the cause of its existence'.[2]

Thus, the fact that early capitalist societies at first assumed a military aspect both in wars and plunder, from which they greatly benefited, does not imply that capitalism's emergence as a system can be explained in mainly military terms. The primitive accumulation by violence abroad and enclosures at home, which inaugurated the English Industrial Revolution, does not fully account for this momentous event. As regards the argument to be considered later that feudalism was as much a military as an economic system, it will be irrelevant to point out that feudal societies and the landlord–serf relationship invariably arose in Europe from conquest or successful resistance to invasion, or, indeed, for its opponents to point out that feudalism did not do so in Japan. In other words, it is essential to

---

2. Karl Marx, *Capital* Volume 1, Moscow, 1961, p. 403. What Marx perhaps also had in mind is that the *origins* of the first appearance of a phenomenon should not be taken as its cause, as well as the first appearance itself. In fact of course neither should be. Languages cannot be fully explained by etymology or the sway of ideologies by the qualities of their originators or first converts.

distinguish between the historical causality of events and the structural causality of societies in which they occur. The previous discussion of the role of warfare in pre-capitalist societies failed to specify the nature of the structural causality governing their history. Once the realm of freedom has also been considered, it will be possible to identify, at least in the crucial case of feudalism, what the role of violence within it might have been.

A pertinent discrimination at this point has been made in his own terms by Althusser, that between dominant and determinant contradictions.[3] A dominant contradiction dominates the history of a social formation at any one time, as Catholic controversy did most of the European Middle Ages; while a determinant one, for Althusser always an economic contradiction, is ultimately determinant both of a society's structure and of its history, in the latter case by selecting which among the various social contradictions is to dominate. Thus a capitalist society may be dominated by a prolonged military engagement, yet the accumulation of capital and the contradiction engendered by it – for Althusser, as for all Marxists, that between the development of the productive forces and the relations of production – must be ultimately determinant, both of its structure and its history, in this case a war.

This distinction refers only to social structures and events, but can be clarified by comparison with the more comprehensive distinction between particular and general causes of events, adumbrated by several thinkers. Montesquieu gave the latter an illuminating formulation for historiography when he said of the decline of the Western Roman Empire, 'If a particular cause, like the accidental result of a battle, has ruined a state, there was a general cause which made the downfall of this state ensue from a single battle'.[4] An instance of this dictum being applied is given by Thucydides's famous judgement on the origins of the Peloponnesian War: 'What made war inevitable was the growth of Athenian power and the fear this caused in Sparta.'[5] The Spartan fear of Athens was the particular cause or catalyst of the conflict, while the general cause lay in the growth of Athenian power. Similarly, while the fears by Britain and France of Germany and by Germany of Russia sparked off the First World War, the growth of Germany's power relative to Britain's and France's and of Russia's power relative to Germany's during the industrialization of the continent and the spread of empire and military readiness in the preceding decades underlay the outbreak of hostilities. Developments in diplomacy

---

3. Louis Althusser, 'Contradiction and Overdetermination', *For Marx*, Verso, London 1977, pp. 87–128.
4. Montesquieu, *Considerations sur les causes de la Grandeur des Romains et de leur Decadence*, Garnier-Flammarion, Paris, 1968, p. 145.
5. Thucydides, *The History of the Peloponnesian War*, Book 1–23.

and mutual perceptions were here precipitants of warfare whose profound causes resided in the respective economies and forms of state of the major European powers.[6]

In the case of those wars arising in the manner Thucydides discerned, it is clear that a specific threat of a military kind engendered a crisis in the realm of necessity, which could, therefore, be said to be dominant within it. The structure of the realm of necessity is determined, however, by those levels contending with more perennial forms of destruction, in general the modes of livelihood and security. A particular famine, to take another example, might *dominate* a particular society in the sense of posing a grave, indeed the gravest possible, threat to its members' lives and thence to its own existence; the structure of its realm of necessity would be itself *determined*, however, by an economic system and social order proving ineffectual against severe drought or other natural calamity, as with certain African states today. In so far as a society is gripped by problems in the realm of necessity, it is possible to discriminate between dominant and determinant instances of them in this way.

In the case of societies coping more or less successfully in their realms of necessity, it could still be possible for some perhaps ephemeral issue to be dominant within them and be determined on some other level by those forces formative of their realm of freedom as a whole. Religious controversy, for example, often preoccupied the surplus attention and energies of medieval Europe, that is, that sphere which existed beyond the cares and activities of the realm of necessity itself and indeed of the province of necessity within this realm of freedom. Religion here could be dominant because of dominant facts of social existence, the comparative clemency of the realm of necessity and the mainsprings of cultural creativity in the society's structure and situation, whatever these may have been. Indeed, the distinction here drawn between dominant and determinant activities in the realm of freedom is analogous to Panofsky's celebrated distinction between iconography and iconology, the former exploring the content or subject matter of a work of art or cultural activity, and the latter revealing its larger meaning within human culture and its underlying social and historical origins.[7]

The dominant issue of the realm of necessity, then, is the problem most critical for the existence of a society or its members, while in the realm of

---

6. See A.J.P. Taylor, *The Struggle for Mastery in Europe*, Oxford University Press 1954, Introduction, pp. xix–xxxvi and Ch. XXII, pp. 511–31, for an examination first of the underlying causes and then of the precipitants of the war, with scarcely a mention of railway timetables.

7. Erwin Panofsky, 'Iconography and Iconology, Introduction to the Study of Renaissance Art' in *Meaning in the Visual Arts*, Doubleday, New York 1955, pp. 26–54, especially table on pp. 40–41.

freedom it is that which in fact engages most attention and concern over and above the necessary preoccupations and activities of social life. The determinant issue in either case is whatever entails that the dominant does indeed dominate its particular realm.

There can, indeed often will, be a dominant issue in the realm of necessity at the same moment as there is a dominant issue in the realm of freedom. During the course of a conflict, they will commonly be the same, namely the problem of ensuring that one does not lose, say, a war in the former case and the problem of how to win it in the other, which is of course the best way not to lose it. They will then share a common origin in the reasons why the conflict occurred, naturally not only its immediate, but also its underlying reasons.

While there may be two dominant levels of social existence, one for each realm, the ultimately determinant dimension of a society's structure and history generally resides in a condominium of its modes of livelihood and production with its mode of security, that is of geoeconomics-cum-economics and geopolitics-cum-politics within the context of its historical environment. In pre-capitalist societies, the economic level can even merge with the mode of security as with fully fledged feudalism, of which more later.

Thus, in the late Middle Ages, the Black Death and its periodic recurrences with their decimations of population alternated with wars and famines in dominating the realm of necessity, while religious developments dominated the realm of freedom. Indeed, these directly interacted with one another, the lugubrious forms of late medieval Christian heresy and art being largely the outcome of the 'dance of death' of the time.[8] Nevertheless, the conflicts that ultimately determined late medieval society were situated at the level of its modes of livelihood, production and security as the fully feudal order broke down. The first was the discrepancy between the development of protocapitalist forms and forces of economic life and the lingering feudal relations of production and changing physical environments in which they unfolded. The second was the discordance between the development of centralizing means of violence, namely artillery and firearms, permitting consolidation of feudal domains into states, and the still fragmented parcellization of sovereignty and reliance upon fiefs based on localized castle defence. These two sources of disruption within European society led to an unleashing of brutal class struggle and wars.

The key point to note is that there will generally be two underlying motors, not merely one, in a society's history. One involves economic,

---

8. J.A. Huizinga, *The Waning of the Middle Ages*, Edward Arnold, London 1924.

military or, indeed, religious means to maintain or increase its security and that of its members in the realm of necessity; the other involves economic or military means to magnify its surplus in the realm of freedom. The former tends to be characterized by improvement of preservative forces in the teeth of destructive ones and the latter by acquisition and enlargement of a surplus through warfare or the development of the productive forces. While the former raises geoeconomic and geopolitical problems, the latter possesses a more 'economist' or Marxist character; although a resort to invasion and plunder, as with nomads and other militarized groups, may long have been more conspicuous than trade and production as a means of amplifying the surplus.

For a Marxist theory, the economic is always ultimately determinant even in pre-capitalist societies. One of the main arguments of this work is that the economic invariably acts with the geoeconomic level and usually also with geopolitical and political levels, and indeed, as with feudalism, can become inseparable from them. While capitalism has presided over an epoch in which geoeconomic and economic levels are ultimately determinant, albeit with the mode of security playing a vital role, under pre-capitalist social orders, especially in epochs governed by the realm of necessity, the modes of production and livelihood allied with the mode of security to confront destructive forces emanating from nature, from other societies and from within societies in a manner permitting an intimate condominium over the structure and history of social existence. This militarization of the realm of necessity then predisposed many societies to geopolitical methods of acquiring the surplus, the indispensable wherewithal for their realms of freedom to thrive.

A theoretical point may be made here, however, of some immediate relevance. Either the realm of necessity or that of freedom can be the crucial realm of social existence in the sense that it comprises its overriding moment in a continuous dialectic between these realms.

The geoeconomic (cum-economic) and geopolitical (cum-political) levels have exercised a condominium over social development for most of history, an alliance whose intimacy and character depends on whether they preside over an epoch of devastation and anarchy in the realm of necessity or one of expansion and progress in the realm of freedom. This reflects the fundamental fact that societies and their history cannot be understood, as has been the wont of Marxism and other schools of thought before it, in terms merely of an interplay between social levels, either material or cultural; they are also the outcome of the interplay between creation, preservation and destruction which has unfolded upon all their social levels.

This perspective, it might be countered, involves a surreptitious return to a unitarian conception of ultimate determination with the insistence on one realm being preponderant. It is important to recognize, however, that a forward-looking expansive economic impulse can escape the embrace of geopolitics, even in the direst epochs, and indeed is usually decisive in bringing them to an end; while conversely a minatory environmental or geopolitical threat of destruction can persist in expansive periods of creative achievement, notably in our own, and its realization often terminates them. It is quite inaccurate and undialectical to insist upon a never-changing primacy of one level in explaining social structures, let alone social change. For societies are capable of shifting from epochs of creation and expansion to ones of destruction and its contention or vice-versa.

The discussion so far has concentrated on the realm of necessity and so implicitly on those dire, even if heroic, epochs when it has preoccupied social life. It is now necessary to consider the realm of freedom, and those happier times when its influence has become pervasive and paramount.

6

The Realm of Freedom

The scope of the realm of necessity is signified by the set of conditions requiring to be fulfilled for social existence to be possible. The realm of freedom denotes that social sphere within which such requirements do not obtain. While the former is necessary for the latter, it does not signify the full range of conditions needing to be satisfied if a realm of freedom is also to exist. For there are several conditions which, although they may be unnecessary for social existence, are necessary for the existence of a realm of freedom. These include the provision of an adequate surplus, whether by production or the exaction of tribute or income from other societies, and the defence of such surplus-creating activities against predatory outsiders. Economics and geopolitics, therefore, often provide essential services for a society to inhabit a realm of freedom at all.

The Province of Necessity in the Realm of Freedom

There may well be several significantly different ways open to a society to fulfil the economic and geopolitical requirements of possessing a realm of freedom. For long historical periods the scope for variation has nevertheless been limited to choosing among the possibilities of gain made available within one social system – say, feudalism or capitalism. Any given type of freedom, such as that involved in feudal or bourgeois civilizations, clearly presupposes the specific social order in question.

As regards the question of why a particular social structure may exist, this may be for more than one type of reason, involving not only the requirements of the province of necessity in the realm of freedom, but also those of the realm of necessity itself. In fact, social orders are likely to be the outcome of the crises of their predecessors in both domains, to whose problems they can provide superior answers. It is a moot point whether, as Marxism alleges, there can only be one candidate system in each case capable of becoming the successor: due to a lack of any conclusive counterfactual evidence, this is difficult to corroborate or refute. The Marxist commitment to a unilinear succession is based of course on the view that the development of the productive forces ordains at a certain moment a step forward in social organization corresponding to it, say from feudalism to capitalism or capitalism to socialism.[1]

The critical and often turbulent periods of social existence in which systems are replaced, however, might allow of several possible outcomes. If there can be reasons of military exigency as well as of economic advance which contribute to causing the formation of a new social order, then it is easier to conceive of a plurality of successor systems. For instance, one could consider the possibility that the Western Roman Empire might have followed the pattern of the Eastern Roman Empire whose territories eventually came under the rule and economic system of the Ottoman Empire, rather than after the Dark Ages being succeeded by feudalism. The fact that Eastern Europe had by 1950 ceased to be capitalist while Western Europe remained so, was not only the unexpected result of the Nazi blitzkrieg eastwards in the early 1940s, but also, it is often argued, of the systemic defence requirements of the Soviet Union, in particular of the need for a cordon sanitaire in reverse.

In other words, societies arise and fall because of the possibilities and problems obtaining in their own and others' modes of security, not just their economic life or their modes of livelihood.

The position being put forward can be clarified by comparing it further with the Marxist position of which it aims to be an amplification. For Marx, a historical society possesses a structure capable of generating progress so long as the latter can fulfil two requirements: firstly, that it can

---

1. A Marxist might wish to contend that a duality or plurality of potential successors is sanctioned by the economic development in question, but this would contravene the spirit of the theory, requiring revision of Marx's notion of historical necessity. This notion is often considered to be deterministic, as by Popper. In fact, it is more akin to the concept of necessity employed here, that is, of conditions needing to be fulfilled to pre-empt destruction; albeit the destruction in question is of the productive gains of a society, not its fruits of civilization in a more extended sense and of its very existence. Two passages reveal this. 'As the main thing is not to be deprived of the fruits of civilization, of the acquired productive forces, the traditional forms in which they were produced must be smashed', *The Poverty of Philosophy*, Moscow, no date, p. 137; and 'In order that they may not be deprived of the result attained, and forfeit the fruits of civilization, they are obliged from the moment when their mode of intercourse no longer corresponds to the productive forces acquired, to change all their traditional social forms', Marx to Annenkov, 23 December 1846, Selected Correspondence, Moscow, 1975, p. 31. It is revealing that Marx speaks as if the transformation is only capable of arising internally, not from without.

reproduce itself, and secondly that it can possess a dynamic or form of productive advance. This at least is presupposed by his view that capitalism is obliged to reproduce wage-labour and the other conditions of capitalist existence and to prove capable of an accumulation of capital. Reproduction of a dynamic system, however, is not merely an economic process: it requires pre-emption of destruction on every social level, and from without as well as within. The renewal of the demographic, environmental and cultural conditions of social existence and, indeed, of any isolated social system, may be more or less automatic. However, the maintenance of military inviolability can often prove difficult; indeed in the founding moments and turbulent epochs of history, it may prove traumatic and either decisive in its demise or formative of its resilience and structure. Reproduction of the mode of security is as problematic as that of any economic mode. Moreover, it has often involved a crucial, if not fatal, dynamic, albeit of a negative kind. This can often come about in a negative interaction of security needs with the mode of production: for the latter's ability to reproduce itself can be sapped by heavy taxes or other burdens upon it, such as when coercive and authoritative means of class domination were undermined in pre-capitalist societies by the ownership of weapons becoming more democratic.

Under capitalism, even military proficiency in the external dimensions of the mode of security has often become an automatic affair, the by-product and even the spur of economic proficiency. But in pre-capitalist societies, the productive forces, it can be argued, were insufficiently developed for this to be so. Economic sophistication of a high order is required for defensive and, indeed, offensive capabilities to be easily provided at low social cost. Even then, some social cost is likely to be unavoidable, as American capitalism is discovering with the financial and other repercussions of sustaining its military-industrial complex.

The military moment in the reproduction of social systems may be so vital that it marks the other crucial prerequisite of their existence in perpetuity, and hence the nature of their dynamic. The motors of such pre-capitalist societies, it can be maintained, can often be interpreted as assuming a geopolitical as well as economic character and can sometimes involve just such a negative interplay between the modes of security and modes of production as was mentioned above.

In order to demonstrate this, it will be necessary in the first place to establish why and how the geoeconomic levels and the geopolitical levels share a condominium over the realm of freedom of recent dynamic societies, although one which, we shall see, has of late undergone a curious inversion in the period of closure of the ecumene. This requires consideration initially of their predominance in the material sphere of the realm of freedom and then, in order to grasp the curious inversion in question, consideration of their formative influence over the cultural sphere of freedom.

2. The Geoeconomic and Geopolitical Components of the Material Sphere of Freedom

The material sphere of freedom consists of four main types of activity: the production of economic luxuries and free time; military aggression and imperialist domination; demographic expansion; and the amelioration of the physical environment. Each of these activities has its counterpart in the realm of necessity: the production of necessaries; external security; reproduction of the population; and environmental custody.

Demographic expansion and environmental improvement are dependent on the existence of a surplus above that needed to reproduce the population at its existing size. Economic expansiveness is, therefore, a vital precondition of these activities, even if not always their raison d'être. Successful wars can also in certain cases prove to be necessary conditions of them, as of European demographic and environmental recovery from the Dark Ages.

The role of demographic expansion in human history has doubtless been profound, even if the great difficulties of estimating sizes and changes in population and related economic variables obscure attempts to theorize its long-term impact. In the early stages of social life before recorded history it may well have been the pressure of numbers upon grazing grounds that compelled the migration of tribes and rendered more probable both trade and outbreaks of warfare between them. Then, a tendency for expanding agrarian populations to outstrip immediately cultivable soils, together with harassment by nomad pastoralists, encouraged the temptation to expand at others' expense and the concomitant propensity for protection under centralized control. Moreover, as populations came into increasing contact with each other and reached critical densities and concentrations in villages and towns, notably in the ancient Near East and China, they became vulnerable to pestilence and other ecological hazards characteristic of expansive epochs.[2]

Fluctuations of population size punctuated by outbreaks of warfare, disease and environmental damage or catastrophe with ensuing famine, could have underlain long epochs of economic activity lasting for several centuries. The Middle Ages in Europe, the Middle East and Asia, as is well known, were interrupted in the fourteenth century by the Black Death

---

2. William McNeill, *Plagues and Peoples*, Basil Blackwell, Oxford 1977 Chs 1–3.

spread by the Mongols, by widespread soil erosion and by ferocious warfare and class struggles, which came between the high noon of the medieval period and the emergence of the modern world. Today, population growth is clearly a crucial dimension of the ecological crisis and warfare afflicting so many Third World countries after their political and economic advances in the early postwar decades. Demographic expansion, therefore, occurring within the realm of freedom, even if it proceeds from more clement conditions in this realm's province of necessity, as the production of foodstuffs and necessaries multiplies, may come to pose severe ecological problems in the realm of necessity, which eventually reverse it. Undue population growth can become a means of social *self-destruction*, against which the domains of necessity are obliged to be on guard.

An interruption to this baleful cycle came with the Industrial Revolution during the very lifetime of Malthus. As Landes has said,

> Where previously an amelioration of the conditions of existence, hence of survival, and an increase in economic opportunity had always been followed by a rise in population that eventually consumed the gains achieved, now for the first time in history, both the economy and the knowledge were growing fast enough to generate a continuing flow of investment and technological innovation, a flow that lifted beyond visible limits the ceiling of Malthus' positive check.[3]

The contemporary ecological crisis of not only the Third World but the planet as a whole, however, has once again revealed the visibility of these limits in the long term. The contradictory needs for great care of the environment to accompany demographic expansion and yet for a generalized affluence to slow the latter down have become, along with avoidance of nuclear disaster, the overriding concerns of our epoch.

Environmental improvements can play a crucial role in expansive epochs of history. The most obvious case is that of the Netherlands whose very existence as a prosperous agrarian and commercial entity depended upon its reclamation of land from the sea by canals and dykes. The economic prosperity they made possible was, nevertheless, the underlying reason for these great endeavours to be undertaken. Yet defence of the community from Spanish oppression was also required, a defence in which, as we have seen, the environmental features of the country played a crucial part.[4] Economics and geopolitics have generally been dominant in

3. D. Landes, *The Unbound Prometheus: Technological Change and Industrial Development in Western Europe from 1750 to the Present*, Cambridge University Press 1969, p. 41.

4. See above, pp. 66–7.

inspiring and protecting environmental improvements and advantages, although aesthetic considerations, such as architecture, parks and gardens, or conservationalist ones, as with zoos, game parks and natural history museums, have also had some significance.

The remaining two sets of activities of the material sphere of freedom comprise the creative dimensions of wider economic activity and of geopolitical life. A society can acquire a surplus over and above that necessary for its survival either by producing it itself or by levying it from other societies. The former method is economic in character and the latter geopolitical but they both pursue an economic end. The mode of livelihood, or the nature of the productive forces and of contention with destruction and their technical modus operandi, can have a decisive influence over both sets of activities, as has already been remarked.

The orthodox Marxist position on the matter, of course, is that the economic level provides the ultimately determinant dynamic in the shape of the *development* of the productive forces. This permits the accumulation of the surplus, conditioning other social development in the process. Cohen argues in favour of this 'developmental thesis' as follows. If certain facts are given, namely scarcity, human intelligence and human rationality, then societies will develop their productive forces since it is rational for them to do so.[5] However, an equally rational course for some societies, although not of course for all, can be that of military conquest and thereby the acquisition of a surplus either by exacting tribute or imposing themselves as a new ruling class.

Engels argues for this primacy of the economic level, and the development of productive forces within it, by pointing to the indispensability of material production to cultural life and social existence. As he said at Marx's graveside,

> Marx discovered the law of development of human history: the simple fact ... that mankind must first of all eat, drink, have shelter and clothing, before it can pursue politics, science, art, religion, etc.: that therefore the production of the immediate material means of subsistence and consequently the degree of economic development attained by a given people or during a given epoch, form the foundation upon which the state institutions, the legal conceptions, art and even the ideology or religion of the people concerned have been evolved, and in the light of which they must therefore be explained.[6]

However, this argument falls to the ground once it is appreciated that

---

5. G.A. Cohen, *Karl Marx's Theory of History: A Defence*, Oxford 1978. pp. 150–60.
6. Frederick Engels, *Speech at the Graveside of Karl Marx, Marx and Engels Selected Works*, Moscow 1968, p. 435.

there are many institutions, language, morality, etc., also indispensable to cultural life and social existence.[7]

Engels elsewhere suggests that the development of the productive forces has priority over that of means of violence in historical explanation since weapons need to be produced, reflecting the level of economic development.[8] This overlooks the fact that production needs also to be defended by military powers and weaponry, whose provision, moreover, in earlier times could constrain and latterly stimulate the level and type of productive advance in question, depending on the quality of the concomitant mode of security. Certain backward peoples, notably nomadic ones, could indeed deploy weaponry capable of yielding tribute from conquered populations, kept in subsequent subjection, which reflected their respective modes of security and modes of livelihood or *types* of production *and* destruction contention, not their levels of production alone. Conversely, military imperatives have in modern times often instigated economic development as a recent precondition and byproduct of security, as with Japan's industrialization and imperialism, after the Meiji Restoration, and Russia's after the Crimean War. The use of military force, which in conquest reflects the mode of security and ultimately geoeconomic powers, is likely to have provided a frequent way class societies were formed and an indispensable means of reproducing themselves, at least before capitalism; above all, this is likely with the onset and during the long predominance of agriculture, which rendered a sedentary peasantry vulnerable to nomadic invasions or to existing class societies. As we have already mentioned, Bloch says, 'Where every free man remained a warrior, liable to be constantly called to service and distinguished from the pick of the fighting-men by nothing essential in his equipment, the peasant had no difficulty in avoiding subjection to the manorial regime'.[9]

Once class societies exist it is not the community which decides collectively whether to attack others, but the ruling orders or classes who do so, usually alone. All that is necessary for the dominant classes in society to overcome scarcity is an effective method of surplus extraction, and they have often been in a position by means of military superiority to enforce such a regime with dispatch, dispensing with the need for economic advance, so tardy and often costly in pre-capitalist times. The essential form of ownership for pre-capitalist ruling classes generally, therefore, was

---

7. G.A. Cohen has pointed this out in 'Restricted and Inclusive Historical Materialism' in *Marx en Perspective*, textes reunis par Bernard Chavance, Ecoles des Hautes Etudes en Sciences Sociales, Paris 1985, pp. 53–76.

8. Frederick Engels, *Anti-Dühring*, (1878), Moscow 1954.

9. Marc Bloch, *Feudal Society*, tr. L.A. Maryon, Routledge, London 1961, p. 248.

that of means of coercion with which to conquer and subdue by the use, or, preferably the show, of force. Repression and intimidation required a more or less exclusive ruling-class monopoly of force, which then permitted the exaction of tribute or the ownership of means of production as a consequence.

Such coercive class systems, nevertheless, have often been harmful to economic development in history, when they have not been able to rely on sophisticated economies for their weaponry and finances. The geopolitical and political or coercive route to surplus extraction and the economic or consensual route have involved quite different social systems and histories, the former leading to slavery and serfdom, the latter to wage-labour and petty commodity production under late feudalism and capitalism. Pre-capitalist ruling strata, such as slave-owners and feudal landlords, strove for rapid ways to enlarge the absolute surplus available to them by amassing estates and land, slaves and serfs; that is, by a geographical and comparatively swift quantitative expansion of the productive forces in league with their modes of security. Their normal method was warfare and the development of the means of violence, although in Europe, and sometimes elsewhere, it also involved encouraging the slower process of deforestation and environmental enlargement. Capitalists have pursued relative surplus extraction in preference by reinvesting much of the surplus in improving or developing the productive forces. As Wood says, 'Before labour productivity becomes the dominant means of increasing surplus, the expansion of property, inside or outside the home country, is a means of increasing surplus. This, incidentally, also means that territorial expansion of an imperialist "kind" may develop as an outgrowth of pre-capitalist economic activity.'[10] Productive improvements could still occur in pre-capitalist times, but they were not essential to the dynamic of social life, while under capitalism they became the raison d'être of the system.

It might be argued, as Wright has recently done, that while the productive forces developed only slowly in pre-capitalist epochs, they did nevertheless grow and so could still form the dynamic of their societies.[11] The development of the productive forces consists in the emergence of superior methods or knowledge, which then enhance the means of production. New techniques of this sort are only rarely relinquished since they can survive physical destruction of the means of production in which they are

10. Ellen Meiksins Wood, *Peasant-Citizen and Slave*, Verso, London 1989. Wood then qualifies this statement by postulating a centrifugal tendency undermining the centralizing one which does not disprove the point above.
11. Erik Olin Wright, 'Giddens' Critique of Marxism', *New Left Review* 138, March–April 1983, pp. 27–8.

embodied.[12] Moreover, ruling classes have always had an interest in encouraging productivity improvements so as to raise the surplus.

However, as Wright admits, exploited classes can often lose heavily from productivity advances, which can bring intensified toil or unemployment in their train, as in the case of the onset of the Industrial Revolution. There may well be vested interests against the improvements of productivity, due not only to peasant or proletarian Luddism, but also to those propertied sectors, such as backward capitalist ones today, which stand to lose by them.

It is by no means clear that modes of production have always induced productive development. Ancient slavery provided an obvious, if sometimes problematic, source of surplus, but was not conducive to technological developments, which were largely absent in antiquity, as Marxist authors have themselves remarked. 'Economically, the slave mode of production led to technological stagnation: there was no impulse to labour-saving improvements within it. Thus Alexandrine technology on the whole persisted throughout the Roman Empire: few significant inventions were made, none was ever widely applied.'[13] Similarly, the absence of secure, private ownership in land constrained advances in Moslem agriculture for centuries, even while commerce and horticulture or handicrafts around or within towns were encouraged by private ownership.

> The corollary of the legal absence of stable private property in land was the economic spoliation of agriculture in the great Islamic Empires. The original Arab conquests in the Middle Ages and North Africa in general seem initially to have preserved or repaired in general pre-existent agricultural patterns, if without adding notably to them. But the subsequent waves of nomadic invasion often proved to be durably destructive in their impact on settled civilization. The two most extreme cases were to be the Hillah devastation of Tunisia and the Turkoman bedouinization of Anatolia. The long-run historical curve in this sense was to point steadily downwards.[14]

Anderson is referring to agrarian production, not technology. Yet in such conditions agrarian technology could hardly develop and in fact stagnated for centuries.

The agrarian-administrative classes and state systems of the pre-capitalist epoch, whose often arbitrary requisitions and fiscal exactions

---

12. This point is made by G.A. Cohen, *Karl Marx's Theory of History* p. 46 and is cited by Wright.

13. Perry Anderson, *Passages from Antiquity to Feudalism*, Verso, London 1974, pp. 132–3.

14. Perry Anderson, *Lineages of the Absolutist State*, Verso, London 1974, p. 449.

upon commerce and industry, together with their frequent ideological depreciation of them, were so deplored by Adam Smith, also constituted crucial obstacles to economic development. In earlier times, the dangers of change frequently motivated a clinging to social stability above all else, as with Ancient Egypt, which after any disruption attempted to restore the status quo ante. Where change was tolerated, moreover, it could involve regression, not advance, as in late Sung and Chi'n and Mongol (Yuan) China. Even in the Ming recovery from 1368 onwards, trade and contacts with foreigners were banned and, while Chinese agricultural productivity continued to grow, there was a relapse of technical progress in the crucial metallurgical industries after advance in the earlier medieval period.[15] China showed much greater technological dynamism than Europe, India or the Near East for centuries, but after the early medieval watershed it began to become less creative.

Some forms of social development can involve actual technical regression and oblivion. A pertinent instance of this was the abandonment of wheeled vehicles with the widespread adoption of the camel for main transportation purposes in Arabia, Spain, Iran and elsewhere in the Middle East in the early and middle centuries of the first millennium. The trades of harness and wagon manufacture fell into disuse and neglect. The extraordinary decline of the wheel into oblivion cannot be ascribed to economic forces alone, although pack camels were certainly cheaper than wheeled vehicles for long-range transport; the vested interests, for example, of the camel merchants lay behind the fiscal law of Palmyra, the caravan centre in Syria, in 137 A.D., whose taxation of competition with camels was prohibitive.[16] In addition it is highly likely that the political dominance of militarily triumphant camel-breeding nomads led to discrimination against wheeled vehicles in Arabia and elsewhere, especially after the Muslim conquests.[17] Stagnation or advance and then some form of relapse were often hallmarks of pre-capitalist civilizations.

A crucial motor of such pre-capitalist societies as were dynamic, apart arguably from feudalism, was not the *intensive development* of the productive forces, which was usually desultory, but rather the geographical expansion and *extensive* amassment of productive forces and the *development* of forces capable of withstanding or perpetrating destruction, such as ditches and dykes and means of violence. The latter development could rapidly and directly assist both a society's defence and its

---

15. See above, pp. 48–9 and William H. McNeill, *The Pursuit of Power*, Basil Blackwell, Oxford 1983 pp. 25–33, who discusses the extensive literature on the matter.
16. Richard W. Bulliet, *The Camel and the Wheel*, Harvard University Press 1975, pp. 19–21.
17. Ibid., pp. 87–110.

environmental or predatory methods of expanding ownership of the productive forces, so meeting the exigencies of the realm of necessity and of provision of an economic surplus in the realm of freedom, in particular for its ruling classes.

A qualification needs to be made here. It is plausible to argue that modes of livelihood, based on hunting, pastoralism, agriculture, extraction, commerce and industry, succeeded each other according to the secular development of the productive forces. The slow improvement in productive, and of course pre-emptive or reparative, forces brought about the supersession of pastoralism by agriculture, and then the marginalization of agriculture by industry. These shifts involved the coexistence of different modes of livelihood and so of different military capacities, leading to class societies and imperialism. Once the main determinant of military capacity and the mode of security is admitted to be the mode of livelihood, then the development of the productive forces remains the long-term dynamic explaining the secular rise and decline of particular *types* of modes of production and class societies. The contention here is that it does so in the medium and short terms only via the mediation of military force and competition between modes of security, which immediately 'select' the property regime or mode of production, before the emergence of full-scale capitalism (and even after it for those such as Japan and Russia which switched to capitalism for mainly security reasons). Pre-capitalist modes of production, then, say slavery or Islamic agricultural economies, arose and fell because of their degree of compatibility with modes of security, whose viability depended on their answering to the development of destructive forces, especially of the means of violence. Nevertheless, modes of livelihood (and so ultimately types of modes of production and security, such as the feudal or Islamic extractive agrarian regimes) arose and declined because of the character and development of the productive forces, including those used to make arms.

None of this is to deny that, even if the economic level is not necessarily decisive in the short and medium terms in developing the forces of production, it can still be decisive in providing the immediate reasons for much geopolitical activity, notably the wherewithal of the ruling classes. It has already been suggested that economic objectives are likely to provide the most powerful rationale for much belligerent conduct and imperialist domination. The expansive and aggressive dimensions of geopolitical existence, therefore, are often predatory or economic in origin.

Nevertheless, the pre-emptive or reparative moments of geopolitical activity have far wider sources which it would be imprudent to ignore, since they comprise important exceptions to the rule of an economic rationale for imperialist aggression. Attack can be undertaken for either of two sets of reasons, the one economic and the other because of modes of security. To resume briefly what has already been said above, military aggression has sometimes been launched from fear of a potential aggressor, that is from the dynamic of the mode of security, not the mode of production. Such preventative belligerence is basically inspired by the need to survive, as, for example, with the Israeli strike on Iraq's nuclear capacity. Yet success in defensive operations can initiate a society into imperialist practices and expansion, notably so in the history of Prussia and Russia. Imperialism can possess either a largely economic rationale, as is characteristically the case with capitalist states, or a defensive geopolitical rationale, as has been primarily the case with the USSR, or a hybrid economic-cum-defensive geopolitical rationale, as with modern Israel. Moreover, internal security can be important or even preponderant in instigating belligerent behaviour; foreign adventures have long been a means of diversion from domestic problems. Wars can be undertaken as a ready method of pre-empting not only external assault but also internal class conflict or ruling-class strife, as well as of seizing economic advantages. Such underlying objectives are likely to be adorned in suitable ideological clothes, whose availability as a result can be a decisive factor in the timing and even the feasibility of their realization.

However, whether due to economics or security, whether aggressive or defensive, geopolitical activity is assisted by proficiency in producing and deploying weapons. This in turn reflects the *nature* of the productive forces in a society's mode of livelihood, although not necessarily their level of development, which can be rudimentary and yet effective for military purposes. Nomads, as we have seen, had a decisive advantage in the age of massed cavalry, despite their primitive economic conditions, because of their mobile mode of livelihood. Military prowess since at least the Industrial Revolution, by contrast, has increasingly been correlated with economic performance and might, as productive development furnishes weapons capable of prevailing almost anywhere. Yet the example of North Vietnam and others has proved that even today the local conditions can favour the less-developed belligerent. In both its rationale and means of equipment geopolitical activity has generally been heavily conditioned and marked by the wider requirements of economic life, whose long-run metamorphoses from one mode of livelihood to another thereby govern the secular possibilities open for modes of security, modes of production and class society.

This argument is in effect maintaining that in pre-capitalist times there was generally a symbiosis or outright fusion, as under feudalism, of the modes of production and security, nurtured by modes of livelihood. The former often reigned in their realms of freedom, but with geopolitics, especially warfare and coercion, as the crucial means of expanding and extracting the surplus from the masses. Moreover, this prominent role of coercion was due to the fact that geopolitics and geoeconomics reigned in their domains of necessity by protecting social existence and the systems of exploitation in question. This can be made clear by examining a particular instance, the crucial one of feudalism, from which capitalism first developed.

3. The Case of Feudalism

Feudalism has usually been characterized in two distinct fashions. For the traditional school of academic history, it was obvious that feudalism was a primarily military system, needing to be analysed in terms of fiefs, military service and gradations of vassalage and sovereignty.[18] Within the Marxist school it has been equally obvious that feudalism was a mode of production, based on serfdom and the manorial economy, albeit one revealing the peculiarity of employing direct coercion to reproduce subjection. For Marxists the economic and the military hence coincided, but with the dynamic of the system remaining economic in character, that is, the development of the productive forces.

Bloch represents something of a synthesis of these two views, but in an openly provisional manner.

> A subject peasantry; widespread use of the service tenement (i.e. the fief) instead of salary, which was out of the question; the supremacy of a class of specialized warriors; that of obedience and protection which bind man to man, and, within the warrior class, assume the distinctive form called vassalage; fragmentation of authority leading inevitably to disorder, and in the midst of all this, the survival of other forms of association, family and state, of which the latter, during the second feudal age, was to acquire renewed strength – such then might seem to be the fundamental features of European feudalism.[19]

This masterly outline of Western feudalism was not completed, however, by an account of the coherence and course of the system.

If the foregoing argument is correct, then the most promising way to clarify the structural and dynamic character of feudalism is to consider both the systemic manner in which it reproduced itself (that is, its conditions of continued existence), and the historical character of its development (that is, the nature of its dynamic). In fact, it will be argued here that feudalism was regulated in its history by two types of motor, one in each of its realms of social existence.

---

18. See F.L. Ganschof, *Feudalism*, Longman, London, 1961, for a classic work of the school.
19. Marc Bloch, *Feudal Society*, p. 446.

Societies usually possess both a dominant mode and motor of production and a mode and motor of security, nurtured by their composite manner of livelihood. Feudalism was characterized by a fusion of these two modes, an analysis of which is required before the nature of its respective pair of motors can be grasped. The two essential preconditions of feudalism for Bloch were that knightly vassals had to be the only professional warriors and that the institution of the fief replaced other forms of authority.[20]

Clearly, economic factors, above all serfdom and secure landownership, need to be brought into the analysis and the conditionality of landholdings related to warfare and the manorial economy. The essential principle of the system was the exchange of land and protection for service – military service by the lord and labour service by the peasant. Lords offered protection for their vassals and serfs in their *persons* as well as their *landholdings* on condition that they performed the relevant service for their rank. In fact protection was usually of the persons of the vassals' and serfs' familial dependants as well as of their own. A complex parcellization of sovereignty was maintained, tolerating some independent allodial holdings by peasants and sometimes certain autonomous towns for burghers, two vital sources of creativity under late feudalism compared with other pre-capitalist societies.

The indissolubility of rank and economics is well depicted by Bloch:

> In the Frankish period, the majority of those who commended themselves sought from their new master something more than protection. Since this powerful man was at the same time a wealthy man, they also expected him to contribute to their support. From St Augustine, who in the closing decades of the Western Empire describes the poor in search of a patron who would provide them with the wherewithal to eat, to the Merovingian formula ... we hear the same importunate cry: that of the empty stomach. The lord for his part was not influenced solely by the ambition to exercise authority over men; through their agency he often sought to lay hold of property. From the outset in short protective relationships had their economic aspect – vassalage as well as the others.[20]

An essential characteristic of such a system was the militarization of the

20. Marc Bloch, 'European Feudalism' in *Mélanges Historiques*, Tome I, SEVPEN, 1963, p. 180. As Lacoste points out, the absence of these two preconditions in North Africa ruled out a feudal development: 'In the Maghreb, the presence of warrior herdsmen and montagnards made it impossible for a professional warrior class to emerge. The vassal system could not emerge because of the strength of tribal structures and the permanent nature of the state structures imposed on them.' Yves Lacoste, *Ibn Khaldun*, Verso, London 1984. p. 109.
21. Marc Bloch, *Feudal Society*, p. 163.

ruling class, a fact which Marxists depreciate or ignore, but which Bloch rightly sees as central. The Roman ruling classes preceding feudalism, like the capitalist ones succeeding them, were exempted from military labour, although certain of their members pursued military or administrative careers in positions of high command or office. The bulk could enjoy their surplus without reciprocal obligations, at least to the community. The feudal warrior nobility, on the other hand, exposed itself to loss of life or limb in the course of its military duties. Death and destruction were its trade and occupational hazards. Most notable families in high feudal times lasted only a few generations. It might well be asked why they exposed themselves to such risks when their predecessors and successors among ruling classes did not have to.

It is Engels's view that:

> The separation of society into an exploiting and an exploited class, a ruling and an oppressed class, was the necessary consequence of the restricted and deficient development of production in former times. So long as the total social labour only yields a produce which but slightly exceeds that barely necessary for the existence of all; so long, therefore, as labour engages all or almost all of the time of the majority of the members of society – so long, of necessity, this society is divided into classes. Side by side with the great majority, exclusively bond slaves to labour, arises a class freed from directly productive labour, which looks after the general affairs of society: the direction of labour, state business, law, science, arts, etc. It is, therefore, the law of division of labour that lies at the basis of the division into classes.[22]

Engels holds that class society arises from the fact that 'labour engages all or almost all of the labour time of society' due to exiguous levels of production. This fails to take account of the fact that however much time has been invested in production, its output and life itself still have to be defended; as we have seen, this explains why geopolitics is as crucial a social level as economics in either realm of social life. In primitive societies the way of life was such that classes did not need to exist, despite low levels of production. If feudalism had a warrior ruling class while other agrarian societies, such as Ancient Roman and Greece, did not have, this is explained not by levels of production, but by questions of security. Feudalism emerged out of anarchy and chaos, both in Western Europe and Japan, due to the breakdown of an imperial order, in the former in the Dark Ages, in the latter with the strife of the early Middle Ages as the samurai class usurped control in the provinces. In each case a privatization of coercive power in the countryside was the result.

---

22. Frederick Engels, *Anti-Dühring*, pp. 333–4.

Feudalism emerged in these situations by installing a decentralized mode of security, not by reconstituting the prior mode of centralized security. As Sartre points out against Engels's position here:

> in the Middle Ages, as Marc Bloch has said, a noble was originally a person who owned a horse; and if the peasants gathered around the castle, accepted the constraints of serfdom, forced labour and the communal kitchen, this was indeed due to a certain division of labour, but not one Engels mentions. The peasant asks the nobles to undertake the labour of war, that is to say, to defend him with violence against violence in the milieu of scarcity.[23]

What particularized the milieu, however, was not scarcity, common to all societies, but the need for defence against unbridled aggression. It was in contention with military destruction that feudalism acquired its peculiar decentralization and concomitant warrior ruling class. The fact that Western European feudalism did so against external destruction from Arabs, Norsemen and Magyars in the Dark Ages, while Japanese feudalism did so from internal imperial dissolution perpetrated by the samurai class itself is important in explaining the origins of the system, indeed its peculiar features, in the respective cases; but it is not crucial in explaining its structure which was, quite apart from the matter of its origins, capable of reproducing itself by reason of the decentralization of violence in the hands of a warrior nobility and hence the need for decentralized protection.

The vassal system permitted a measure of order to be retained within the decentralization of the mode of security: but feudalism possessed no mechanism to ensure unity, as opposed to conditional allegiance, upon its fragmented parts so long as proper state-powers were lacking. Vassals could withdraw their allegiance if their liege could not protect them, a custom that fostered the perpetuation of the generalized insecurity justifying it. The decentralization of feudalism, so peculiar among social systems, was therefore clearly interlocked with its other idiosyncrasy, its tolerance, indeed encouragement of warfare among its ruling class. Its fusion of production and security systems entrained a further peculiarity of feudalism, the fact that its lords participated in the village community as owners of watermills and other machinery and as dispensers of justice and enforcers of internal peace; the coercive role in exploitation of the serfs, which Marxists underscore, was a perennial concomitant, since security of person and peasant property made for security of general property.

The argument so far has stressed the exchange of protection and land

---

23. Jean-Paul Sartre, *Critique of Dialectical Reason*, Verso, London 1976 p. 145.

on the one hand for service on the other, whether by vassal or peasant. This analysis could be extended to consider the role of guilds, at least in Europe, and the priesthood in both Europe and Japan. Guildmasters provided maintenance and protection as well as tools and training to their apprentices, who reciprocated with their labour services. Priests provided magical forms of protection for their flocks and their patrons in exchange for mundane protection and upkeep, indeed in the case of monasteries for lands and estates. Yet this reciprocity of exchange, which was the hallmark of feudal society, only organized the domains of necessity. Feudal societies also posssessed their realms of freedom, largely the preserve of their ruling orders and classes, the warrior nobles and the leading priests. The province of necessity in the feudal realm of freedom furthered the exploitation of the serfs within the manorial economy or by the acquisition of new manors and estates. The Marxist analysis of feudalism is appropriate at this level, illuminating the process whereby the privileges of the ruling strata were obtained and reproduced. Feudal society did not only inhabit the realm of necessity, engaging in an exchange of necessary equivalences, as its advocates were wont to argue; it possessed an inegalitarian realm of freedom, as well as one of necessity, within both of which exploitation occurred.[24]

Feudalism possessed two types of motor, one in each of its realms of social life. For Marxism, the dynamic of capitalism is twofold: the accumulation of capital at the level of the property regime, or production relations; and the development of the productive forces. For feudalism, the two corresponding forms of creative dynamic in production were: the accumulation of estates and towns by warfare and dynastic, usually nuptial, alliance; and the development of the forces of production and means of war. This conception of creative dynamic needs to be enlarged to take account of the geographical expansion as well as development of the productive forces and so of the development of pre-emptive and reparative forces and of land reclamation to contend with natural destruction of areas brought under cultivation from forest, marsh or sea.

Feudalism was also characterized, however, by a twofold preservative dynamic in its realm of necessity: firstly, the enforcement of security, both internal and external, by extension of vassalage, law and order; and secondly by a geographical expansion and development of the means of security, that is of weaponry and fortifications, in contending with destruction from external assault or other feudal manors or domains. The

---

24. Exploitation takes place in the realm of necessity by allotting different classes or groups different life-spans, as was markedly the case with feudalism; exploitation occurs in the realm of freedom by reason of the privileged classes' or groups' enjoyment of the surplus.

first type of motor set off the second, the accumulation of estates and towns by some entraining the need for their defence by others. Indeed, the two types of motor of the two realms of social life interlocked, by reason of the military-economic fusion of the system, the accumulation and securement of estates and towns being furthered by both the expansion and the development of the productive forces and the means of security – castles and weapons were used for attack as well as defence. These two types of motor in fact only clearly disassociated as the properly feudal age of vassal networks became anachronistic for the purposes of security. This was due to the emergence of nation-states or centralized modes of security towards which feudalism had been fitfully tending since its birth in generalized insecurity. It took place under the impact of the development both of productive forces in the towns and countryside and of means of security, as artillery undermined local castle defences. Europe possessed in its fragmented, yet continental-wide, geography a great advantage over Japan in urban development: towns could more easily escape the control of lords and princes as a multiplicity of state sites permitted independence, at least for some, such as those of the Hanseatic League and the Low Countries. Indeed, as economic life progressed towards capitalism, relations of production eventually came into dis-junction with modes of security, which precipitated the bourgeois revolutions from below or above.

The mode of mundane security of feudalism, therefore, was at first decentralized and so generative of the insecurity it was its duty to curb. In Western Europe, the curbing and eventual resolution of this contradiction became an indispensable historical boon, without which the productive forces would never have recovered from the Dark Ages or begun to expand or advance towards the Industrial Revolution. Crucial assistance in the continent-wide regulation of the system was given by the mode of magical security – Christendom, centred on the Papacy in Rome. Christian conversion was vital in civilizing and taming the barbarian hordes assailing from without, whether Norsemen or Magyars; while holy war against the common foe, Islam, was essential to the Spaniards in generating the enthusiasm needed to turn the tide of the jihad, and then later to the crusaders, to the accompaniment of heresy-hunting. This gave the continent a fragile unity for a time. Moreover, Christian doctrine and 'peace movements' may have had some deterrent effect on resort to violence; although it must be accepted against this view that the reality of the afterlife was so evident and important to the true believer that it made death a less intimidating threat, even for its perpetrator, so long as penance and absolution were made.

Roman Catholicism, then, was not a contingent carapace of feudalism in the West, but the unifier of its realm of necessity as the guarantor of the

European mode of security; feudalism in Japan could do without such a support because of its insular compactness and isolation. Nevertheless, the stronger the feudal domains of the leading countries, the more dispensable the Papacy itself became; and, indeed, it was periodically dispensed with by king or emperor until eventually Christianity was sundered by the Reformation. The heresies, which had earlier given expression to mass forms of discontent, were taken up by princes themselves. A component of the realm of necessity at its outset, once Europe had entered into an epoch of expansion and creative development, Catholicism became dependent upon the economic and geopolitical fortunes of classes and states.

This analysis of feudalism is itself of course a highly schematic one. It is, however, of use to the extent that it shows how modes of production and security can interlock in history and are both of crucial relevance to understanding social structures.

Economics and geopolitics can share a condominium in the material sphere of freedom, which is conterminous with the realm of freedom's own province of necessity. Their role in the cultural sphere of freedom will now be explored.

4. The Economic and Geopolitical Preconditions of the Cultural Sphere of Freedom

It is plausible to suppose that economics and geopolitics play a decisive role in cultural life. New cultural departures require to be financed and defended and are rarely oblivious of the debts which they incur in the process, if they wish to succeed. Luther benefited from the Peasants' War of 1525 by his support of the princes and vituperation of Müntzer and the rebels, where the Lollards and the Hussites, mainly rebellious peasants, had failed.

Prosperity in the material sphere of freedom and a class structure capable of using its economic wherewithal for non-productive purposes remain necessary conditions of a flourishing and active realm of freedom. A thriving economy is usually a prerequisite and asset to cultural and social life as a whole. A related, but not always concomitant, feature of great importance is that there should be an abundant surplus available to be deployed for non-economic purposes, as in slave antiquity. A class differentiation allowing diversion of the surplus to non-economic activities has long been a necessary, even if not sufficient, condition of cultural vitality, apart from the popular arts of oral poetry and music. A separate warrior caste can provide the means and protection for a vibrant culture. In the great epoch of Athenian civilization for instance, its Greek hinterland was poor compared with Asia Minor; yet its culture was sustained by imperialist wars and tribute.[25]

Another instance, the Carolingian Renaissance, was financed by exactions of tribute after a successful military imperialism, which afforded it, however, only a brief respite. The Italian Renaissance was made possible by the commercial and agrarian prosperity of Quattracento Italy and then undone by its fratricidal divisiveness and vulnerability to external occupation. In each epoch an efflorescence of cultural life was feasible only because of the provision of a protected economic surplus capable of being deflected to non-economic activities.[26] These boons required in turn the existence of a class society in which non-productive or prosperous strata could be supported by a productive population, feudal and urban princes, landlords and warriors and mercantile orders being necessary to extract the surplus and to expend it in part upon social luxuries and in part upon defence. In either case, a sophisticated class society and mode or modes of production were necessary permissive conditions of the vitality of the cultural sphere of freedom.

While material conditions are necessary for the realization of the cultural sphere of freedom, it does not follow that culture is as subordinate

---

25. G.E.M. de Sainte Croix, *Class Struggle in the Ancient Greek World*, Duckworth, London 1981, p. 119.

26. It is notable how many vibrant imperialisms and so great cultural epochs in history were made possible by the profits of precious metals. Ancient Egyptian imperialism and civilization were financed by the goldmines of the eastern desert. In the Ancient Greek world, Athens's naval and imperial pre-eminence in the Aegean and further afield would have been impossible without the Attic silver mines; while Macedonian expansionism was premissed on the early annexation of the Thracian gold mines, with all its huge implications for human culture.

In the modern world, the Spanish dominance of Europe in the sixteenth century, the Golden Age of Spain, was based on the supply of American silver and gold; while Swedish imperialism and court-culture in the seventeenth and eighteenth centuries were founded on the copper and iron industries of the Berslagen; Perry Anderson, *Passages from Antiquity to Feudalism*, pp. 40–45, *Lineages of the Absolutist State*, pp. 71–2, 182–3. What seems relevant here is the ease of appropriation of mining profits and output by the state compared with the difficulties involved in diverting funds from customary revenues, already earmarked for existing expenditures. Such a source of ready funds, therefore, was at least an unusual inus condition of early imperialisms and often a necessary one (an inus condition, it can be recalled, consists, put simply, of a necessary component of a sufficient condition of something).

That imperialist expansion has not always required even any financial basis as a necessary condition is shown by the case of Pan Chao, the great commander and creator of Chinese Turkestan in the first century A.D.; due to eunuch opposition at the imperial court he was unable to obtain finance for troops from China other than a few officers when he embarked in 80 A.D. on his second expedition to the region. He gained such troops and material as he needed from the allied states and rulers themselves against the recalcitrant ones, since the former cherished the memory of the peace and order which he had introduced there on his first mission. His army eventually reached Samarkand, securing passage for the commerce of the Silk Road and the transmission of Buddhism to the Far East. See C.P. Fitzgerald, *China: a Short Cultural History*, 4th Edition, Barrie, London, 1976, pp. 194–201.

to material life as even the most latitudinarian Marxism implies. The Renaissance, for example, diverted resources and energies into construction of public and religious buildings on a massive scale, when investment in the economy could have had a more substantial effect on productive development. Of course such diversions might be interpreted by Marxism as necessary for legitimating class society, even if economically and militarily otiose or harmful. Yet the cultural sphere of freedom has absorbed surplus expenditures on a scale which has often far exceeded that useful or necessary for class harmony. The resources and human energies diverted from productive employment and invested in Egyptian pyramids, Inca and Aztec temples, the monasteries of Tibet and the religious buildings of the medieval and Mughal world outstripped what on even the most generous allowance for the specific needs of social harmony seems likely to have been necessary.

Just as the realm of freedom as a whole possesses considerable autonomy from that of necessity, so its cultural sphere possesses a wide – sometimes beneficial, sometimes damaging – leeway with regard to the material sphere of freedom encompassing its own province of necessity. The epoch of the Renaissance, to return to our earlier example, gave rise to the scientific revolution of the seventeenth century, which in turn made possible the Industrial Revolution over a century later. The profound discoveries and inventions in the spheres of knowledge and communications, which were the long-term consequences of the mental emancipation begun by the Renaissance, can hardly be explained as the product of capitalist development *on its own*, even if obviously indebted to it; the expanding urban capitalism of Tokugawa Japan, for example, manifested no tendency to induce anything comparable. A conjunction of favourable conditions in the material and cultural spheres of society, the prosperity of late medieval Europe, the rise of nation-states and the recovery from destruction and oblivion of Europe's technological and cultural patrimony made possible first the Italian and then the European Renaissance and later the 'European miracle' in their aftermath.[27]

It is possible, nevertheless, to argue that the Industrial Revolution has itself inaugurated an epoch of continual, even if periodically crisis-ridden, expansion, in which the economic level has become its perpetually determinant moment. Economic strength increasingly provides the means for military strength, environmental control and scientific or cultural

---

27. See Perry Anderson, *Passages from Antiquity to Feudalism* and *Lineages of the Absolutist State*, for a Marxist classic on the subject. The technologies of classical antiquity stood more in need of revival than its cultures since much of the latter were widely diffused during the Middle Ages, from Arab lands and other sources. It was the technological heritage, moreover, which was to have the profoundest influence on the incipient Industrial Revolution of the West.

discoveries and advances. The dependence of such achievements on technology is broadening with the growing complexity of the productive forces of society. The impact of the microelectronics revolution on culture and education, for example, promises to be profound. From merely providing the means of activity in the cultural sphere of freedom on request, the economic level is increasingly shaping and determining the nature of the demands which are made upon it. The industrialization of science and the services sector testifies to the ubiquitous expansionism of capitalism, as it refashions and develops the conditions of possibility for human existence as a whole, whether in the sphere of sport, leisure, art, knowledge, communications or education.

7

Ideas, Ideals and Material Forces: The Interaction between the Realms and Provinces of Freedom and Necessity

Human history has witnessed a long interplay between ideas, ideals and material forces, whose course has been deflected by the simultaneous interaction between the realms and provinces of freedom and necessity. While consideration has already been given to the terms within which the latter can be understood, the same is not yet true for the former. A brief clarification of the categories involved can form a preliminary to assessing the significance of what they denote for the theory of history.

1. Introduction and Explication of Terms

Those espousing materialism, such as Marxists, environmentalists and geopolitical thinkers, have tended to emphasize the role of economics or military affairs in human history where their idealist opponents stress the role of ideas and ideals. Yet the material activities of the former kind are saturated with ideas and values: the very notion of action, however physical its result may be, presupposes that intentions and choices of value intervene in the process; while ideas and ideals in turn depend upon material conditions. It is necessary to consider what could be adjudged as either materialist or idealist phenomena or explanations before assessing their comparative importance for any theory of history.

It is usually possible to interpret historically significant activities in terms of the intentions of their agents, whether conscious or not, and of certain ideas about the world on which they impinge. Moreover, at least some of these activities involve or reveal value preferences. Consequently, any investigator highlighting the role of agents as the prime movers of historical change might seem to be committed to an idealist theory of it. Vico's famous dictum of 'verum factum' is a notable instance of this anthropocentrism, leading him to the conclusion that human history is easier to comprehend than nature, since we made the former but not the latter.[1]

For those, such as Hegel, for whom a divine agency is at work, history needs to be interpreted in theological terms. Yet the idealist emphasis is just as marked, even if human history manifests not humanity's aims and goals alone, but also those of God, who is the ultimate author of all. Marx's claim that 'men make their own history, but they do not make it just as they please; they do not make it under circumstances chosen by themselves, but under circumstances directly encountered, given and transmitted from the past',[2] accepts the same productivist problematic as Vico and Hegel; its qualifying clause indicates the need to redress an idealist creationism in favour of a materialist one.

An alternative approach is to found a materialist theory, or at least the materialist moment of a realist theory, on a rejection of the proposition that the action relevant to understanding history is itself always human. Vico is mistaken in claiming that human history is wholly created by humanity since nature also makes a contribution. It is not only human action, but the action of nature as well, which plays a crucial role in the fate of our species. Nature itself can act, indeed its creation of homo sapiens is what led to the human story in the first place. Marx of course admitted these obvious facts, but couched them, as we have seen, in a productivist framework. The ongoing activities of physical nature, whether destructive with entropy and natural disasters or creative with the fertility of the soil and the other resources of the planet, have had a profound effect on the development of civilization.

It has already been argued above that human communities must first avoid their destruction in their realms of necessity before engaging in free activity. In an abstraction from relations between societies, it is possible to conceive human history as unfolding in two arenas of activity: in the first, the realm of necessity, nature acts on mankind and then mankind back on nature (a reaction to which nature in turn reacts); and only in the second, the realm of freedom, does mankind originate the action and nature the reaction.

There is, however, a third possibility to be considered, one which admits of activities between and within groups. Nature and mankind do not exhaust the sources of agency even if God is excluded from the purview. For structures of nature and social behaviour or institutions can also be created or activated, albeit via the action of natural entities and

---

1. G. Vico, The New Science, N2–331.
2. Karl Marx, The Eighteenth Brumaire of Louis Bonaparte, p. 1.

human beings or groups. The marital exchanges between primitive tribes can abide by rules and structures of exogamy unknown to their members. Similarly, the languages of human groups, such as primitive or nomadic tribes, can be governed by rules of grammar of which its practitioners are quite ignorant. In such cases, it can be argued, a collective unconscious, with its own teleology, can be posited as active, as in different ways with Lévi-Strauss's depth structures or Chomsky's transformational grammar. But, in yet other cases such as the role of DNA in inheritance or of the capitalist market-place in economic development, a general structure can appertain to natural or human relations or activities which cannot be ascribed to any collective consciousness, or unconscious, among the parties involved. The role of structural agencies of this sort in explaining social or economic expansion or crisis, due, for example, to the extension, amelioration or impairment of the hidden hand of the capitalist market-place, has been considerable in human history. No theory that ignores it can do proper justice to the complexity of the subject.

Nature can act and humans can act and structures can be activated by both of them. Indeed, each social level manifests activity of each of these three kinds. Nature provokes and contributes, along with labour, to production, and does so within structures of ownership and distribution which can help or hinder the process; meanwhile environmental degradation has to be offset by preventative or reparative activity within a more or less suitable mode of livelihood.[3] In the cultural spheres of social existence nature can be mute or passive and the activities involved can issue from human beings within the structures of their coexistence, such as languages and public mores.[4] The question arises of the relationship obtaining between the material and cultural spheres and how it is to be explicated.

Just as any given historical event or process, such as the provision of military capabilities, often does not exclusively inhabit either the realm of

---

3. On the map of social existence on pp. 26–7, it can be seen that the total and partial disasters of columns (A) and (B) consist, in the case of its material levels of forms of natural destruction, while in column (C) the activity pre-empting or repairing them is undertaken by mankind within various modes of social life designated by column (D), which are also capable of organizing the creative activities in the realm of freedom of column (E). The military activities of the mode of mundane security represent an exception, since it is other societies, not nature, which are capable of committing the disasters of columns (A) and (B). This is of less importance than it might appear, once it is recognized that the destruction perpetrated by human beings in warfare is as dependent as production on geographical and demographic conditions.

4. On the map of social existence on pp. 26–7, it can be seen that the total and partial disasters of columns (A) and (B) consist in the cultural spheres of cultural phenomena, such as amorality, aphasia and oblivion. Nature might contribute to them, as with the destruction of a society's cultural patrimony in an earthquake or a war, but only when a disaster has taken place in the material spheres of social existence.

freedom or that of necessity, so certain structures or sets of events cannot be identified as exclusively material or cultural in character. This is a fact which Marxism above all must concede since communism itself is supposed to be a civilization at once materially and culturally superior to bourgeois society, which in its turn has encompassed both a capitalist economic structure and a network of cultural institutions.

This fact does not, however, exclude the possibility of *explaining* historical phenomena primarily in either materialist or cultural terms. It is necessary to distinguish between historical events, actions, structures or processes on the one hand and explanations of them on the other.

A materialist explanation of a phenomenon needs to account for an explanandum in terms of a materialist explanans; while an idealist explanation needs to do the same in terms of an idealist or cultural explanans. The explanandum itself can be either materialist or cultural or a combination of the two. A structural explanation can be considered either materialist or idealist depending on whether the structure it invokes as the explanans is itself materialist or idealist. This latter usage is at any rate employed by Marx, for whom an explanation of social life in terms of economic structures is materialist, since such structures appertain to a set of relations between and among agents and things engaged in material activity.

A materialist explanans can consist of material entities or a structure of such entities, such as a geographical location or change or a demographic trend. Alternatively, it can comprise an activity, event or process trans-forming or preserving nature or physical entities, whether it emanates from nature itself or from human society; while within a society a require-ment or interest can be said to possess a materialist character if it furthers physical survival or well-being.[5]

An idealist explanans can also assume several forms. The older school of narrative historians, of whom Carlisle was a prime example, high-lighted the conscious intentions of great or prominent personalities and the quirks of character animating them, including predisposition to ideas of one sort or another; while a more sophisticated liberal historiography has concentrated upon the emergence and spread of ideals and systems of ethical or political thought, such as the rise of Christianity in Ancient Rome and the European Middle Ages and of Protestantism in northern Europe or the rise of civic freedoms and representative government in

---

5. These rubrics, as they have been expounded, are somewhat arbitrary. Space forbids an extended defence of them, but it should be remembered that there is no objection to characterizing a phenomenon, such as a sluggish growth of population, as a material explanans, simply because it might itself in the role of explanandum be capable of being explained by an idealist phenomenon, such as religious prohibition of early marriage.

England according to the Whig interpretation of history. The frequency with which the totalitarian regimes of the twentieth century are attributed to their ideological antecedents in nineteenth-century systems of thought, in particular those of Hegel, Nietzsche and of course Marx, indicates how widespread is the influence of what may be called an ethicocentric idealism. Yet again, an idealist explanans can consist of the discovery of new knowledge, such as the scientific revolution of the seventeenth and eighteenth centuries, to which the Industrial Revolution has been partly ascribed.

For Marxism cultural values and ideals need to be understood in terms of the institutions which embody them and the requirements and interests they serve in the economic base of a society. The property system and the vested interests it involves are ultimately to be explained in their historicity by the long-term development of the productive forces; and this, as we shall shortly see, is not as unambiguously materialist a phenomenon as might be supposed. While Marxism is inconsistent with an ethicocentric idealism, it is by no means incompatible with a knowledge-centred idealism, albeit one which can admit, unlike Hegel's, an ultimately materialist foundation. This type of point, however, can only be made intelligible after drawing certain further distinctions.

An explanation can assume a form which is neither exclusively materialist nor idealist but what may be termed meta-materialist or meta-idealist. A meta-materialist explanation possesses a triadic structure in which a materialist explanans (which can be a composite one) accounts for an idealist explanandum which then forms the explanans of a materialist outcome. Thus, an earthquake might engender traumas among the survivors, which in turn bring about psychosomatic disorders and disease. A complication could well exist in which the adult victims of the earthquake with their knowledge of what was happening and of death itself suffered traumas whereas the infants did not.[6] While an earthquake can be the precipitant of traumas, the post-infantile age of the surviving victims can be another permissive condition, forming part of the composite explanans. The middle term of the sequence is itself idealist, but only to make possible a materialist explanation of a higher order, a meta-materialist explanation.

An idealist explanation of an event is often merely what could comprise the latter stages of a meta-materialist explanation. Thus, while the rise of Islam can account for the Arab subjugation of the Middle East, the

---

6. The survivors rescued from the Mexico City earthquake of September 1985 have been often prey to severe psychological problems, a free-floating anxiety and nightmares of being buried alive; but, significantly, among the babies, psychic impairment has apparently been negligible or non-existent. *The Times*, 28 April 1986, p. 12.

Maghreb and Spain in the sense of being an unusual, but necessary, component of a sufficient condition of such an event, it is possible to offer explanations of Islam's own emergence and early characteristics in terms of the geopolitical and geoeconomic requirements of the Arabian peninsula in the seventh century, that is, the need for unity between its nomadic and sedentary populations if the north–south trade was not to be irretrievably ruined and the need for an outlet for the peninsula's surplus population.[7] Such an explanation might be empirically inadequate and its functional cast be impugned on theoretical grounds for failing to stipulate any mechanism whereby the religious event was uniquely related to social requirements.[8] But so long as it is admitted that the rise of Islam could have explained why Arab conquests took place and that it is possible to offer some type of materialist explanation of the rise of Islam, if only an oversimplified one – such as that it issued from the covetous designs of Arabian merchants on the trade of the Fertile Crescent – then it is simultaneously recognized that a meta-materialist explanation of the Arab conquests could be made in which religion provides the middle term.

An explanation is meta-idealist if it possesses a triadic structure in which the first term is an idealist moment, the second or middle term a materialist one and the third term again an idealist one. A pure instance of this type of explanation is that offered by Christians of their founder. The immaculate conception of Christ by the Holy Ghost is the original idealist moment; Christ's birth to the Virgin Mary is the materialist moment of the incarnation of God as flesh and blood Messiah; and Jesus's apotheosis after the resurrection as the saviour of mankind is the culminating idealist moment.

A more complex example of meta-idealist explanation is found in Hegel's philosophy of history. The Logos or world-spirit induces the emergence of world historical individuals and nations – such as Alexander's Greece or Luther's Germany – spirit giving rise to material manifestations, whose exploits then engender new epochs of cultural life and thought – Alexandrian science and philosophy or the Reformation and the Protestant world-view. A pervasive idealist explanans accounts for a material explanandum, which in turn explains an idealist event.

The longstanding dispute between materialism and idealism has usually been conducted in the form of dyadic arguments ignoring these higher-order possibilities. It might of course be asked why even higher-

---

7. See pp. 96–9 above for an explanation along these and other lines.
8. Jon Elster has made an incisive critique of functionalist explanation, which will be considered later; *Ulysses and the Sirens*, Cambridge University Press, Cambridge 1979.

order arguments should not be deployed. It is not only the explanans of an explanans which can be given, but the explanans of this meta-explanans and so on. But a certain asymmetry enters into the story at this point, in that meta-materialist arguments commonly reach a literally natural terminus before meta-idealist ones, so long as resort is not made to notions of a transhistorical Logos or universal mind. It is this fact which permits a materialist perspective to be given a certain priority, even if this priority itself needs to be historicized; it can then be seen that at least cognitive ideas are assuming an increasingly decisive role in the emergence of a truly world history.

2. The Role of Ideas in Production, Destruction and Destruction Avoidance

It is now possible to assess the status of various claims concerning materialism and idealism put forward by Marx and his followers or opponents. The core of human history for Marx consists of the development of the productive forces and the successive economic structures within which such development has taken place. This is usually conceived to be a pre-eminently materialist perspective, the hallmark of historical materialism. A corollary of this approach is that the economic structure or 'base' of a society determines the character of its political, legal and religious life in its 'superstructural' institutions; that is, that what may be called its ideals or ideology, manifested in its politics, laws and religion, assume forms helpful, or at least non-harmful, to its economic structure in its task of developing the forces of production. The secular movement of history is governed ultimately by the dynamic of the productive forces.

This section will concentrate upon this fundamental claim concerning economic development while considering the impact upon the latter of advances in human knowledge; appraisal of the interaction between ideals and economic life will be left to the subsequent section. Objections to the Marxist theses have already been considered above. What is in question at the moment is not only their truth or falsity in general but their status as materialist or idealist propositions. Thereby we shall be better placed to assess in what way they are pertinent to historical explanation. The basic contention, then, consists of the allegedly materialist thesis that the forces of production develop within successive economic structures, whose order of progression is determined by their ascending capacities to preside over such productive development.

Yet the brunt of the development of physically productive, or indeed preventive and reparative, powers resides in the advance of knowledge, in particular of technical knowledge; on the face of it this is an idealist development even when productive power is in question. Cohen argues tellingly to this effect in support of Marx:

> the development of the productive forces is very largely the growth in knowledge of how to control and transform nature, and that is a development of labour power. Marx writes that 'the handmill gives you society with the feudal lord, the steam mill society with the industrial capitalist', but those economic structures may be inferred from the presence of those means of production only because the latter give evidence of particular and different levels of technical knowledge. Destroy all steam engines but preserve knowledge of how to make and use them and, with a bit of luck in the matter of material resources, you can soon return to the *status quo ante*. Destroy the knowledge and preserve the engine and you have a useless ensemble of metal, a material surd, a relic of the future (unless the producers have enough skill left to rediscover the engine's *modus operandi*, but that they could, with *sufficient* general knowledge, do so is a way of making our point). The productive forces must include labour power because the centre of their development is a development of labour power:
> '... the accumulation of the skill and knowledge (scientific power) of the workers themselves is the chief form of accumulation, and infinitely more important than the accumulation which goes hand in hand with it and merely represents it – of the *existing objective* conditions of this accumulated activity. These objective conditions are only nominally accumulated and must be constantly produced anew and consumed anew'. The 'objective conditions' are instruments of production, and also raw materials in so far as their productive versatility increases with advancing knowledge. One may say that the source of the development of the productive forces is subjective, but that it needs an objective medium, which the stated conditions supply.[9]

This argument has several interesting implications. The motor of human history is, for Marx, the development of the productive forces; but this in turn derives, at least for recent human history, from an advance in knowledge, that is in ideas about producing things. Marx here is rejoining the classic problematic of German idealist thought on the subject, which was summarized in Lessing's characterization of human history as 'the education of the human race'. Marx, unlike Lessing and other idealist thinkers, has in mind the scientific and technological education of humankind, not its moral and religious improvement. This view, it is true, involves maintaining that ideas concerning how to make physical entities

---

9. G.A. Cohen, *Karl Marx's Theory of History*, pp. 41–2. Cohen's own quotations are from Marx, *The Poverty of Philosophy* (1847), Moscow no date, p. 122, and *Theories of Surplus Value*, III, Moscow, 1972, pp. 266–7 and cf. 295. As Cohen adds, the 'objective conditions' are elsewhere described by Marx as the 'power of knowledge objectified', *Grundrisse*, Berlin 1953, p. 706.

have priority over other types of ideas, those belonging to the super-structures of a social order. Yet it remains to be demonstrated how this can be rendered compatible with a materialist conception of history.

It might be said that this view consists primarily of a productivist theory of history. Indeed, it could be seen as an example of material productivism, since the production of things is in question. However, an explanatory theory is presumably to be judged idealist or materialist not on the basis of whether the effects are ideational or material but on whether the alleged causes are; for example, psychosomatic theories of disease or recovery from disease are idealist by reason of the putative mental causes, not materialist by reason of the physical effects. Of course, even if the 'objective conditions' of production are described as the power of knowledge objectified, materials for their manufacture and transport must exist for them to be provided and for production to take place. Yet the key factor in promoting the *development* of the productive forces remains ideational for Marx, that is, the advance of knowledge; and it is such development, not production itself or even the development of production, which is held to be crucial in history. Marx's theory is thus capable of being interpreted as a productivist one, albeit with an ideationally anthropic emphasis.

However, a further elucidation could be that the ultimate reasons why productive forces exist or are developed have to do with material require-ments or facts. This requires an enlargement of the perspective beyond productivism.

Once account is also taken of contention with destruction, then the prime forces under consideration should be those of destruction and its prevention, reparation or perpetration, rather than just production. The destruction wrought by nature cannot be deemed idealist and since its minimization remains the first task and rationale of social existence, then a certain type of theory invoking its primacy qualifies as a meta-materialist one. For while the advance and diffusion of knowledge might account for much economic and technological development, the former can be explained to some degree by their necessity for the alleviation or elimin-ation of destruction, not only by nature but, as a consequence, also by other societies seeking to alleviate natural pressures upon them at the expense of others. The spontaneous growth of population from earliest times, while periodically checked by disease and famine, provoked different societies to expand the scale of their productive activity or to improve their ability to coerce others so engaged. This, as has already been argued, required them to concentrate upon the geographical expansion and *extensive amassment* of productive forces and the *qualitative development* of forces capable of withstanding or perpetrating destruction, such as ditches and dykes and means of defence and violence.[10] It did not necessarily require them to improve their forces of production, so long as new areas for settlement or new prospects for conquest remained available.

A difficulty with this type of explanation for our present purpose is that it is concerned by definition with the realm of necessity. Once the survival of societies has been explained by the requirements of contending with destruction, there remain the questions of what social level is most responsible for deciding the character of their realms of freedom and of what role is played by ideas and ideals in the process. It must be remembered that institutions inhabit both realms of social existence simultaneously and, therefore, that if it can be shown that their general character has been determined by the requirements of the realm of necessity, as with societies rapidly modernizing under military threat, then this explanation will largely account for the character their institutions assume even in their societies' realms of freedom. Nevertheless, developments in a society's realm of freedom cannot always be explained as responses to what has come to pass in its realm of necessity. While a justification can be made for the paramountcy of economic and geo-political activities in the realm of necessity, it has yet to be shown how these levels predominate in the realm of freedom. Why is it, for example, that economic activity has become expansive and pervasive in societies such as our own where the realm of freedom predominates over the realm of necessity? Is this to be accounted for by the development of knowledge, an idealist phenomenon? If this is the case, an idealist explanation of at least modern history would seem to be inescapable.

In arguing earlier that economic and geopolitical activities exercise a condominium governing the character of the realm of freedom, certain reflections were made that can assist us here.[11] Cohen maintains that the forces of production tend to develop in human history – the 'development thesis' – for several related reasons. Given the intelligence and rationality of homo sapiens and the scarcity of resources and goods, it is rational for societies to develop their productive forces. An objection that can be made to this thesis, however, is that given these assumptions it is just as rational for some, if not all, to embark on military aggression and extraction, both of necessaries and a surplus, from others. The development of military prowess can be, indeed traditionally was, the main means whereby societies expended the surplus available to them in their realm of freedom. And the advance of military technique, as of economic technique, has long been subject to improvement by the application of ideas about making,

10. See pp. 120–22 above.
11. See pp. 118–25 above.

maintaining or destroying things developed without duress in the realm of freedom. The Welsh crossbow and the Swiss pike, for example, in all probability developed as a result of the practice of highlanders' sports and martial arts, as has already been remarked above.[12] Artillery and firearms were greatly enhanced by the scientific revolution of the times, as were of course naval warfare and air power more recently. The dependence of progress in military technology upon advances in scientific knowledge scarcely needs to be demonstrated in the nuclear age.

This fact, however, is not incompatible with a broadly materialist account in at least certain circumstances. When an individual society needs to be militarily prepared, not only to survive in the realm of necessity, but also to attain room for manoeuvre in the province of necessity in the realm of freedom, then its very adoption of knowledge and skills vital for warfare can be explained as a rational strategy for the improvement of its chances in the *domains* of necessity.[13] The imperatives of these domains of necessity comprise a materialist explanans of a society's cognitive and cultural progress, which in turn becomes the explanans of its economic and military development, an ultimate explanandum within a meta-materialist explanation.

For example, by the nineteenth century, military force had come to depend overwhelmingly on technological prowess, the latter in turn requiring large expenditures, which have only been possible, at least in the longer run, for economically advanced states. It was realization of this fact that lead to the spread of cultural and then economic modernization in the nineteenth and twentieth centuries: Japan, Germany and Russia all embarked on rapid expansion of their scientific and technological capacities in order to furnish themselves with modern industry and the means of military development. Once committed to industrialization and modernization their social development, it can be argued, became governed by their economic history. Economic requirements in the realm of freedom became paramount, not least because economic advance had already given them a military preparedness in the realm of necessity, which could be used for imperialist adventures in the realm of freedom. Whether economic or military in character, the dynamic of their social development lay in a transformation of their conditions of material life; and the scientific and technological expertise they acquired in the process can be functionally explained as being required by this dynamic. It was

---

12. See pp. 69–70 above.
13. The *domains* of necessity comprise both the realm of necessity and the province of necessity in the realm of freedom, those areas of social life in which the struggle for social existence unfolds, see p. 76, fn. 59. The *domains* of freedom comprise the realm of freedom and the province of freedom in the realm of necessity.

precisely because of their effect upon material life that new ways of thought and ideas concerning methods of organization were adopted.

While this form of explanation can account for the rapid adoption of more advanced knowledge and expertise within a given society it remains to be demonstrated how it can account for the advance of knowledge as a whole, for the universal development, rather than the diffusion of science and technology. And this in turn, according to Marx's argument cited earlier, is what underlies the worldwide progress of the productive forces, as indeed, it may be added, of the means to withstand or perpetrate destruction. Marx's theory can be seen as applying not so much to individual societies, but to civilizations and to the world as a whole. In these terms the key difference between earlier and later stages of human history can be seen to reside primarily in the advance of knowledge and technology, which has travelled in the form of ideas across boundaries from one country or zone of the world to another. The international transmission of cognitive ideas, which has been accelerated in recent times due to improved means of duplication and communication, has speeded up the advance of knowledge. The course of world history, as opposed to that of a national history, remains explicable in terms of the global advance of knowledge and the wider powers that humanity has created to deal with and benefit from nature.

It could, of course, be argued that the wider advance of knowledge and expertise has still come about because of its utility in economic and military affairs. While novel ideas and the universal advance of knowledge have had profound effects on economic and military developments, it could be claimed that this is precisely why they have taken place, the latter developments, therefore, remaining the ultimate explanans. A functional explanation of the advance of science and knowledge as a whole could be postulated to bolster a functional explanation of their diffusion to certain societies.

A difficulty with this global form of functional explanation, however, is that there is no obvious agent capable of operating on a world scale to select and promote advances in knowledge and expertise. While individual states can choose to develop their scientific and technological capacities, as indeed Meiji Japan and Wilhelmine Germany did, there is no world government that has promoted the universal advance of knowledge.

One answer to this difficulty could be that universal knowledge has developed as a byproduct of the strivings of individual states and smaller units, such as firms and individual inventors. While the latter have concentrated upon local efforts to improve scientific and technological capacities, the sum total of their efforts has been to promote the diffusion and advance of sciences and technologies as a whole. Indeed, the struggle for social existence, taking several forms, can comprise the mechanism whereby this unintended consequence has occurred, akin to the way in which the evolution of species has issued from the struggle for existence between them.[14]

There is, arguably, a great deal of truth in this argument when applied to the modern world. The desiderated mechanism, indeed, can consist of the struggle for social existence and, as we shall shortly see, of the struggle for existence in several other guises as well. The international development of science and of technology is clearly promoted today by the competition between East and West, as with the space and missile races, and by competition between different advanced capitalist powers and multinational companies. Indeed, different nations now co-operate directly to promote scientific research, as in the CERN physics institute in Geneva and the ecological, agronomic and medical efforts of various United Nations organizations. A functional explanation of recent scientific, technological, ecological and medical progress, therefore, is plausible, stipulating both international concertation and diffusion of the results of research and international rivalry between social systems, nations or high-technology firms, as the means or mechanisms of functional adaptation, of ensuring that the development and diffusion of knowledge and expertise takes place in general as well as in immediately useful aspects.

A necessary condition of these forms of universal progress, indeed, has been that advances in knowledge increasingly often require collective organization and planning. Successful research and diffusion of its results in the natural sciences need huge teams of scientists and expensive physical facilities and materials. The public acceleration of science and technology is only possible because of the inherent socialization of intellectual creation. There still remains scope doubtless for maverick thinkers in science and technology. Yet, the development of new knowledge is not so dependent as in former times upon unconventional pioneers, such as Aristarchus of Samos, Copernicus, Galileo, Lamarck, Faraday, Darwin and Wegener, who were prepared to confound religious or secular authority; nor is it so dependent upon the ingenuity of individual craftsmen and inventors, such as Watt, Stevenson, Fulton, Daguerre and Edison, working in the wake of the scientific visionaries.

The emergence of modern science itself cannot be so easily explained in functional terms. The discoveries and inventions of the great scientific pioneers were not required by their societies when they were made, even if later generations put them to practical use. They cannot be accounted for

---

14. Elster has argued for the need of some mechanism other than the explicit agency of powerful actors to account for how functional explanations can be valid, see Jon Elster, *Ulysses and the Sirens*, pp. 28–35.

on the other hand simply by the arrival of great geniuses, for even the greatest of them depended upon the achievements of their predecessors. To Newton is attributed the saying, 'If I have seen a little farther than others it is because I have stood on the shoulders of giants.'[15] The origins of the creative epochs in human thought have to be sought in the worldly and cultural predispositions of their societies.

The emergence of Greek and Hellenistic science and then of modern European science in the seventeenth and eighteenth centuries, on which the Industrial Revolution to some degree came to depend, owed a great deal to the economic dynamism and city- (and then nation-) state rivalry of the times, which encouraged patronage of new ideas and devices. However, the city-states of the Phoenicians or Etruscans in antiquity and of Spain and central Europe in the Middle Ages and Renaissance attained no comparable cultural dynamism. The original achievements of the Grecian cities have been generally attributed by historians to a cultural vitality, precipitated by the impact of Babylon and Egypt upon them; similarly, the mingling of cultures in the wake of Alexander the Great's conquests stimulated science and technology in the Hellenic world. The revival of the cultural and technical achievements of classical antiquity by the Renaissance courts and scholars in Italy, France, the Low Countries and England provoked the scientific revolution of the sixteenth and seventeenth centuries; the works of Euclid, Archimedes, Aristarchus of Samos, Hero of Alexander, Vitrivius and many more were translated and transmitted by medieval monks and scribes and by Arab scholars to generations of Renaissance thinkers. These latter either, like Copernicus, found encouragement and ancient warrant for their ideas or, like Alberti and Galileo, found fresh stimulus for their own departures from the medieval world-view. Each of these epochal triumphs depended upon necessary conditions of a geopolitical or economic kind, but were conjured into existence by an unusual communion of cultures, in the one case across space and in the other across time. The unusual necessary component of a sufficient condition of scientific development was in each case an idealist, not a materialist, phenomenon. The interaction of old and new ideas in the cultural sphere of the realm of freedom would appear to have been decisive for cognitive and so to some degree for social progress.

It can be questioned, nevertheless, whether the practical arts of technology were stimulated by the development of science itself, even if few doubt the debt of the latter to the former. Technological innovations abounded in China and Korea in the first millennium A.D. and for some time thereafter, including the inventions of paper,printing, gunpowder,

---

15. E.T. Bell, *Men of Mathematics*, Simon and Schuster, New York 1965, p. 93.

the pound-lock, the compass and other aids to navigation and transport. Yet this technical creativity was not accompanied by a corresponding growth of scientific knowledge, at least as the modern world understands it. Chinese science was classificatory rather than causal in character, or, as Needham puts it, Vincean rather than Galilean. Taoist and Confucian reverence for nature and its vicissitudes confined the scope of its generalizations, exceptions to which were curiosities to be marvelled at rather than challenges to established paradigms.[16]

The absence of a scientific revolution in the Chinese world comparable to the type of technological transformation it experienced in early times indicates that these developments were neither necessary nor sufficient conditions of each other. Yet the continuation of technical progress into a fully fledged industrial revolution might still have depended upon a scientific revolution. Europe's industrialization, several centuries later, eventually advanced much further than the Chinese performance, although remaining indebted to it for some of its best ideas and devices. This success may well have been partly due to Europe's development of a modern scientific outlook, with a capacity for learning from practical innovators and providing them with guidelines and abstract criteria for further advance, as with the interplay of ideas between Newcome, Watt and the originators of thermodynamics and modern steam engines or between Ørsted, Faraday, Clerk-Maxwell, Hertz, Marconi and Edison. In this manner science created the *disciplines* of technology in place of the lore of the craftsmen, handed down from generation to generation. The latter, by eschewing abstract formulation and relying upon precedent and accumulated experience, was inherently conservative and ill-suited to the emergence of ideas to tackle new problems or indeed old ones in a new way. With the development of science technology could become more abstract and so capable of genuinely new directions.[17]

Such a conclusion cannot be inferred from the conjunction of the absence of a scientific revolution in China and the abortion of its early technological advance, however. Other factors in the Chinese experience can also account for the latter, including pressures from the northern nomads, environmental disasters and a conservative and security-conscious officialdom and state, which proved burdensome on entrepreneurial activity and prohibitive of foreign contacts and trade.[18] It nevertheless seems reasonable to suppose that the intellectual illumination

16. See S. Nakayama, 'Science and Technology in China', in *Half the World*, pp. 143–4. For the wider significance of this for Chinese social development, see P. Anderson, *Lineages of the Absolutist State*, Verso, London 1974, pp. 543–4.

17. See A. Pacey, *The Maze of Ingenuity*, Allen Lane, London 1974, pp. 18–20.

18. On the fate of China's early iron and steel industries see pp. 48–9, 122 above.

brought by the great scientists found various paths through to the practitioners in the workshops and engineering laboratories of the early industrial world, fostering a permanent technological revolution within them.[19]

If the emergence of modern science since the Renaissance has been, indeed, an essential precondition of at least the continuation of the West's remarkable technological prowess, then an idealist phenomenon must be admitted to have proved decisive in changing the whole course of human history. And this development of ideas in turn cannot be attributed merely to the inspiration of early technological and industrial advance, since, as we have seen, China had the latter without engendering the former.

At least one unusual precondition of Western advance, therefore, lay in the peculiar cultural heritage from its classical past, which was reactivated during the Renaissance and the scientific revolution that ensued. Another crucial peculiarity of European achievements, it has already been suggested, resided in the rich possibilities of its *historical* geography. This proved capable, unlike China's, of being deforested by farmers, at least in the north, with a fertile, disasterless and disease-free countryside as the outcome; it has been blessed with uniquely favourable means of riverine and marine transport and rich in potential resources of energy and raw materials; the fragmented coastline of its compact topography encouraged a diversity of states and cultures and a fruitful intercourse and competition between them. The emergence of feudalism and then capitalism within this zone can be largely explained by these facts, even if space does not permit adumbration of this point here.[20]

Any such explanation assumes at this stage both idealist and materialist aspects. A set of idealist conditions conjoined with a set of materialist ones can account for the Western ascent. The argument can be pushed further back, however, by seeking the explanans of these explanans themselves.

The historical geography of the European world on the eve and during the course of its great transformation was the outcome of the spontaneous activity of nature and of the alterations which mankind implemented or

---

19. This claim has however been disputed. Many studies have been undertaken to show that even in modern times the contribution of science to technology has been exaggerated. These studies, however, tend to focus on immediate influences, which may often have been absent, even while the spread of a scientific ethos and a mathematical proficiency did tend to encourage new technological ideas and an increasing rigour in their development. For a critical summary of the literature, which makes this point, see Alexander Keller, 'Has Science Created Technology?', *Minerva* XXII, summer 1984, pp. 160–82.

20. For an environmental and geopolitical interpretation, along these lines, of Europe's rise to pre-eminence, see E.L. Jones, *The European Miracle: Environments, Economies and Geopolitics in the History of Europe and Asia*, Cambridge University Press, 1981.

provoked in the light of its improving technological knowledge. The ulterior explanans, therefore, of the materialist explanans of Western development possessed a double significance itself, consisting of earlier historical geographies and bodies of technological knowledge.

The other crucial precondition, the heritage from classical antiquity, cannot be ascribed only to the rise of sophisticated city-states based on free peasant and slave labour which nourished their cultural advance in Greece and Rome. For these from the Milesian school onwards were to some degree indebted to the earlier civilizations of Mesopotamia and Egypt; Thales and Pythagoras, Plato and Euxodes possibly travelled there for enlightenment, as certainly did Herodotus and of course the later luminaries of the Hellenic world in Alexandria. In the field of technology, in particular, much of the achievement of classical civilizations consisted in transmitting local Middle Eastern techniques to a wider public, such as the Archimedean screw (possibly indigenous to Egypt before Archimedes's time), the wadi irrigation system of the Nabateans which the Romans spread across North Africa and the qanats of Persia that were used in Spain, not to speak of the horizontal water wheel, which was used in the Near East in early times and spread through the later Roman Empire.

Earlier cultural and technological achievements, however, can be attributed in the long run to the emergence of civilization itself, which, with its introduction of specialization and its fostering of arts and skills, made possible an advance beyond the slow improvement and diffusion of techniques among conservative and often widely dispersed communities of tribes. Agriculture and the succession of bronze, iron and steel ages superseded the long sway of stone age hunter-gathering. At this level of explanation, the explanans relevant to accounting for technical progress consists, it has already been argued, of the struggle for social existence. Hunter-gathering bands gave way to agricultural communities during the course of the eleven millennia B.C., as they were displaced from their hunting and foraging grounds by the vicissitudes of nature or the encroachments of the agriculturists, who also often doubtless worsted them in battle.[21] Agrarian tribal societies then engendered at a certain point the formation of states, towns and civilizations; the first territorial states, such as those of Egypt and Mesopotamia, mobilized more resources than smaller communities could muster and so proved victors in competition over them. The advance of technique, then, remained subject to the pressures of social competition in nature.

The originality of the Greek achievements lay in their liberation of

---

21. For a discussion of this epoch of struggle for social existence, see pp. 77–82 above.

abstract thought, not only in science but in philosophy and mathematics as well. Whatever its antecedents, this represented something new in history and of the profoundest importance. For a body of universal knowledge was established and codified – notably by Aristotle and Euclid, Archimedes and Hero of Alexander – within which criteria were available for the evaluation of further progress, whether new departures or improvements to the existing canon. The Greeks gave rise to self-conscious universal reason.

It is at this point in history that the group selection in nature which had propelled, as it continued to propel, cognitive as well as social advance, was joined by a further form of struggle for existence. Once it is accepted that cognitive ideas need to be tested by being submitted to experiment or natural demonstration and the play of criticism, then an advance of objective reason becomes possible. Scientific theories are obliged to predict certain experimental or natural results as well as to confirm or refute those already established in the corpus of the science. If they survive this initial ordeal, they still remain subject to revision or eventual refutation in the light of further theories and experimental or natural results.

This process has been explicated by Popper in terms of his famous theory of falsifiability. Ideas in physics and elsewhere which concern nature, however autonomously conceived from material *interests*, nevertheless aim to correspond to material *truth* or verisimilitude. The elimination of unsuccessful hypotheses leaves the rivals in charge of the field, to become the better established the more attempted falsifications they have survived. Thus, Popper's falsification theory of scientific discovery has its affinity with Darwin's theory of natural selection. Nature in both cases selects the winners, in the first case by survival of experiments or natural observations, in the second, by survival of material destruction.[22] Just as human institutions in the realm of necessity respond to nature's exigencies, so then, do ideas about nature even in the realm of freedom.

---

22. Karl Popper, *The Logic of Scientific Discovery*, London, 1933, for the principle of falsifiability. Popper himself draws the parallel between survival for theories and natural selection: 'The tentative solutions which animals and plants incorporate into their anatomy and their behaviour are biological analogues of theories; and vice-versa: theories correspond (as do many exosomatic products, such as honeycombs, and especially exosomatic tools, such as spiders' webs) to endosomatic organs and their ways of functioning. Just like theories, organs and their functions are tentative adaptations to the world we live in. And just like theories, or like tools, new organs and their functions, and also new kinds of behaviour, exert their influence on the first world which they may help to change.' Karl Popper, *Objective Knowledge: an Evolutionary Approach*, Oxford University Press, 1975, p. 145. Popper's 'first world' here is the world of nature. There are of course problems, into which it is unnecessary to enter at present, concerning the manner whereby successive theories for Popper can, given his rejection of induction, acquire increasing verisimilitude.

Actual Greek practice by no means achieved this ideal of objective science. The Greeks were slow to recognize the vital role of experiment, although they did make observations of nature to test their astronomical and other hypotheses and these proved increasingly accurate as to the sizes and distances of the sun, moon and planetary bodies, for example. Their tardiness in experimentation might have been partly due to their numinous view of the cosmos, in whose workings the gods were capable of intervening for their own purposes. Be that as it may, the sciences of mathematics and nature had begun their odyssey towards the rational illumination of reality. The arbiter of the struggle for ideational survival became nature in its historicity, as it already was of species and societies in their struggle for existence.

Thus, a meta-materialist explanation of general cognitive advance can be given, which recognizes its pre-eminent role in promoting technical and social progress, even when this advance has not been functionally required at the economic or geopolitical levels. However spontaneous the speculations of the Greeks and later the Renaissance thinkers, they became subject to a struggle for existence with each other and with traditional ideas of nature. These 'naturally selected' ideas had in turn a profound impact upon nature as they contributed to its human transformation.

The immediate imperatives of the struggle for social existence often accounted for the timing and tempo of the introduction and development of ideas within the sphere of technology. Military applications were for these reasons frequently made earlier than civilian ones, although the former could lead to the latter. Belisarius, for instance, initiated the use of floating mills on the Tiber during the siege of Rome in 537 A.D. when the Goths broke the aqueducts and put the city's watermills out of action.[23] This is a rare example of inventiveness in the Roman and Byzantine worlds, which tended to exploit and spread the inventions of others, notably the watermill itself from Alexandria.

The 'military-commercial complex' in the Renaissance helped to promote a wide-ranging number of innovations – in mining, metallurgy, navigation, shipbuilding, clock manufacture and engineering science – which largely accounted for the incipient industrial progress of the time. The 'military-industrial complex' more recently has been an inspiration behind much of the Industrial Revolution, ever since the massive increase in the state's demands on the civil economy which was temporarily associated with the Napoleonic Wars and then permanently with the arms

---

23. This story is told in Procopius, who is quoted by L. Sprague de Camp,. *Ancient Engineers*, London 1977, pp. 231–2.

races of the nineteenth and twentieth centuries.[24] Today, the micro-electronics revolution has stemmed from the missile and space races between East and West. Competition between ideas, states and now whole systems has propelled economic and military development.

3. The Interplay of Ideals and Material Forces

The preceding discussion has concentrated upon the interaction between ideas and economic and geopolitical affairs. There has also been a far-reaching interaction throughout human history between religious and other ideals on the one hand and economic and military development on the other.[25] If the latter was more truly fundamental than the former in both realms of social life, then one would expect that ideology, whether religious or political, would have generally reflected the requirements of the economic and geopolitical interests of a people.

Yet, the survival of certain religions, such as Hinduism and several forms of Buddhism, has long been considered an obstacle to economic development or military preparedness in India and elsewhere. The Buddhism of Tibet might seem a striking instance of this desuetude of a surviving religion to latterday requirements.

It has already been maintained that the primary functions of religion and of theocratic forms of rule have been to provide magical and mundane security in one. And this has not necessarily been helpful to economic and military innovation. Indeed, by offering consolation for economic and military disasters, whether hunger or defeat, religion can often thrive in epochs of general adversity, as with Christianity in the Dark Ages. The moments when new religious affiliations and mass conversions have been made have characteristically been those of widespread crisis, such as the third and fourth centuries in Rome for Christianity, the seventh century in

---

24. See W.H. McNeill, *The Pursuit of Power*, Basil Blackwell, Oxford 1983, for the 'military commercial complex', pp. 117–43, and for the 'military-industrial complex', Chs 7–10. As an instance of the 'military-commercial complex', during the Dutch War of Independence Prince Maurice of Orange set up a military academy which was to become a model for the rest of Europe; Stevin, its most famous son, was responsible for advances in ballistics, fortification and navigation as well as in mathematics and science. As an instance of the 'military-industrial complex', the French state founded the Ecole Polytechnique to promote military, but also technological, prowess; the descriptive geometry of Monge and the projective geometry of Poncelet, who were respectively teacher and pupil at the Ecole Polytechnique, had a profound impact on the engineering of the nineteenth century.

25. There can also of course be economic and military ideals, those of 'conspicuous consumption' and 'chivalry' for instance. 'Ideals', however, will be used to refer to non-economic or non-military values; and 'ideology' will refer to an imaginary or magical resolution of mundane problems.

Arabia for Islam and the epoch of the Aryan invasions for Hinduism in India. This is not surprising since these times were characterized by a novel intensity of destruction, against which new religious answers might well appear necessary. The early or eventual development of these, as of other, religions that have survived, nevertheless, has proved increasingly well-suited to wider social requirements than merely consolation for an unusual scope of destruction. Even in such cases as Poland and Tibet today, it can be argued, the tenacity of religion serves the goal of safe-guarding the independent survival of a people's whole culture and way of life from outside destruction.

In general, the religious and political ideals guiding a society can be seen to reflect certain basic requirements, to which they usually offer, if not a uniquely satisfactory, at least an adequate response; the exceptions occur in instances where societies have eventually perished instead. New ideals emanating from either the realm of necessity or the realm of freedom itself are likely to take effect in history only if they are sponsored by powerful material interests, such as states and wealthy patrons or powerful institutions, whereupon they can assume great importance in both realms of social life. Ideals may not be so subject to physical destruction as material things, but they remain vulnerable to something quite as deadly, namely neglect and oblivion. It could be argued that only those ideals which promise to or actually do further the interests of the realm of necessity and of the province of necessity in the realm of freedom, especially of their economic and geopolitical spheres, are likely to prosper and prove efficacious in changing history.

In the case of liberal-democratic states there have been great advances over the last century in civic freedom and public welfare, notably in the successes of feminism today. The ideals behind them, nevertheless, have arguably only prevailed because they have responded to the needs of capitalist development. Liberal scholarship itself has recently come to recognize the role of economic structures in the triumph of liberal democracy.[26] In the modern capitalist world at least, economic life benefits from the education and health improvements of the working population and the assimilation of women into the upper reaches of the labour force, which liberal reformism has brought about. Even the pressure upon wage rates exerted by free trade unionism compels productivity advances and the spread of consumerism.

However, a further question arises of how notions, such as those of liberal democracy, and their attendant institutions actually do prevail. Since there is no automatic mechanism to adapt the cultural sphere of

---

26. I am referring to Barrington Moore Jr's justly famous work, *The Social Origins of Dictatorship and Democracy*, Allen Lane, London 1967.

freedom to underlying social requirements, such as those of the modern West, how can it come about that the ideals and institutions characteristic of a society answer to its underlying needs?

There are two sets of reason which have been proposed why ideas, ideals and institutions embodying them can prevail when favourable to material requirements, proving that their time has come. Firstly, that they are perceived to be favourable by powerful interests, either lucidly or in self-deception, and are therefore acted upon or encouraged. Secondly, that they just win out because of their superior abilities in performance and competition with other less suitable rivals, so long as their implementation has at least begun. The latter is a form of Darwinian explanation. Destruction of ineffectual rivals in this case paves the way for creative advance, as with the evolution of species. A combination of these two types of rationale is also of course possible, indeed likely, with a variety of humanly selected notions and institutions being subjected to the trial of the wider world.

This then sets off a third type of reason why ideas, ideals and indeed cultural activity and institutions generally, can respond creatively to material requirements. Human ideas and activity can change in the course of struggle against adversaries, acquiring a drive and momentum to conquer them. The challenge of competition improves all-round performance: hence the winners survive not just because of their initially superior qualities, but also due to their accentuation or to new ones acquired in the process. This consists of an inheritance of desired acquirable characteristics, a 'neo-Lamarckian' inheritance complementing 'Darwinian' survival. The dynamic of ideas, ideals and structures of social life in competition with others, then, generates its own responsiveness to the needs of survival. These three forms of causation characterize the struggle for human social existence.

Thus, Mohammed became the prophet of a worldwide religion because certain Medinians and then Meccans saw the worldly advantages for them in becoming Moslems, with no doubt a large mixture of self-deception involved, and secondly because Islam proved to be triumphant in war, establishing a brilliant combination of a unified, militant mode of mundane security with a monotheistic, evangelical mode of magical security for Arabia's contentious, pagan tribes. His rivals, of whose parochialism he was aware, the prophet, Maslama, of the Hanifa and the prophetess, Sajah, of the Tamun, underwent eventual eclipse as advocates of less suitable creeds for unifying them.[27] This is not to deny that had

---

27. Maxime Rodinson, *Mohammed*, Allen Lane, London 1971, p. 272. It is possible that Maslama or Sajah as monotheists could have played a similar role, but unlikely. The former believed in chastity after the birth of a son and the latter was a woman and ex-Christian, facts which were hardly likely to commend them throughout Arabia. Moreover, Mohammed was an able general and politician as well as an ideologue of genius.

Mohammed never lived or had he been killed at the battle of Badr in 624, the history of the Arabian world, the Middle East and elsewhere would have been altogether different.

These three types of causal relationship for bringing ideas into line with material requirements are very similar to those considered by Cohen as means of functional explanation.[28] While his forms of functional explanation are designed to account for the correspondence of Marx's superstructures to the economic base, they can be invoked to account for the adaptation of ideas, freely conceived, to the realm of necessity. The cultural sphere of the realm of freedom does not exist in a vacuum; its ideas and initiatives, whatever their autonomy in creation, are likely to improve their chances of survival before the tribunal of posterity if they minister to certain necessary interests. While they may not inhabit the realm of social necessity, they must contend in their own realm of testamentary necessity with the neglect and oblivion befalling unpopular ideas. Gifted ideologues and creeds have not despised the arts of exemption from reproof, as with the indulgences sold by the Papacy in the Dark Ages and the 'Islamic Rents' of Middle Eastern banks not allowed to charge interest. None are more ready to be flattered by exclusion from anathema than the vigilant interests of the realm of necessity. The solicitude of religious founders in the US for the needs of commerce has had fruitful results.

The adaptation of successful religions and ideologies to mundane requirements in the long run, therefore, is not so surprising, since their own survival has been thereby facilitated. Cultural activity comes to reflect the diversity of needs of social life as a whole.

4. The Cunning of Reason

The development of religions or other ideologies and of scientific or philosophical truth, then, responds to material exigencies, albeit in different ways. While the drive towards truth accounts for most scientific progress, the technological applications of pure research aim, not to reflect the truth of the world, but, rather, to devise means of transforming it. The truth of how to transform the world and prevent its destructive transformation is the goal of engineering and allied technologies. Nature as a result is undergoing great changes. Its historicity, once an independent force, is now increasingly, if not largely, the product of the human species. Of course these powers of mind over matter have mainly been exercised to

---

28. See G.A. Cohen, *Karl Marx's Theory of History: A Defence*, Oxford 1978, Chs 9 and 10, especially the latter, pp. 278–96.

further the interests of the realm of necessity and its province in the realm of freedom, the elimination of labour from the production process, the combating of disease and so on.

The end result of this development, however, has been an enlargement of the realm of freedom in the advanced capitalist countries, and the growth of leisure and leisure pursuits. Technological progress is increasingly achieved in the service of play and diversions, such as computer games and music. Ideas, then, are now more potent in improving inessential, as well as essential, activities. The eventual upshot of the process may doubtless be automation or near automation and the life of human liberation which Marx and others have postulated as the goal of social development, communism, the 'riddle of history' solved, albeit still contending with some persistent or novel destructive powers. Be that as it may, ideas and ideals are shaping the prospects for human history to an appreciable degree, even if their very prominence in this respect can be attributed in large part, as we have attempted to do above, to the underlying logic of material developments.

Any admission of ideas and ideals to the rank of prominent historical agents must confront the problem of the ruses of which history has shown itself perennially capable, deflecting ideological and other movements to fates that they never anticipated or might have scorned or feared. What Jesus and Mohammed or Marx and Lenin would have thought of the impact of their ideas is a moot point; but it is scarcely disputable that their upshot has baffled, if not disappointed, many perceptive observers and adherents. Similarly, technological or artistic novelties can have quite unexpected effects or byproducts. It was earlier argued that while the realm of necessity confronts the destructive forces of nature and of humankind relaying these onto others – the vampire of reason – social life as a whole is governed by the ruse of reason, the subtle reversals of history out of which progress can still come. It was also promised that a materialist basis could be provided for this hitherto obdurately idealist notion. Indeed, it was claimed that material developments themselves were encouraging the ruse of reason to extend its sway.

As was pointed out, the ruse of reason is a notion which Hegel derived from a close study of Smith and his famous 'hidden hand' of the capitalist market-place.[29] An efficient and fruitful allocation of resources can come about from the blind pursuit of individual interests. Thus, a ruse of reason has operated to develop the forces of production despite the losses, bankruptcies and unemployment befalling inefficient and laggard firms and their workers. This idea has evident affinities, as Marx and others have remarked, with Darwin's theory of natural selection. Darwin himself

---

29. See p. 24, fn. 17.

was inspired by his reading of Malthus's *Essay on Population*, which puts forward a simple notion of the struggle for existence, akin indeed to that of capitalist competition. The conceptions of Darwin and political economy reveal a world governed by an evident ruse of reason. Creation emanates from blind destruction. An evolution of species proceeds from the decease of nearly all species. The author of this process is nature itself in its historical vicissitudes. Natural selection determines the course of life; and its devastations and havoc are ruses of natural reason. The struggle for existence can be seen as the avatar of the laws of reason in the animal kingdom, which have issued in its highest product, homo sapiens itself. Homo sapiens not only emerged from natural selection, but has proved capable of conscious choice and rational deportment.

The various forms of functional explanation, cited by Cohen, and the reasons why ideas and institutions tend to minister to the interests of the realm of necessity invoke these very forces of natural selection, conscious choice and self-improvement through struggle. Just as the ruse of reason can manifest itself in natural selection, and the triumph of homo sapiens, so can it do so in the means whereby human ideas and institutions come to conform blindly as well as wittingly to the interests of the realm of necessity. Societies have prospered or failed by virtue of the viability of their modes of livelihood and security in the struggle for social existence, those geoeconomic and geopolitical institutions which are reminiscent of animals' powers of contending with nature and other forms of life. The difference for human beings lies in the group character of the selection in question and in their concomitant scope for conscious rational choice of means to advance and secure survival, to reject failures and to bequeath knowledge and ideas to their offspring, a faculty characteristic of human evolution.

One form of society which emerged primarily not out of warfare and contention with nature in the struggle for social existence, but spontaneously in the realm of freedom was capitalism, which internalizes however, the principle of competition in its starkest form.[30] The exception here proves the rule that more and more sophisticated forms of group selection continue to govern the evolution of human society into its civilized phase, the cunning of reason remaining operative in the creative work it makes of the destruction wrought by the vampire of reason. The vampire of reason, indeed, is but a ruse of reason itself, without which homo sapiens would never have emerged or, once evolved, would have languished for want of a spur or challenge.

---

30. For a perceptive account of this see John Torrance, 'Reproduction and Development: A Case for a "Darwinian" Mechanism in Marx's Theory of History', *Political Studies* 1985, vol. xxxiii, pp. 382–98.

This perspective can be seen to be consonant with the direction of German idealist thought on the subject. Reason for Hegel in its pristine form consists of the laws of nature, whereas for Kant reason is constitutive of them. On either reading of reason's status, it is epitomized by the 'laws of nature'; in Hegel's case this is because these laws are rational and reason in its first guise and in Kant's case because they are constituted by nature's own highest product, homo sapiens, which can in its practical history realize nature's hidden design of rationality. Thus, the 'cunning of nature' in Kant's philosophy parallels the 'ruse of reason' in Hegel's.[31]

The idea of reason invoked here is somewhat different from that of either Hegel or Kant. Hegel's notion of reason suffers from ignoring the fact that while nature is rationally intelligible in terms of certain laws, these laws themselves need not manifest any rationality in nature as, for instance, with the second law of thermodynamics postulating that entropy tends to increase in a closed system or the laws governing irrational behaviour itself, such as those of hysteria. A madman's actions may be intelligible, but this does not mean that they are necessarily rational. Kant's notion of reason is confined to human perception or transcendental apperception.

A rationality can, nevertheless, be discerned in nature beyond either of these conceptions of it. Nature has manifested a tendency towards an ever more complex and expansive order. This increasing order has been promoted in the case of living things by natural selection and in the case of human beings by means of the higher forms of struggle for existence which we have been considering above as studied in their respective fields by Smith, Darwin and Popper.

The presentation of a very similar form of argument to those of Kant and Hegel in both Smith and Darwin allows them to be given a latterday vindication. If a rationality is expressed by nature in its historical develop-

---

31. Kant anticipated Hegel's concept of the ruse of reason in his argument for political progress in the *Idea for a Universal History* and in *Perpetual Peace* where he assigned to nature the hidden design of promoting advance and, in his own day, enlightenment by wars, devastations, exploitation and rampant self-interest. Eric Weil has called the principle Kant invokes here the 'cunning of nature' on the parallel of Hegel's 'cunning of reason', in *Problèmes Kantiens*, Paris 1962.

For Kant even if reason constitutes the *laws of nature*, reason and *nature* are distinct; hence the need for the distinctive term, 'the cunning of nature'. For a most perceptive account of the argument that the concept designates and the shifting character and role of this argument in Kant's thought, see Yirmiahu Yovel, *Kant and the Philosophy of History*, Princeton University Press, 1980, pp. 8–9 and Part II, 'The Vehicles of Progress', pp. 125–200 passim. For the later Kant political progress and social existence stemmed from the antagonistic conflict of different tribes, not from survival or property requirements, although an antagonism which the philosophy of the Enlightenment could mitigate and even partially replace in the political sphere and wholly in the ethical sphere governing modern human history.

ment, commencing in the operation of natural selection and continuing in the struggle for social existence – indeed under capitalism in the competition between capitals – the history of nature and a fortiori reason can be credited with its own cunning on properly scientific grounds. The cunning of reason in human history for Hegel and the cunning of nature in political history for Kant can be seen as intimating the operation of progressive forms of natural selection.

These ideas of German speculative thought have not escaped the rigours of ideational competition themselves. The leading role of ideas in human activity has itself been subject, as we have seen, to the pressures of the realm of necessity, and, in the decisive spheres of science and cognition, to a natural selection of its own. Just as Darwin's natural selection and Smith's hidden hand can further the interests of a higher rationality, so can Popperian attempts to falsify theories; however, in the two latter cases, unlike the first, the participants in the process since Smith and Popper can in principle become aware of their own incitements to progress even when they fail.[32] Our knowledge of the external world is forever growing on the corpses of our false conceptions of it. Thus, ruses of reason can unfold in biology, economics and scientific advance alike. Indeed, given that societies are themselves subject to a struggle for existence, human history as a whole can be marked by the ruses of an ascendant reason. The human species has been the instrument of an increasing sophistication in the forms and workings of selection between organisms, groups, ideas and social institutions or societies themselves, while being the most conspicuous product and ruse of reason of all.

The advance in rationality, promoted by struggle within nature and society, has made possible a progress in human freedom, when this is defined as increasing avoidance of destruction in the realm of necessity and concomitant enlargement of the realm of freedom. The ever more complex and expansive order achieved by rational development has transformed human prospects both for survival and for non-survival creativity. This has permitted an increasing adaptation of means to ends, within an instrumental rationality, and the attainment of more complex and numerous, because more consistent, ends, within a normative rationality. Advances in cognitive rationality accompanied and sometimes occasioned

---

32. The realization that failures of ideas could play a progressive role actually long predates Popper, and indeed emerged under the influence of 'political economy' itself. As Bentham says of the capacity of entrepreneurs to learn from past failures, 'the career of art, the great road which perceives the footsteps of projectors, may be considered as a vast and perhaps unbounded plain, bestrewed with gulphs, such as Curtius was swallowed up in. Each requires a human victim to fall into it ere it can close, but when it once closes to open no more, and so much of the path is safe to those who follow.' This judgement is not widely known, although quoted by Keynes in *The General Theory of Employment*, Macmillan, London 1964, p. 353, who calls it Bentham's noblest passage.

these forms of progress, the careers of science (knowledge of what) and of technology (knowledge of how) for instance informing each other in promoting an instrumental rationality.

We have already considered how improvements in medicine and ecology as well as in production have lengthened human life-spans and reduced the incidence of disease and disaster, although they have of course far from removed them. Human beings tend to live longer than formerly with greater exemption from hunger or disease and with more leisure and means to enjoy it. A greater order prevails in the realm of necessity and a wider and ever-expansive order in that of freedom, as new means of creativity emerge and proliferate, especially, but not exclusively in the advanced Western world.

The character of the realm of freedom has in the process undergone a significant change. From being more or less blindly concerned with non-survival activities, it has increasingly come under conscious control and direction. A fuller freedom than merely that of successful destruction avoidance has come about, at least in embryonic stages. Indeed, the conscious choice of new departures has become important in both realms of social life. The spread of democratic freedoms and participation means that in at least the advanced world a measure of self-determination obtains, both where governmental policy has to answer to the needs of an electorate and where individuals themselves have civic rights in the limited sense of protection against army or police coercion. Attempts at self-determination, however, whether at a social or individual level, can be frustrated by intractable problems of the realm of necessity, such as economic stagnation and the difficulty of controlling population growth. All societies remain subject to forces they only imperfectly understand and, therefore, cannot bring under control. Indeed knowledge itself is not sufficient in many instances, as with the global problems of pollution, environmental hazards and the threat of nuclear warfare. Nevertheless, a far wider scope of activities than was the case before can now be consciously improved under the impact of medical, ecological and other forms of knowledge of nature and of society.

The advance of the productive, destructive and destruction-minimizing powers of mankind has led to a complex interaction between them, some of whose rhythms we have already attempted to elucidate. The formation and maintenance of classes and status groups, based on their unique positions within modes of production and modes of security, has, it has already been indicated, been an accompaniment of this complex process.

The destructive forces rife in the world have met with unequal responses from human groups, some of whom have been able to relay the destructive pressures assailing them onto others, as with ruling classes and dominant nations. The varying abilities of societies to contend with destruction have been subject to a long process of selection, the inferior ones giving way in time to those better adjusted to their tasks. This has taken place within the struggle for social existence, leading to ever more complex and pervasive social orders, slave societies, continental empires, feudalism and now capitalism with its global reach. Indeed, with the emergence of socialism, the struggle for social existence has taken on a novel kind of form between not just different societies but different social systems, the significance of which cannot be appreciated without a long analysis of its own, out of place in the present enquiry.

Setbacks in the development of productive and other powers have often taken place, periodic long-run crises afflicting the economies and polities of individual states. Indeed, the torchbearer of progress in one epoch of human history, such as Greece, Rome, the Arab world, Renaissance Italy and in turn France, Holland, Britain, Germany, the United States and now perhaps Japan in the latter half of the second millennium A.D., has held the stage for a while and then found its leadership eclipsed by some other centre of vitality, better placed for social, geographical or other reasons to exploit new technologies and avenues of power and expansion. The factors favouring a society in its ascent to primacy persist for only a period before others or another jealous of its role either expose some novel vulnerability, as did the barbarian tribes with the later Roman Empire, or prove to possess superior characteristics to develop the former's own technological and organizational advances, as did Imperial Germany and the United States with late Victorian Britain. These vicissitudes in the struggle for social existence have their own rationale in furthering human knowledge and technological prowess. For each society enjoying an ephemeral leadership can, once its creative powers have flourished, be sacrificed to permit a new order to prove itself, much as the mammals eclipsed the dinosaurs. The vanguard of advance of human reason can shift from place to place the better to develop the various potentialities of the human race across the globe.

Instead of the Logos of Hegel or Marx's development of the productive forces comprising in a closed dialectic the prime motor of human history, it has rather been the open interplay of creation, preservation and destruction in nature, knowledge and human society, which has accounted for creative development through local setbacks and disasters. Yet, as Hegel himself has said,

> The particular has its own interests in world history; it is of a finite nature, and as such it must perish. Particular interests contend with one another, and some are destroyed in the process. But it is from this very conflict and destruction of particular things that the universal emerges, and it remains unscathed itself. For it is not the universal idea, which enters into operation, conflict and danger; it

keeps itself in the background; untouched and unharmed and sends forth the particular interests of passion to fight and wear themselves out in its stead. It is what we may call the *cunning of reason* that it sets the passions to work in its service, so that the agents by which it gives itself existence must pay the penalty and suffer the loss.[33]

The universal idea, one may say, has itself fallen victim to the cunning of reason. It is struggle for existence within nature in its increasing historical sophistication which has propagated the ascent of science and civilization. First, the biological struggle for existence compelled the evolution of life; then, with nature as the foil, homo sapiens and its primitive and civilized societies struggled for social existence; nature was installed, with the emergence of capitalism, as the canvas of its endeavours and the arbiter of the 'hidden hand', all the while foiling human conceptions of itself by refusing to disclose its true identity without further experiment. One need look no further than struggle within nature in its historicity to find the true begetter of the ruse of reason. Yet who can claim to know its secrets?

There is one branch of human thought and endeavour which has often claimed to answer this question. No area of social life has been less tractable to the realm of necessity nor less prepared to limit its claim than religion. Yet in being so, the great world religions have not escaped the attentions of the ruse of reason. Ancient religions can provide magical security against forces of destruction, indeed thrive on them and reveal not merely the secrets of nature but those of mankind in their antiquity. Humans are unlike animal species in having the capacity to console themselves for misfortunes and their knowledge of death by belief in an afterlife. This in turn can have profound effects on political and social life. While other social levels have been constrained by the struggle with nature, religion, and under its sway sometimes politics, have been released from the full brunt of natural and social selection, at least in imagination, permitting for a while the most curious developments. It is to them, therefore, that it is now necessary to turn.

33. G.W.F. Hegel, *Lectures on the Philosophy of World History*, tr. H.B. Nisbet, Cambridge University Press 1975, p. 89.

8

The Power of Religion: The Mode of Magical Security

Religion has had a far more powerful role in human history than might on rational grounds seem warranted. The central place which it has occupied in primitive and civilized societies and the still potent sway which it exerts over many throughout the world presents a paradox for any rationalist enquiry.

Religion has so far been referred to as a mode of magical security to withstand destructive forces and social disorder. It concerns itself, it will be argued, with the destructive, but also the creative, powers of nature, and indeed of the cosmos as a whole. Fully fledged religion, according to Fraser, originally involved belief in a supernatural world, whose power is conceived as being much stronger than that of human beings or of the earth itself, indeed is conceived as the divine source of them. This numinous vision has its own rationale in primitive societies gripped by destructive or creative forces which they can scarcely comprehend – drought, flooding, pestilence, earthquakes, lightning and storms, entropy and decay, or sunshine, rivers, abundant vegetation and wildlife, fresh vegetables and fruits, fire, wind and rain.

As Fraser says,

> I am more than ever persuaded that religion, like all other institutions, has been profoundly influenced by physical environment, and cannot be understood without some appreciation of those aspects of external nature which stamp themselves indelibly on the thoughts, the habits, the whole life of a people.
>
> The spectacle of the great changes which annually pass over the face of the earth has powerfully impressed the minds of men in all ages, and stirred them to mediate on the causes of transformations so vast and wonderful. Their curiosity has not been purely disinterested; for even the savage cannot fail to perceive how intimately his own life is bound up with the life of nature, and how the same processes which freeze the stream and strip the earth of

vegetation menace him with extinction. At a certain stage of development men
seem to have imagined that the means of averting the threatened calamity were
in their own hands and that they could hasten or retard the flight of the seasons
by magic art. Accordingly, they perfected ceremonies and recited spells to make
the rain fall, the sun to shine, animals to multiply, and the fruits of the earth to
grow. In course of time, the slow advance of knowledge, which has dispelled so
many cherished illusions, convinced at least the more thoughtful portion of
mankind that the alternations of summer and winter, of spring and autumn,
were not merely the result of their own magical rites, but that some deeper
cause, some mightier power was at work behind the shifting scenes of nature.
They now pictured to themselves the growth and decay of vegetation, the birth
and death of living creatures, as effects of the waxing and waning strength of
divine beings, of gods and goddesses who were born and died, who married
and begot children on the pattern of human life.[1]

The supernatural soliciting of sorcery (equivalent to Fraser's magic) gives
way to fully fledged religion, in which a cosmology is elaborated with a
divine hierarchy of power.

Human beings in civilized as well as primitive societies remain different
from animals in being able to conceive the future in extended terms and to
work out relations of apparent or real cause and effect by trial and error.
They know that they must inexorably perish. The ageing process in
humans, moreover, that harbinger of death, is far more evident to them
than with animals, due to hairlessness and conscious loss of faculties,

---

1. Sir James Fraser, *The Golden Bough: A Study in Magic and Religion*, Part IV,
'Adonis, Attis', Vol. I, Preface I–V. This passage not only gives an account of religion in
terms of managing creative and destructive forces, it also expresses the fundamental
distinction between magic and religion that underlies Fraser's work. For him the primitive
magician is akin to the modern scientist in thinking himself able to change or preserve the
course of nature directly by his own intervention in its play of forces, by means of spells,
charms, taboos, etc.; whereas religion involves belief in a higher power or set of powers
capable of explaining fundamental questions about the cosmos and needing to be
propitiated to influence nature's course. Malinowski expresses a similar distinction when he
points out: 'Religion refers to the fundamental issues of human existence while magic
always turns round specific and detailed problems', B. Malinowski, *A Scientific Theory of
Culture and Other Essays*, Beacon Press, Chapel Hill 1944, p. 200. This distinction is
perfectly acceptable in itself and is given fruitful employment by many historians, such as
Keith Thomas in his excellent book, *Religion and the Decline of Magic*, Penguin, Harmondsworth 1971. It might seem, indeed, to vitiate the notion of religion put forward here as a
mode of magical security, since this could by definition only apply to primitive sorcery or its
residues in advanced religions or popular beliefs.
Nevertheless, 'magic' can refer in a broader sense to non-rational and imaginary means
of acquiring knowledge, even of the most fundamental issues, and of acting upon the world.
In this case sorcery, or magic in Fraser's sense, and religion are both essentially magical as
opposed to science and rational enquiry. This distinction does not preclude the possibility
that magical means of knowledge and activity, whether sorcery or religion, can sometimes
prove valid or efficacious, whether due to insight, to chance or to the psychic momentum
and drive which such means can generate in true believers, as with the Islamic jihad, a point
to be expanded upon later.

revealing the passage of time and the ultimate frailty of all organisms. In addition human beings can remember the vicissitudes of fortune and the unexpectedness of past disasters, whether experienced by them personally or not. They are aware of the vast range of fickle powers assailing them.

Epicurus observed of religion that it emanates from fear, primarily of death or the unknown.[2] In the virtual nescience of primitive societies religion became a talisman for averting evil or misfortune, for recovery from it if it occurred and for achieving creative goals; it employed magical means of forfending destruction and ensuring preservation and prosperity (or security of aim in black magic to the malevolent purposes of its practitioners). This magical world-view has been elaborated in the development of the great world religions, assuming more sophisticated forms. As we shall shortly see, the magic of supernatural pre-emption, recuperation, reassurance, creation and destruction, has been evident in the ancient systems of religious doctrine, whether as worship of the divinities of the natural elements, as with animism, or of the other chance forces at work in the struggle for existence. Religion's provision of magical means to contend with human destruction by invoking supernatural powers of creativity and preservation can come to dominate the province of freedom in the realm of necessity, the space within which choice and change in the performance of destruction contention remains possible. It, thereby, can lead societies down most deluded paths. Religion can offer an antidote to destructive forces outside the pale of rational enquiry, to the pristine vampire of reason itself, which it promises to exorcize or attenuate.

This supernatural activism and anti-destructivism, however, debouches on to a larger set of reasons why religion plays so crucial a role in human existence. For it is not merely physical creation or destruction, but moral and existential anguish and, indeed, as Fraser says, wonder at the universe and natural transformations, that religion can dispel or direct. The security it offers is not only of spiritual reproduction by life after death or reassurances amid havoc and ruin, but also the certainty of knowledge about life and the world and the human plight within the cosmos. The great questions that arise in the strange and mysterious predicament of conscious, reflective existence are given confident answers. Kant has said that the prime interests of speculative and practical reason consist in:

1. What can I know?
2. What ought I to do?
3. What may I hope?[3]

---

2. Christ seems to have concurred: 'Be not afraid, only believe', Mark 5, 36.
3. Immanuel Kant, *Critique of Pure Reason*, tr. Norman Kemp Smith, Macmillan, London 1964, p. 365.

Answers to the first can endow confidence of knowledge, to the second morality and meaning to life and to the third release from fear, if the answers are positive and believed in. These positive answers minister to the urgent or transcendental imperative to engage the future and to prevent wonder, uncertainty, anguish and fear about the future from destroying human self-confidence and assertion; Kant's categorical imperative is a response in the sphere of morality to the second question. Indeed, over and above this religion can offer transcendence of human facticity or abandonment of human being in the world, the bedrock of the transcendental imperative.[4]

The transcendental refuge from mundane fear and anguish, however, can beget fear of God and hell and dread at what may come to pass from transgressions. Even if doubts are entertained, human beings can still be persuaded into subordinating their outward behaviour to religious norms by fear, if not of religious authority, then yet of God and damnation. As Kant says of the sceptic, he has an interest in not offending religion, even if not fearful of religious authorities or possessed of moral beliefs:

> for although, through lack of good sentiments, he may be cut off from moral interest, still even in this case enough remains to make him *fear* the existence of a God and a future life. Nothing more is required for this than that he at least cannot pretend that there is any *certainty* that there is *no* such being – and *no* such life. Since that would have to be proved by mere reason, and therefore apodeictically, he would have to prove the impossibility of both, which assuredly no-one can reasonably undertake to do.[5]

Hence, fear might restrain the sceptic as it does the believer from the outbreak of evil sentiment.

Religion then, offers for its believers an all-embracing refuge of security and consolation without which for many their lot would have been unendurable, and for unbelievers fear and cause for restraint. It can thereby become a salient means of social cohesion and survival, a question to which attention will soon be given. It is possible for it to acquire prominence within the province of freedom in the realm of necessity.[6]

The oldest living religion is Hinduism which exemplifies these charac-

---

4. Transcendence and facticity are prime categories of Sartre's ontology in *Being and Nothingness*. The permanent possibilities of dread and anguish inherent in the domains of freedom of a conscious for-itself can be kept at bay by a religious set of answers transcending them.

5. Immanuel Kant, *Critique*, p. 651.

6. The province of freedom in the realm of necessity comprises the scope for change and choice in meeting the requirements for survival in the realm of necessity: religion can become one main way to contend with social destruction, as we shall see.

teristics remarkably aptly. Hinduism, as Chaudhuri has pointed out, has retained a persistently animistic character.[7]

To sum up, Hinduism in its fundamental aspect is a civilized amplification of the primitive man's way of living in the world by accepting the conditions which he believes are inexorably laid down by the supernatural spirits who really own and govern it. It is also an elaboration of the primitive man's corollary to the main proposition that by accepting the conditions it is possible to establish a relationship of mutual dependence which will be stable. In modern terms, the collaboration between man and the supernatural spirits might be called religious feudalism based on the principles of fealty, service and protection.

But above the elemental aspect of Hinduism there is another which is not less fundamental. This has been created by the geographical environment and historical evolution of the Indo-Aryans [who] had to face the difficult problem of surviving with their culture intact in an environment which was hostile in every way. For this they had to create a way of life which would serve multiple purposes, resist the enmity of the aboriginal inhabitants whom they looked upon as savages, as well as the temptation to fraternize with them; compensate for the decline of vitality inevitable in a tropical environment; check erosion of morale; and withstand the destructive impact of the environment on their institutions.

This security could not come from social life, which itself had to be saved.

These handicaps would have created serious difficulties in the way of social and cultural survival even in a favourable geographical environment. But the environment was wholly hostile, because in India nature in all its aspects was in arms against men. Therefore to win the battle against nature they had to seek the help of the supernatural in everything. A pattern of life had to be created in which the supernatural would be able to reinforce human strength.

The caste system based on superiority over the untouchables, protected the conquerors from the disease-ridden aboriginals; while taboos on cow meat and cow slaughter protected animal husbandry from the disasters of depleting reproductive stock in a famine.[8]

It is significant that it was within Hinduism that the cosmological idea of a perennial interplay between creation, preservation and destruction was given an explicit statement in the Gupta period with the trimurti of Brahma, god of creation, Shiva, the god of destruction and Vishnu or

---

7. Nirad C. Chaudhuri, *Hinduism*, Chatto and Windus, London 1979, pp. 21–4. Chaudhuri argues that Hinduism is strongly Indo-Aryan in origin, the original inhabitants contributing little to what remained a conqueror's religion. His work is a most thoughtful and sober evaluation of the complex phenomenon of Hinduism.

8. McNeill points out that most of India with its tropical climate and monsoon humidity was certainly rife with disease and pestilence throughout historic times, even more so than southern China, a notorious plague zone. W.H. McNeill, *Plagues and Peoples*, Basil Blackwell, Oxford 1977, pp. 73–5 and 91–5.

Krishna, the god of preservation. This conception of the relations between these gods was esoteric, characterizing the 'way of knowledge' of such thinkers as Samkara, rather than the 'way of action' of the masses, for whom these gods assumed different forms and avatars, Shiva being the protector for his devotee with his escort, Kali-Durga, the mother-goddess and goddess of war. Brahma's cult underwent a notable decline, far fewer temples being dedicated to his worship than those for Vishnu, Shiva and Kali, the demotic trinity of Hinduism.[9] Brahma once his work of creation was accomplished retired from the scene, leaving the universe to the struggle between destructive and preservative forces or divinities; while Vishnu or Shiva assumed responsibility for further creation.[10] This of course was not inappropriate in a country where nature, as Chaudhuri says, was essentially hostile to human beings and where little creative development proved possible – except perforce in Hinduism, with its proliferation of cults and castes above the untouchables.

For both Fraser and Chaudhuri, religion provides security for the faithful: and both the physical environment of a people, and their way of life within it, profoundly influence the forms it assumes. In other words, the mode of livelihood in its historical geography and demography strongly conditions the mode of magical security. While the adverse and adventitious physical conditions of a people may make necessary some form of belief system to contend with them, several alternatives or variations could suffice. Religion thrives in a society's province of freedom in the realm of necessity, becoming capable thereafter in the manner by which it fulfils necessary cultural requirements of decisively influencing its course and history.

Religion for Marx is the opium of the people, which consoles them in their subjection and reconciles them to their lot. This latter function, however, is derivative on religion's original function for man as the talisman of avoiding evil, of his apotropaic anxiety and dread. Thankfulness for divine creation and supplication to avoid divine displeasure anthromorphically mime the human plight within primitive societies and early civilizations in their subjection to forces of creation and destruction beyond their ken. This original utility of religion is the source of its narcotic utility in advanced civilizations. It is by consoling human beings for their inevitable death and suffering that a religious world-view can also compensate for socially induced misery and resign oppressed races and classes to dolorous abjection. In addition, religion can issue penalties for

---

9. K.M. Sen, *Buddhism*, Penguin, Harmondsworth 1961, p. 59 ff.
10. Brahma is depicted in the Mahabharata as the offspring of Vishnu, 'creating a lotus from his own navel, of his own will, from which Brahma was born', Kalpana S. Desai, *Iconography of Vishnu*, Abhinav Publications, New Delhi 1973, p. 24.

anti-social behaviour, helping to ratify the prevailing codes of morality and to assure the unity of the higher orders and the general harmony without which any social order risks being destroyed. Indeed, religion is as much the opium of the aristocrats as of the masses. Religion ministers in class or caste societies to the needs of the province of necessity in the realm of freedom, ratifying the subjection of the masses and ensuring privileges for and loyalty by the higher orders.[11]

Yet it is by no means only acquiescence to public morality and class harmony which are reinforced by religious beliefs. Bravery in battle, for instance, is more likely to be attained if the warrior can face death with equanimity due to his certainty of survival into another world. The power of Islam was greatly indebted to the boons which it promised the faithful in the cases of either success or failure in the jihad or holy war, the saviour or survival of souls. This magical means of justifying imperialism and instilling courage in combat began as an idiosyncratic movement of nomadic tribes, but became militarily necessary, as we have seen, for their neighbours' survival, hence the rapidity of its spread. For religious zealotry in such a situation becomes an indispensable weapon in the realm of necessity, without which a society perishes. The rise of a proselytizing Catholicism in medieval Spain was vital for its resistance to the Islamic invasion; while it later proved as serviceable as it had for the Arabs in promoting audacity and valour in imperialist adventures of its own. Religion, therefore, can be a compound of opiate and stimulant for competitive prowess, transforming its devotees into nightmarish sleepfighters, while providing a talisman for the avoidance of evil forces or ill luck.

Religion's narcotic functions as opium and as stimulant of the people are later accretions, characteristic of class and warmongering societies, which have partly displaced or at least qualified its role as talisman of averting evil and quelling anxiety or anguish. For those primitive religions which entertained unduly extravagant ideas about the prophylactic or apotropaic qualities of their creed could put the believers at a severe disadvantage in the struggle for survival with those enjoying a faith more blessed with a social rationality. Their economic development and military performance could become fatally impaired. The death obsessions of Ancient Egypt and Mesopotamia, the contemplativeness and quietism of Tibetan lamasaries and the religious wars and human sacrifices of the Aztecs, all gave their believers a severe handicap in confronting those with

---

11. The province of necessity in the realm of freedom is the sphere in which various imperatives must be satisfied if the realm of freedom is to exist at all, namely the provision of a surplus and the protection of the surplus-extraction process. In other words, it consists of what has to be done in society to achieve what need not be done, beyond what has to be done for sheer survival.

172 THE VAMPIRE OF REASON

a more mundanely rational cast of mind. Tibetan charms against missiles proved unavailing in the face of British and Chinese bullets and Chinese tanks.[12]

The history of the Aztecs illustrates this point particularly clearly. Their religion at first stood them in good stead in contending in their environment with other tribes but then assumed a suicidal self-centredness. As Peterson says, 'the Aztecs and other Mexican Indians concentrated on spiritual methods to meet the challenges of life, rather than mechanical methods. They used mixtures of magic and religion to obtain good crops, long life, health, wealth, prestige, children and happiness.'[13] The Aztec conception of the world dictated these preoccupations. As is well known, they worshipped a sun-god who was locked in struggle with the forces of evil and darkness. Since they were the chosen people, they were required to replenish him with sacrifices of animal blood, without which he would have been unable to continue the fight and would have remained in the nether regions after dusk, bringing about the destruction of the world. 'The idea that they were fulfilling a transcendental duty and that on their action rested the possibility that the world might continue to exist, enabled the Aztecs to undergo the hardships of their migration, to settle in a place that the richest and most advanced peoples had rejected, and to subjugate their neighbours.'[14] The province of freedom in the realm of necessity permitted the magical mode of security to transform the mundane mode of security and hence, as their change of abode shows, even the mode of livelihood itself. Geopolitics and economics were changed at the behest of religion.

Nevertheless, the underlying natural conditions of Aztec life in their new habitat provided the challenge which altered the course of their religious development. Their eventual mode of livelihood helps to account for why their most bizarre institution, extensive *human* sacrifice, took hold. They became agriculturalists in the parched Mexican plain, forever in contention with the vicissitudes of nature. The seedbeds of Aztec religious evolution are to be found in these harsh conditions, where 'war, famine and pestilence' were only too frequent, devastating attempts at productive and social advance. The Aztecs and other Indians practised extensive *animal* sacrifice to their gods.

---

12. Britain invaded Tibet briefly in 1904; China occupied it in 1908–11, withdrawing after the revolution of 1911, and then returning after the 1949 Communist Revolution in 1950.

13. Frederick A. Peterson, *Ancient Mexico*, George Allen and Unwin, London 1959, p. 125.

14. Alfonso Caso, *The Aztecs: People of the Sun*, University of Oklahoma 1958, p. 94. The Aztecs migrated from the north to a swampy island near Tenochtitlan avoided by others, where they engaged in fishing and eating snakes.

In Mexico, human sacrifice on a large scale was instituted by the Aztecs, probably around 1450, when bad weather destroyed all the crops and caused four years of national distress. The Aztecs thought that Huitzilopochtli was angry with them for not feeding him sufficiently. In order to secure sacrificial victims for the sun, the Aztecs engaged in ceremonial battles with their neighbours, called Xochiyaoyotl (Flowery Wars or Wars of the Flowers). These were not fought for territorial advantage, but only to take prisoners for sacrifice. The drought and famine disappeared in time and the Aztecs thought their god was pleased and decided to continue mass sacrifice in order to keep Huitzilopochtli happy.[15]

The religious aspect of their imperialism did not preclude its possessing an expansive and exploitative character as well. Not all wars were merely ceremonial and by the late fifteenth century the Aztecs had constructed a tribute-paying empire over Mexico from the Pacific to the Atlantic. As is well known, their subsequent defeat by the Spaniards was due not only to the disaffection of subject peoples under tribute and human sacrifice, but also to their fatal belief that Cortes was the god of light, Quetzalcoatl, expelled several centuries before by previous inhabitants of Tenochtitlan, to whom he vowed a triumphant return. The illusory character of the religious moment in the 'mystico–militaristic' symbiosis that gripped Aztec society was to prove its undoing.[16] Its mode of magical security, which gave such comfort to its people in distress as a means of escape, eventually undermined the mundane mode of security of its imperialism.

Religions which abide by the requirements of the domains of necessity tend to displace those which do not. It must be remembered that almost as many religions as societies have become extinct, although the former can linger more easily than the latter. Nevertheless, surviving religions have tended to conform to the Marxist characterization of them as opiates of the people, being generally pre-emptive of social conflicts while eschewing unduly irrational beliefs about the world which they perforce inhabit. This increasing suitability of religions to the stern tasks of the domains of necessity (that is, the realm of necessity and the province of necessity in the realm of freedom) is but one instance of how enterprises in social life either conform to the limitations the former impose on them or perish.

Thus, religion is ambivalent in its fortune or fate. It can possess, at least for a while, remarkable autonomy from immediate economic and geo-

15. Frederick A. Peterson, *Ancient Mexico*, pp. 145–6. The flesh-eating ceremonies which seem to have accompanied the human sacrifice could have had an obvious rationale in a famine, although this is a moot point. See Marvin Harris, *Cannibals and Kings*.

16. The phrase comes from Miguel Leon Portilla, *Aztec Thought and Culture*, Oklahoma Press 1963, p. 94.

political imperatives, ministering as it does to a more fundamental set of needs, providing reassurance against death and destruction, anxiety and dread, and responding to the transcendental imperative. Hence its extraordinary influence over history in certain turbulent epochs, notably the conversion of the late Roman Empire to pre-Roman Catholic Christianity, an event which for Gibbon clinched its doom. Christianity, indeed, survived the demise of Rome. Yet this remarkable resilience, it can be argued, was due to its 'pre-adapted' characteristics as a magical carapace of security and unity for the turbulence and disintegration of Europe through the Dark and Middle Ages; the papacy, in Hobbes's celebrated phrase, 'was no other than the ghost of the deceased *Roman Empire*, sitting crowned upon the grave thereof'.[17]

The mode of magical security may either correspond successfully to the needs of the modes of mundane security and of production, as has been argued was the case with Islam, or prove detrimental to them, as with the Aztecs and the late Ancient Egyptians. The fact that their societies perished is not without significance. Those societies with counter-productive or obsolete religions expire or are transformed into those with more suitable creeds for economic and military survival.

The revival of Islam in the modern world is an apparent counter-example to the mundane determination of the magical. Iran's Islamic revolution has doubtless to be understood originally as a profoundly nationalist and anti-imperialist movement; its all-embracing attempt to restore the fundamentals of ancient Islamic society can be seen as a task of reparation of the destructive activity of Western imperialism over the last century. Without this context of external encroachment on its ancient culture Khomeini's triumph would have been inexplicable. In this instance, the realm of necessity has come to be dominated by a geo-political and political project of rejection of a social order imposed from without and involving an abrasive economic development; while the realm of freedom has correspondingly come to be dominated by the rehabilitation of an ancient religious nation and way of life, which is assuming a passéiste sway over society.[18] While cultural security has been advanced, economic development, however, has regressed. The geopolitical level of warfare and mundane security dovetail with the religious level of magical security to share a condominium over Iranian society, displacing economic development from its primary place. Hence the stagnation of the productive forces in contemporary Iran. It remains to

---

17. Thomas Hobbes, *Leviathan*, Oxford University Press 1946, p. 457.
18. A further analysis would have to consider the especial appeal of Shi'ite funda-mentalism to the working class and peasantry; it is among the workers in the Gulf states that Shi'ite militancy is most common.

be seen, however, whether the surrounding world of Arab and Western capitalism can reclaim it for their own, in which case the primacy of the economic in the contemporary epoch will be vindicated.

The occupation of Afghanistan by the Soviet Union in January 1980 provides a further instance of the primarily geopolitical reasons for Islamic revivalism in the present. An avowedly atheist regime cannot but disturb the susceptibilities of a profoundly religious people, especially when instituted by the ancient enemy of the country. As in Tibet and Poland, socialism enforced by armed might merely encourages a fierce anti-communism and religiosity. Once their mundane mode of security has been breached, the people fall back the more tenaciously on the magical means where they can preserve their separate identity and continuity with their past.

One counter-instance which could be raised against the thesis being proposed here – that magical modes of security tend to conform over the long run to the interests of the domains of necessity – consists of the history of Judaism in the diaspora. For once Jews were settled in foreign countries, their loyalty to Judaism became a handicap for them, exposing them to periodic expropriation and pogroms. As often wealthy aliens in Europe, subscribing to the very religion whose authorities had brought about the crucifixion of Christ, they made themselves the object of popular envy, suspicion and hatred.[19] Conversion to Christianity obviously stood to improve their mundane security. Yet, despite a seepage of conversions, Judaism has survived and even spawned a militant nationalism in Zionism, recreating a state in its original homeland. The magical mode of security here outlasted for millennia the loss of its abode in 70 A.D. when the Temple of Solomon was desecrated and the diaspora was greatly accelerated. Despite imperilling the worldly security of its flock, it finally triumphed, realizing its long-cherished belief of a return to Palestine and Jerusalem. Indeed, the disasters befalling old Israel, its defeat and occupation, were all prophesied in Exodus and confirmed rather than undermined Jews in their faith. The possession of, so far, a remarkably prescient holy text in the Old Testament has been one reason for the tenacity of Judaism. Also significant, however, was that the Jews of the diaspora were mostly settled in towns as merchants, shopkeepers, craftsmen and moneylenders; and it is arguable that the advantages

---

19. Indeed, Jews in their own land had provoked Roman repression due to the exclusivity of their faith before the rise of Christianity; Hadrian's attempt to rebuild Jerusalem as a Roman colony with a temple of Jupiter Capitolinus in 130 A.D. led to the last great revolt by Shimon Bar Kosiba, whom many saw as the Messiah. Its suppression took four years, involving three to four legions and causing over half a million casualties. Fergus Millar, *The Roman Empire and its Neighbours*, Weidenfeld and Nicolson, London 1967, p. 206.

accruing from a tightly knit religious cohesion outweighed, even in worldly terms, the disadvantages of periodic pogroms. The creation of the state of Israel in 1948 owed much of course to Jewish and worldwide realization after Hitler's Holocaust, that a Jewish state was necessary for mundane survival.[20]

With the exception of Islamic fundamentalism, Zionist Judaism, Polish Catholicism and other embattled currents and creeds, contemporary religions nevertheless show signs of being on the wane in advanced societies, with significant effects upon their public morality, work discipline and economic performance. This secular decline is explicable once its original prophylactic or talismanic function is appreciated. For the growth of science and technology has enabled some destructive forces to be tamed or at least understood, particularly diseases and death. Many destructive forces of the natural environment can be more easily avoided, while our knowledge of the cosmos and its likely destiny is continually advancing, even if new mysteries are also revealed in the process. The dependence of religion's function as opiate and as stimulant on its fundamentally talismanic stance is shown by the impairment of the former as a result of scientific development's subversion of the latter. Religion, as a mode of magical security, it might be argued, is increasingly relieved in civilized states by the advances in social security and medicine. Yet, modern societies have introduced new insecurities of their own stemming from new destructive forces, such as air disasters, terrorism, viruses, pollutants, environmental deterioration and nuclear emissions or fallout, about which information is continually being disseminated. The popularity of horror films attests to the fascination these destructive powers exert over the minds of contemporaries. Religion, therefore, while its larger claims are arguably being undermined by scientific advances, is as a mode of magical security also being reinforced by them. The pertinacious mystery of the cosmos and of the place of life within it cannot be wholly dispelled by science. Its intractability to complete rational explanation and the persistence of certain stubbornly destructive forces which cannot be avoided, above all old age and death, may afford it a long lease of future life.

---

20. The history of modern Israel is primarily, moreover, that of its struggle to survive. See Conor Cruise O'Brien, *The Siege: the Saga of Israel and Zionism*, Weidenfeld and Nicolson, London 1986.

9

The State and the Mode of Mundane Security

There is one level which has so far not been considered at the length it deserves, namely that of the political community or mode of mundane security, whose apex in most societies is the state. The mode of security, today the state, has expressed the unity of society, literally defining in most cases the boundaries of social existence. After initially considering the chief objectives of the political community, it will be possible to investigate in the first section the mundane means employed to achieve them. This will lead in the second section to an assessment of the magical reinforcement so often obtained from religious forms of legitimation of political power. The third section will broach the complex question of power and freedom and their significance for politics, leading in the fourth section to consideration of the momentous issues of class and status. Next, an assessment of nationalism and the forms of subjectivity with which the political community is associated will be in order, followed by a cursory account of international modes of security.

1. The First Functions of the State

The classic objectives of the polity were expounded by Hobbes when he said that people found a state to 'defend them from invasion of foreigners and the injuries of one another, and thereby to secure them in such sort as that by their own industry, and by the fruits of the earth, they may nourish themselves and live contentedly'.[1] A state, in other words, can aim to curb violence to person and property in the domains of necessity and so provide the security for the realm of freedom to thrive.

---

1. Thomas Hobbes, *Leviathan*, Oxford University Press, 1946.

In Hobbes's theory, the minimization of threats to property has a class-neutral character; everyone benefits from the curbing of crime, whether it be theft or violence against the person. In fact not everyone does benefit from a successful rule of law. Criminals and would-be criminals may frequently be losers. Even among the law-abiding population those with little or no property benefit least; and in so far as the state protects the existing distribution of income and wealth from their claims for more worldly goods, they may well lose out compared with their prospects under an alternative social order or property regime. As Smith says, 'civil government in so far as it is instituted for the security of property is in reality instituted for the defence of the rich against the poor, or of those who have some property against those who have none at all.'[2] The state in this guise can be defined, in a paraphrase of Marx's dictum, as the 'executive committee of the propertied classes'.

Neither Hobbes nor Smith mention yet another crucial objective of the state, which is coming into increasing prominence today but has often had a central significance, and that is the protection of the population and its environment against depradations, such as soil erosion, natural disasters, macropredators and micropredators and changes in climate and access to water. The famous thesis of Wittfogel that eastern autocracy was the result of the need for centralized irrigation works was greatly exaggerated; yet, irrigation control in the great riverine civilizations of the ancient world was clearly fundamental to their survival.[3] Contention with pestilence and wild animals, and with drought or flood and consequent famine have been major preoccupations of great polities in history.

Local initiatives are often foremost in this regard, as with the villagers near the Sundarban forest in southern Bangladesh, who operate armed vigilante squads to guard against man-eating tigers. But co-ordination among widely scattered populations against major dangers threatening them requires the intervention of the state or equivalent polity, as with, for example, control of the deforestation that swells the seasonal inundations of the Brahmaputra and Ganges and sometimes floods the lowlands of Bangladesh. The emergence of the contemporary crisis of the environment – as pollution and global warming call for concerted state measures on an international scale – testifies to the ubiquitous need for states to be involved in countering natural destruction.

What the various objectives of the state have in common, therefore, is the avoidance of destruction, whether of a society as a whole or of its property system, its civilization or its members, which is perpetually

2. Adam Smith, *An Enquiry into the Nature and Causes of the Wealth of Nations*, Oxford University Press, 1926, p. 715.

3. Kurt Wittfogel, *Oriental Despotism*, Yale University Press, New Haven, 1957.

threatened by its situation in nature and among other communities. Outside destructive forces or the fear of them, including in certain societies metaphysical forces, persistently menace or haunt societies, which need to resist them if they are to survive, not least by containing internal ones, such as internecine strife among the ruling orders. Thus, the initial raison d'être of a political community comes from the need to promote social order and synergy in the face of forces destructive of existence.[4]

The responsibility for preventing internal dissension and external encroachment has rested with the mode of mundane security. In most but not all historical societies this mode of security has consisted of a state, which with its various branches has formed the legislative centrepiece and executive arm of the mode of mundane security, the main exceptions being tribalism and feudalism with its decentralization of sovereignty. International modes of security can also exist, however, as with NATO and the Warsaw Pact countries today, although they will not be our first concern.

Different modes of security have been responsible in history for preventing their subjects from instigating whatever is destructive, not just of society's existence, but of its members, for example, by resort to organized or individual violence. As a result, the state (tribal chieftain or feudal authority) has been required to establish and then maintain some form of the rule of law. It is essential if human beings are to live in communities that arbitrary violence and robbery of personal effects be curbed. Murder and violation of the person by rape and rapine are enemies of any form of civilized existence, as Hobbes pointed out, requiring the firm hand of a strong authority to curb them. The institution and operation of a powerful rule of law were difficult historical tasks in early civilized societies and even more so in empires, lacking as they did the technological means of surveillance and law-enforcement available today. The imposition of law and order by Rome and their reimposition by feudalism after the anarchy and devastations of the Dark Ages were necessary for European societies, without which Roman and medieval achievements, either in material or cultural fields, would have been impossible.

So long as societies possess neighbours it is also necessary for them to maintain external security. An exercise of means of violence is clearly

---

4. John Pym gave his own interpretation to this notion in a famous speech: 'Those commonwealths have been most durable and perpetual which have often reformed and recomposed themselves according to their first institution and ordinance, for by this means they repair the breaches and counterwork the ordinary and natural effects of time', John Pym, cited in S.R. Gardiner, *The History of England*, 1603–1642, Vol. VI, Longman, London 1884, pp. 313–4.

crucial for both purposes. In state forms of society, the state assumed a monopoly of legitimate use of violence within a given territory, in Weber's famous definition, as a prime requirement of the domains of necessity, as fundamental as economic and reproductive activities or as geopolitical activity with which it clearly overlapped for long historical periods.

The state in its primary functions, then, has to be defined as the central directorate for enforcing a mode of security over society both for internal and external reasons. External dangers, moreover, make internal security even more necessary; and so it is hardly surprising that if a state performs well in external terms, it can thereby attract a general support and legitimation for its authority, even in deeply class-divided societies. Respect for the power and effectiveness of a state in its external policies can give it authority at home. The co-ordination of authoritative resources, for Giddens as for many other sociologists, determines in at least non-capitalist societies their mode of integration and change.[5] This is better understood as a concomitant than a cause of efficient state power, whose rationale primarily lies in a more decisive form of activity: defence against destructive forces. In pre-capitalist societies such forces would principally be natural calamities, foreign invasion, dissension among the ruling orders, and unrest from below.

2. Religious Legitimation

While impressive deployment of means of violence is clearly the first prerequisite for the establishment of a state and its authority, a second crucial requirement in most epochs of history before the modern world has been the invocation of religious sanctions and legitimation. The mode of mundane security has often been powerfully reinforced by the mode of magical security, notably in primitive tribes, in early agrarian civilizations such as Egypt and Mesopotamia, and in Western feudalism and Eurasian despotisms. The divine kings of tribal Africa, the god-kings of Egypt, Persia, Meso-America and South Asia, the monarchies of Mesopotamia, China and Japan and the Divine Right of European monarchies have exemplified in different ways the efficacy of the principle of invoking metaphysical legitimation for mundane power and authority, and of magical sanctions for enforcing security. Indeed, according to the world-view of the state religion of several societies, for instance in Ancient Egypt and the Mayan and Aztec realms, religious observances were crucial in withstanding the destruction of the cosmos itself. If the pharaohs

5. Anthony Giddens, *A Contemporary Critique of Historical Materialism*, Macmillan, London 1982, p. 4.

defaulted on the obligations incumbent upon them, then 'matt' or cosmic as well as social order was placed in peril. As we have seen, the Aztec state religion came to involve belief in the necessity for human sacrifices to feed the sun with blood and ensure its diurnal return. These views, once held, justified extraordinary measures of social mobilization, pyramid or temple construction and warfare. Other ancient civilizations tended to be less extravagant in their cosmic claims. It was very common amongst them, nevertheless, for a monarch to possess some unique ability to contend with natural destruction, say by reason of his rain-making, river-protecting or drought-dispelling powers.

It might be argued that the religious carapace of state power even here had its main raison d'être in enforcing class domination. That this is not so, however, is demonstrated by the prevalence of divine or social forms of kingship or chieftainship in tribal societies, forms which then survived into the epoch of class society and states. They originated according to Fraser in a far more ancient contention of human societies with natural destruction.

Sorcerers are found in every savage tribe known to us; and among the lowest savages, such as the Australian aborigines, they are the only professional class that exists. As time goes on, and the process of (social) differentiation continues, the order of medicine-man is sub-divided into such classes as the healers of disease, the makers of rain and so forth; while the most powerful member of the order wins for himself a position as chief and gradually develops into a sacred king, his old magical functions falling more and more into the background and being exchanged for priestly or even divine duties, in proportion as magic is slowly ousted by religion. Still later, a partition is effected between the civil and the religious aspect of kingship, the temporal being committed to one man and the spiritual to another.[6]

Early sorcery and taboos gave way to sacrifices and prayer, in other words to religious forms of magic seeking intercession by divine spirits or gods. In Africa and elsewhere, the regal role in providing security was such that a ritual killing of kings took place if they failed to bring rain or good crops. The mode of magical security here usurped the mode of mundane security at its peril.

With class societies, a proper state power evolved with complex institutions, but the residual functions of divine or sacral kingship in protecting society against nature and internecine strife, particularly among the ruling orders, were often crucial to its working. The mortuary religion of the divine pharaohs, as we have seen, was concerned to maintain 'matt'

---

6. Sir James Fraser, *The Golden Bough, A Study in Magic and Religion*, abridged edition, Macmillan, London 1923, pp. 105–6.

or cosmic and social order. While the Mesopotamian monarchs were not themselves divine, their legitimacy derived from their sacred functions in protecting society against inundations of the Tigris and Euphrates and against civil strife. Hammurabi's laws in Babylon were held to be divinely inspired: his reign coincided with exaltation of Marduk, Babylon's divine proprietor and protector, the ultimate guarantor of legal right. Hammurabi's reorganization of Mesopotamian society into a service military order, with soldiers stationed on landed estates, gave the legal and ideological innovations a solid basis.[7]

In the long run, developments in the mundane mode of security can dislodge religious sanctions from their central place. This was first evident in the democratic polities of Ancient Greece and Italy. Nevertheless, even after the emergence of their republics, the union of a royal title with priestly functions remained a common practice in both countries. As Frazer says,

> at Rome and in other cities of Latium there was a priest called the Sacrificial King of the Sacred Rites and his wife bore the title of Queen. In Republican Athens the second annual magistrate of the state was called the King and his wife the Queen: the functions of both were religious. Many other Greek democracies had titular kings, whose duties, so far as they are known, seem to have been priestly, and to have centred around the common Hearth of the State. At Rome the tradition was that the Sacrificial King had been appointed after the abolition of the monarchy in order to offer the sacrifices which before had been offered by the kings. A similar view as to the origin of the priestly kings appears to have prevailed in Greece.[8]

The deification of the Roman Emperor as the protector of his subjects began as early as Augustus, although Roman civic traditions and cynicism concerning the proliferation of membership of the pantheon diluted its intensity, which never reached the exaltation of worship of the contemporary god-kings of Sassanid Persia.[9] Christianity of course relegated emperors and monarchs to a lowlier status as secular representatives of one extramundane God; by the early fourth century the imperial cult had almost become secularized and Constantine himself, no doubt for reasons

---

7. W.H. McNeill, *World History*, p. 62.

8. Sir James Frazer, *The Golden Bough*, p. 9.

9. 'In Ammianus' version of their correspondence in 358, King Shapur II of Persia and the Emperor Constantius II could call each other "brother"; but Shapur, in his arrogant letter to Constantius, styles himself "king of kings, partner of the stars, brother of the sun and moon", whereas Constantius, in his haughty reply, is content to describe himself as "victor by land and sea, perpetual Augustus" (XVII.V.3.10)', G. de Ste Croix, *Class Struggle in the Ancient Greek World*, Duckworth, London 1981, p. 379.

of its obvious expediency, made only desultory efforts to suppress it, confining himself to banning images of his person in pagan temples.[10]

The spread of Christianity in post-Roman Europe went hand in hand with the formation of territorial states by the barbarian tribal settlers of the Dark Ages, sanctioning the supersession of clannic by centralized modes of security and social organisation.[11] In Visigothic Spain, the kings received 'most holy unction', as one of them, Enrig, calls it, and were 'preoccupied with ensuring by state action that the orders of the Church were carried out'; this religious form of monarchy seems, as Bloch suggests, to have had a profound influence via the Spanish diaspora of the time on the Carolingian kings, who, unlike their Merovingian predecessors, were annointed with holy oil at their coronation, so acquiring a sacred character. This Carolingian invocation of religion gave sanction to the new proto-feudal relationships of protection, serving to 'consolidate the public peace, which was at once the most cherished and the most fleeting object of their dogged ambition'.[12] The Anglo-Saxon monarchy in turn seems to have acquired its sacred character in imitation of the Carolingian one.

In eastern Europe, the conversion to Christianity went hand in hand with the institution of sacral kingship and the consolidation of territorial states. Vaclav, founder of the Bohemian kingdom in 915–29, Mieszko I in Poland in 966 and Stephen the First, Arpad monarch of Hungary, in 996–7 (assuming his kingly title in 1000 like Mieszko, from Rome) converted to Roman Catholicism; while Vladimir, the Rurik prince who completed the Varangian realm in Kievan Russia, was converted to Orthodox Christianity in 988 in order to marry the sister of the Byzantine Emperor Basil II.[13] The strengthening of the European monarchies in the late Middle Ages and the early modern period was accompanied by the elaboration of the doctrine of the Divine Right of Kings, later to be the target of the English Puritans and the French revolutionaries.

The secularization of society and thought involved in the post-Enlightenment world marginalized the religious legitimation of European monarchies, although the monarchs of Britain and Holland remain leaders of their national protestant churches to this day. The general disassoci-

    10. A.H.M. Jones, *Constantine and the Conversion of Europe*, Hodder and Stoughton, London 1948, pp. 212–3.
    11. E.A. Thomson, *The Visigoths in the Age of Uffila*, Oxford University Press, 1966.
    12. The quotations are from Marc Bloch, 'A Contribution towards a Comparative History of European Societies', in *Land and Work in Medieval Europe*, tr. J.E. Anderson, Routledge, Kegan and Paul, London 1967, pp. 52–3.
    13. Perry Anderson, *Passages from Antiquity to Feudalism*, Verso, London 1974, p. 232.

ation of the mundane from the magical modes of security has been a characteristic of the rise of liberal bourgeois societies.[14]

The theocracies of the modern world, moreover, have tended to prove cumbersome in contending with more secular states and hence tended to disappear, the last of these to do so being the Mahayana Buddhist theocracy of Tibet under Chinese occupation. The revival of Shi'ite Islam in Iran, however, attests to the continued possibility of a resurgence of theocratic forms of state, at least in Third World countries. This, however, still conforms to the rule that the military quality of a theocratic order is decisive for its fate, Islam being generally capable in this regard, except in relation to the militancy of Zionist nationalism. Judaism shows, as we have seen, that a religion can not merely legitimate a people's state, but maintain its cultural identity even when it has disappeared and then recreate a state form for it thousands of years later. The mode of magical security, if it is articulated in a sufficiently rich, cohesive and apparently prescient religion, such as Judaism, can survive the dissolution of its mundane equivalent to aspire for its eventual redemption. Religion remains capable by virtue of its magical durability of secreting the strangest atavistic phenomena.

Religions, then, can compose magical carapaces of security to reinforce, and even rehabilitate the mundane functions of the state in providing protection of its people and civilization. The state, however, is not only a guardian protector. It can show a Janus face to its wards and subjects; for it can itself become a destructive force for the population and civilization of a society unless internal checks and balances operate to curb its arbitrary power. Hence the importance of the growth of liberalism, which cannot be interpreted, as Marxism is wont to do, as merely a class ideology.

3. Power and Liberty

The role of liberalism in countering the internal power of the state can be understood in terms of the negative freedom which the state's successful pre-emption of destruction assures its individual members, but which it

---

14. The decline in the belief in the therapeutic powers of the royal touch was one symptom of the general loss of mystery and magic suffered by European monarchies after the Reformation in the north and epochal bourgeois revolutions. See Marc Bloch, *The Royal Touch: Sacred Monarchy and Scrofula in England and France*, tr. J.E. Anderson, Routledge and Kegan Paul, London 1973, p. 217. The last recorded instance of the royal touch in Britain is of Queen Anne in 1712 touching the thirty-month-old infant who grew up to be Dr Johnson.

can then easily infringe itself. Negative freedom is complemented by positive freedom.[15]

Negative freedom for individuals consists, inter alia, of the ability to exercise their positive freedom, created by the successful pre-emption of its incipient or definitive destruction, whether by outside forces or the state itself. Positive freedom consists of the scope for exercise of powers of autonomous activity and creation, whether by individuals or the state, which includes the conditions making possible negative freedom. Liberalism emphasizes the role of negative freedom for the individual, especially freedom from the state's interference. On the other hand, socialism or liberal-democratic theory has underlined the role of positive freedom for individuals in a community, that is democratic positive freedom, for instance through the state; for only at the group level can many activities be undertaken which possess a liberatory potential for all, such as cultural and educational advances.[16]

The analysis here depends on the crucial notion of power, in terms of which positive freedom and so negative freedom have been defined. The state itself has sometimes been defined as the epitome of social power, and human history as the outcome of competition for power. 'Power', indeed, is one of those concepts, such as 'state' and 'freedom', that are as contentious to define as they are indispensable for explanation.

A common predilection of those who invoke power as a key category of analysis is to consider it in its social form for agents, whether of individuals or of collectives. Michael Mann, for example, distinguishes thus between collective and distributive power: collective power is exercised by communities over each other and over their environments, while distributive power is expressed in the allocation of power within human communities between individuals and groups.[17]

This distinction, however, needs to be supplemented to show how 'power' can be ascribed to properties of nature as much as to those of mankind, such as the manifold power of the environment over human communities. Indeed, the emergence of our species and the evolution of life itself have attested to the power of natural selection.

'Power' in a general sense can provisionally be defined as the ability to

---

15. The most eloquent exponent of these liberal concepts is Isaiah Berlin, *Two Concepts of Liberty*, Oxford University Press, 1956. The ideas behind them originated in the epoch of the French Revolution, being given an exposition by Benjamin Constant amongst others.

16. In Sartrean terms, the point can be put by saying that positive freedom on a communal scale can change those conditions which constitute the facticity of any individual freedom, its being-there in the world. The intimate rupture involved in exercising such collective freedom can be highly oppressive as well as liberatory; indeed in some cases it can become both in different aspects of experience.

17. Michael Mann, *The Origins of Social Power*, Cambridge University Press, 1987.

create, destroy, consume, preserve or repair. The productive powers accessible to society, which for Marx are synonymous with the productive forces, debouch on to those of nature, such as the natural fertility of the soil and the procreativity of the animal world. The destructive powers of nature include entropy, earthquakes and lightning; its preservative and restorative powers encompass biological immune systems, forest canopies and solidified lava. It is in a creative tension with these fundamental transformative and preservative powers that human history has unfolded.

Human power can in turn be defined as the ability to (realize human intentions or potentialities to) create, destroy, consume or preserve such things as independence and authority in the political sphere, or wealth in the economic, or might in the military sphere by intervening in these powers of nature. Collective power benefits from the synergy of combining individual powers in the process; while distributive power registers the allocation of abilities to create, destroy, consume and preserve within the framework of this synergistic power, this allocation being to structures, such as the market, law, or parliamentary democracy, and to roles that individuals can play within them, for instance, as electors.

An objection which could be raised against our provisional codification is that the terms employed in definition are more complex than that of power itself, thereby abrogating Occam's Razor. However, even if Occam's Razor is applicable to definitions as well as explanations, there is not necessarily a contravention of it when a cluster of terms can be used to define not just one concept but a series of concepts. While the defining terms may be more complex than any one concept individually, they may be simpler than the series. Thus, if the terminology of creation, preservation and destruction, which has been deployed here, can elucidate not just power, but also forms of historical explanation and of freedom, then its common invocation may permit a simplification on a wider scale than was previously feasible.

The notions of power and freedom can be related, then, in a common problematic. Human power can be defined as the ability (to implement intentions or potentialities to) create, destroy or preserve some order (of authority, legality, independence, wealth or military might) by intervening in the transformative and preservative powers of nature, which includes the human species itself. Positive freedom consists of the scope for the exercise of human powers on either an individual or collective scale; while negative freedom consists of the scope for exercise of positive freedom without interference from others, including the state.

The provision of justice and order, that is of individual negative freedom so dear to liberalism, is heavily weighted by class interests, one law prevailing in most societies for the rich and another for the poor. A too flagrant misuse of state power by the privileged is, nevertheless, likely to weaken its legitimacy, otherwise so serviceable for social and class domination, unless it is buttressed by a powerful inegalitarian ideology, such as Hinduism or Confucianism. A consideration of status and class can now be made.

4. Status Groups and Class Society

The stratification of a society, either in a primitive or civilized stage, is determined in the first place by its perpetual contention with destruction, which desiderates a division of labour and a hierarchy of tasks and social orders, whether officials, warriors, lawyers, priests, workers, farmers or tradesmen. In the second place, it is determined by endeavours in the realm of freedom as a whole, including those of particular status groups, actors, sportsmen, writers and artisans, etc. The division of labour does not by itself necessarily create a class system, as the example of primitive societies makes clear. It rather fosters differences in order or status. Classes only appear in history when certain status groups obtain private property of pre-emptive, reparative and productive forces or of the surplus generated from the economy, whether by owning the means whereby it is produced or by reason of their military and political power. It is possible, as in socialist societies, that the status groups from which class developed can persist after the abolition of private property and class society.

Status, then, appeared long before class in history and requires prior elucidation. It is essential to discriminate between definitions of status and class and explanations of them. While comparative status is defined in pre-capitalist epochs by the locations of individual members of a society in both its mundane and magical modes of security, that is the varying degrees of respect and protection accorded to them, its explanation was to be found in their roles in social life in any of its various modes, including the modes of security themselves. Individuals were customarily graded in terms of their degree of indispensability in the struggle for social existence and their degree of renown and achievement in the realm of freedom.

Thus in primitive societies, hunters or farmers, warriors or witch-doctors, women or children, chiefs or officials were given differing degrees of importance in the network of due protection and esteem, including in the afterlife, depending on what type of destruction contention was required of them and on whether they were able to shine in creative activities. Warriors would be accorded immense prestige in warlike tribes and witchdoctors in those requiring sorcery and magic to combat natural forms of destruction, while hunters or farmers could come into their own in more tranquil circumstances. Warriors, priests and chiefs usually of course occupied privileged positions even in quite pacific tribes, being able to wield means of authority and intimidation internally, whether weapons, damnation or proscriptions, lacking to the farmers, womenfolk and children. In the post-glacial foraging societies, warriors, priests, chiefs and officials were often buried in separate types of graves with their own distinctive ornaments, denoting a privileged status in the afterlife.[18]

The first steps towards class societies were taken when the social differentiation based on status and primitive wealth became compounded by distinctions of ownership of means of production and destruction contention. Just as status is *defined* by location in the modes of security, so class is by that in the property regime or mode of production. While status remains *determined* by the roles which individuals perform in the modes of livelihood, security or other means of social life, class can be *determined* either by the dictates of productive development alone, as often in capitalist societies, or by those of both production and security, as under feudalism.

Indeed, as we have seen, historical societies before capitalism were not in general characterized by secular productive development, with the major exception of the Middle Ages.[19] The structure and changes in their class system could not have been due to it, as Marxism has claimed both of them and, with more justice, of capitalism. The objection here is not that a variable cannot be explained by a constant, for it sometimes can; rather, it is that the Marxist claim to explain a class structure and its changes, a constant and a variable, by the dictates of productive development, a variable, is vitiated by the fact that the alleged explanatory

---

18. Marek Zvelebil, 'Postglacial Foraging in the Forests of Europe', *Scientific American*, May 1986, pp. 90–91. Zvelebil reports on the existence of carved objects of wood, bone or stone in such graves, probably indicating considerable social differentiation and a primitive form of money as store of value for times of famine. As Trigger points out for one of the predynastic Egyptian civilizations, 'increasing social stratification can be traced in the varied size and design of Gerzean tombs and in the grave goods being put into them'. B.G. Trigger, 'The Rise of Egyptian Civilization', in B.G. Trigger et al., *Ancient Egypt: a Social History*, Cambridge University Press, 1983, p. 36; see also p. 48. Among the warlike tribes which conquered the Western Roman Empire, status was closely bound up with military life. As Contamine says, 'the arms carried varied with the social rank of their owner to such an extent that archaeologists think it is possible to recognize rank from graves according to the arms and jewellery they contain. From excavations of Alamanic remains in the Würtemberg region, it has been concluded that graves with a sword and sax are those of the free men, graves with spears, arrows or axes are those of the half-free and graves lacking arms those of the unfree', Philippe Contamine, *War in the Middle Ages*, Basil Blackwell, Oxford 1984, p. 179.

19. Duby even claims that, 'a great change in productivity, the only one in history until the great advances in the eighteenth and nineteenth centuries, occurred in the countryside of Western Europe between the Carolingian period and the dawn of the thirteenth century', Georges Duby, *Rural Economy and Country Life in the Medieval West*, Edward Arnold, London 1968, p. 103. Even if this is exaggerated, it is not so mistaken as to fail to support the above generalization, to which the major exception would be China, at least until late medieval times.

variable was often missing. Also, no argument has been adduced of how the often static needs of production alone could account for different class structures and changes, given that the same mode of livelihood (material mode of production and destruction contention within nature) is compatible with several property regimes (in the Marxist sense of modes of production). It is here of course that security needs can play a crucial role, since the development of new weapons and means of defence against them has, unlike that of production, been almost perennial in history and prima facie comprises a good candidate for helping to explain variations in class structures, in conjunction with more or less static productive needs.

It has already been argued that the modes of livelihood and so production and class structures of a society can emerge and succeed each other in history in answer to the requirements of its struggle for existence. This may well involve, as with the spread of agriculture in northern Europe, certain societies forsaking their mode of livelihood, in this case hunter-gathering, and adopting another, agriculture, in imitation of others for reasons of their contention with nature, as some vital hunting resource, such as oysters or seals, dwindled away. Alternatively, this may have happened for reasons of contention with other societies, say as loss of territory to agriculturalists took place. Either production or security needs, then, propelled forward a shift towards a new mode of livelihood and so production with its class system, a pattern which was repeated with the different routes to capitalist industrialization by latecomers. Again, it is possible, however, for some societies to change their modes of livelihood and production quite spontaneously without being compelled to do so by their struggle for existence, as with those first into agriculture or industry; a development of the productive forces here is unambiguously responsible for a new mode of production and class system in a classic Marxist fashion.

It is not just the spread of new modes of production which can owe a great deal to security factors, something which many Marxists would doubtless be prepared to concede, but also their evolution and character. Status can often play a decisive role in determining class, rather than vice-versa. This commonly happens through the mediation of the state, which can remain, as it began, the executive committee of the ruling status groups.

Such a position might, indeed, be thought to be not incompatible with Marx's own reflections on the nature of class relations in pre-capitalist societies. For Marx the 'essential difference between the economic forms of society, between for instance, a society based on slave labour, and one based on wage-labour, lies only in the form in which surplus labour is in each case extracted from the actual producer, the labourer'.[20] Marx also

20. K. Marx, *Capital*, Vol. I, p. 217.

considers that the labour regimes of pre-capitalist societies were characterized by the use of extra-economic coercion in extracting the surplus out of
the producers so that they rendered 'direct forced labour'.[21] Coercion,
therefore, was recognized by Marx as central to pre-capitalist class
society.

Nevertheless, this general premise can lead to divergent arguments,
depending on what other premises obtain. It might be contended that
coercion was important in societies of pre-capitalist productivity levels for
several reasons, not just to extract the surplus but to compel the producers
to engage in the unpleasant work involved since the advent of agriculture
or industry and to develop the forces of production. Under these
historical circumstances, the exercise of violence becomes functionally
necessary for toil and technological developments, as well as for the
generation of the surplus. This is, then, compatible with the Marxist
primacy thesis that the development of the productive forces is the crucial
dynamic explaining both the class system (or the relations of production)
and social life as a whole.

However, the producers of agrarian pre-capitalist societies could still
subsist even without coercion, as was shown by the independent farmers
on allodial plots or mountainous terrain in Europe and the early European
settlers of North America, engaging in 'primitive commodity production'.
Moreover, as we have seen, it is implausible to contend that productive
development was the dynamic of such social orders since technical
innovations were comparatively rare within them, excepting during the
expansive periods of the European Middle Ages.

It is more plausible to explain the centrality of coercion in pre-capitalist
agrarian societies by imperatives of security and distribution, which, when
coupled with those of production, can explain the nature of class and
social development. In the first place, once a social order exists then it
needs to be defended by some means or other against internecine strife
and its members against violence upon person and property. This was true
of primitive societies before class society and, a fortiori, of more stratified
agrarian societies. Secondly, if the strata privileged in terms of status were
to enjoy their consumption, some means became necessary to squeeze the
surplus from the rest of the population. In other words, coercion was both
a means of satisfying a prime requirement of the realm of necessity and
one of the province of necessity in the realm of freedom.[22] It was neverthe-

---

21. K. Marx, *Grundisse; Foundations of the Critique of Political Economy*, Pelican,
London 1973, p. 245.

22. The province of necessity in the realm of freedom, it may be recalled, consists of
those conditions which must be fulfilled over and above the necessary conditions of social
life if a realm of freedom is to exist; generally at least the provision and protection of a
surplus-generating system.

less just a means, not the only one available. Religion could and often did minister to the preservation of social order and the provision of the surplus, moreover often with facility, persistence and harmony. A third reason for the prominence of coercion, however, often obtained, namely its *necessity* for external defence for societies in proximity to others. This then made it more likely that it would be employed in the service of satisfying the first two requirements. This was the more so, since resort to force or its threat would greatly strengthen non-coercive means of securing social order and surplus provision. Perennial religious sanctions for these ends could be given powerful reinforcement in times of crisis. Of course, external security is only necessary if societies threaten assault: and acquisitive intentions have often motivated belligerence. This indicates a fourth reason for the prominence of coercion, namely its indispensability in waging war in order to extract booty and tribute. In pre-capitalist societies in proximity to each other, coercion could prove vital both for external defence and for external enrichment. Its use in these respects could then deflect the internal social order into either a repressive or democratic pattern depending on security needs. Moreover, the development of means of violence could then acquire a priority, and its implications for social change become pervasive. For this reason coercion was often formative of pre-capitalist societies.

It has already been argued earlier that possession of costly weaponry and the privileged status and exploitation it conferred and required explains why the invasions of charioteers during the mid second millennium B.C. led to the aristocratic empires of the Hyksos, the Aryans and the Kassites and how the development of infantry and naval warfare with the onset of the Iron Age changed military conditions in the Eastern Mediterranean.[23] In ancient Greece and early Republican Rome an independent peasant class emerged and persisted by reason of its citizenship and participation in civic life, itself the reflection of its vital role in military life. The infantry phalanxies of Athens and other Greek states and the rowers of the Athenian navy were drawn from the peasantry and urban poor, giving them a crucial status in democratic assemblies, where they were able to limit levels of taxation and rent and to protect their landholdings and crafts from encroachment by the wealthy. Their civic status reflected their contribution to the defence and advancement of the state; which then assured them economic freedoms.[24] The eventual decline of their position and the eclipse of Greek democracy were linked to military developments, especially that of the mercenary armies of the Macedonian rulers. Similarly, the Roman Republic, with its independent peasant class

23. See pp. 85–6 above.
24. Ellen Meiksins Wood, *Peasant-Citizen and Slave*, Verso, London 1989.

subject to the call-up, gave way for military reasons to imperial autocracy, a professional army and a degradation of peasant status, leading to the new class relations of the colonate. The organization and deployment of means of violence within the mode of security determined status and, therefore, class and relations of production, not vice-versa; the development of the means and organization of violence, not of production, were responsible for social transformation, albeit within a predominantly agrarian mode of livelihood.

Alternatively, status could continue to stratify society rather than class. The aristocratic empires of the Ancient Middle East and Asia, for instance, appear to have conformed to a status rather than a class pattern of power. A warrior aristocracy led professional soldiers into battle, as in Ancient Egypt and Persia.[25] The elite owed its position not to landowner-ship, but to comprising the groups of leading warriors, bureaucrats and tax collectors surrounding the monarch, who, at least in principle, owned all land. The state, here, extracted the surplus from the peasantry itself with the assistance of these privileged strata, whose income or upkeep was dependent on service to the king. They formed, therefore, a principal elite status group within the mode of security, not an independent class. Mundane security was buttressed by magical security. The panoply of state was characteristically supported by a socially cohesive religion conferring divine or unique sacerdotal status on the monarch himself. Massive temple construction and a group of priestly officials, an aristocracy of service warriors, administrators or tax collectors and peasant villages dependent directly on the king were characteristic of such societies.[26]

It could be argued that whatever the legal relations, in reality a consid-erable degree of effective ownership of land devolved on to local warrior nobles or tax farmers. This was certainly true of Mesopotamia and Ancient Egypt for long periods, rendering the Sumerian and pharaonic dynasties vulnerable to aristocratic usurpations. But here, as elsewhere, the nobles owed their position firstly to their privileged status in the mode of security to which their acquisition of full class power was due. In general, the power wielded over their domains by Mesopotamian, Egyptian, Assyrian and Persian rulers was of a far greater magnitude than that of the feudal sovereigns of medieval Europe, where the notion of royal landownership was commonly diluted by de facto aristocratic

---

25. For the constitution and cavalry cum-infantry armaments of the Persian armies of Cyrus and Darius the Great, see Arthur Ferrill, *The Origins of War*, Thames and Hudson, London 1985.

26. The Islamic world, several centuries later, reveals a somewhat similar picture, albeit with an imamate, rather than a priesthood.

ownership – not just tenure – of estates, which were passed from generation to generation in a manner which the monarch could not suspend or only at the risk of rebellion.[27] This again was due to their centralized organization of military force compared with the decentralized pattern of feudalism. Class, where it existed before capitalism, stemmed from status, not vice-versa.

Status, indeed, can prevail over class even under capitalism. A striking instance of the dominance of status over class and of the mode of security over that of production is given by South Africa. The different gradations of status defined in racial terms under the apartheid system confer different degrees of protection and respect in the state's security network whose durability ultimately rests on the monopoly of means of violence enjoyed by the regime. It might be argued that it is the white ruling class's ownership of the means of production which accounts ultimately for this monopoly and so apartheid. But in fact the state is not the possession of the ruling class alone, which would benefit from further relaxation of apartheid to placate world opinion, to prevent sanctions and to develop the economy. It is the white masses which command the state and man its apparatus of security. It is they who benefit in particular from the confinement of the franchise to whites: status has fostered a vast cleavage between the white and black working classes and confirmed white farmers and landlords in their possession of the best soil.

Liberals have persistently argued that economic development would inevitably erode the system. But this has proved illusory, apartheid remaining in its political essentials unchanged. Certain reforms of course have been conceded, such as the abolition of the pass laws and with it the dismantling of the restrictions on labour mobility and training. But the franchise remains restricted, since its extension to blacks would clearly threaten the privileges of the whites. What is at stake here is indeed the security of consumer privileges; yet these are not merely the consequences of the capitalist nature of the economy, but also of the particular security system prevailing – a system whose characteristics are not explicable as furthering development of the productive forces, but as furthering the interests of a small, but distinctive, racial minority. Security needs quite clearly prevail over production needs, as does status over class.

None of this is to deny the fact that class can sometimes, indeed today usually, be dominant over status or that this is now due to production's primacy over security. The class structure of modern bourgeois societies is primarily determined by the division of economic labour and the requirements of productive development, while military factors play a smaller,

---

27. As is graphically displayed by Bolingbroke in Shakespeare's *Richard II*.

although not negligible, role. The class systems of the United States and the British dominions, comparatively isolated countries and bourgeois almost ex nihilo, have clearly developed overwhelmingly for economic reasons. Under pre-capitalist regimes, therefore, coercion and geopolitical factors combined with the dictates of the divisions of labour to determine class structures and their evolution, while under capitalism the latter can often exert a more independent sway over social life.

5. Nationalism and the Role of Subjectivity

We are now in a better position to understand something of nationalism and its offshoots. The necessity of retaining geopolitical inviolability helps to explain why nationalism and other forms of collective solidarity have played so important a role in history and have so often prevailed over class conflicts. Since societies are perennially afflicted with destructive pressures, a communal solidarity is an imperative of social life: a clinging to old customs which have assisted survival in the past often has a rationality in the present, particularly in moments of immediate danger, as in wars or catastrophes, when it becomes vital and can be easily seen to be vital by the population as a whole to remain united. This is so even supposing that the society in question is the obvious aggressor, for any form of warfare involves an element of chance and peril. Conversely, if the social order is revealed as incompetent to defend the community at such a time, it becomes vulnerable to internal change. Defeats in wars and manifest ineptitude in disasters have triggered off the great revolutions and social transformations of history, which are, nevertheless, long prepared by internal strains of a kind richly illuminated, if not quite fully grasped, by Marxism.

For the internal dialectic of class and economy to which Marxism ascribes revolutionary situations is often only one side of the story. Social orders can enter a critical stage, not only because their dominant mode of production impedes further economic development, but primarily because geopolitical institutions are exposed as inadequate to the requirements of their survival. Thus, while the great English and French revolutions may generally have abided by Marxist criteria, the spread of bourgeois society and state forms, indeed of industry itself, on the European continent and to Japan was due to the geopolitical vulnerability of the latter to the more industrial powers. In Japan the whole class structure and economic system was changed by the threat of imperialism from 1854 onwards, as the Japanese undertook an imitation of the West. A bourgeois industrialization became a sine qua non of its national independence. Similarly, the Risorgimento and Bismarck's revolution from above were necessitated by the vulnerability in the European state system of a disunited pre-bourgeois Italy and Germany. It was the international development of the productive forces eclipsing the emergence of a rudimentary local capitalism which gave the decisive impetus towards these upheavals, with the impact of the former being mediated through the geopolitical sphere in a conscious imitation of England. A Marxist analysis in terms of economic development and a geopolitical analysis in terms of the wider reaches of the realm of necessity need to be combined in order to understand modern history.

One objective of such a synthesis should be to clarify the basis of class relations under different modes of communal solidarity. One striking feature of class society for much of its history has been the external determination of its structure, rather than its exclusively internal one. This has been particularly the case for societies existing in close proximity to one another. Their realms of necessity have then contained the need for a strong social solidarity against any potential intruder. The struggle for existence between societies in an exacting world gives them reason to be apprehensive of each other's intentions. Societies are defined, not just positively by their modes of production, reproduction and cultural life, but also negatively by their fears and solidarity against an enemy or putative enemy. Ruling classes throughout history have been able to legitimate their domination by invoking a genuine or fictitious foe as the source of some imminent threat to all society. Moreover, such an enemy in the struggle for existence can lend a crucial dynamism to social and economic developments, justifying and facilitating measures of austerity at the same time as a faster tempo of labour and consequently an increase in surplus extraction.[28]

In the case of a genuine enemy a more successful mobilization of the realm of necessity in these terms has a quite rational foundation. In the case of the 'satanization' of an opponent, the greater dynamism of society can impel it more successfully towards its creative projects, even if these are of a partly deluded kind. The Nazis perfected this latter form of social mobilization, of which the Islamic jihad is the prototype, and produced its modern theorist, Carl Schmitt, whose conceptualization of the necessary adversary can be freely translated as the existential enemy.[29] The decisive

---

28. For the speedy modernization of British industry and agriculture provoked in 1915–18 by the trauma of the Great War, see Correlli Barnett, *The Collapse of British Power*, Alan Sutton, Gloucester 1984, pp. 112–7. This modernization was of course to prove short-lived by the complacent 1920s once victory had been won.

29. Carl Schmitt, *Der Begriff des Politischen* 1937, Vorwort and Drei Corollarien, Berlin 1963. For a more explicitly geopolitical work, *Volkerrechtliche mit Interventions-Verbot für raumfremde Mächte*, Berlin 1939. I am indebted to the late Nicholas Krasso for the term 'existential enemy', which is a free translation of Schmitt's concept of the absolute adversary, to be distinguished from a conventional one, as in the case of one democratic party in relation to another.

ruptures of social organization, undertaken by ruling classes themselves, particularly those undertaken on an international scale, have been accomplished by the invocation of an existential enemy of a genuine or factitious kind, which has maintained a framework of negative self-identification to hold society or a group of societies together, while the work of internal transformation has proceeded on its way.

The first form of the existential enemy in human history was doubtless that of the rival tribe. The great empires of domination which superseded tribal existence were often in contention with one another, as was Carthage with Rome and Late Period Egypt with Persia. The existential enemy could assume the form of barbarian nomads and outsiders, notably for Persia, Imperial China and later Japan. Alternatively, it could take the form of an evil deity or cosmic force, such as Seth, the evil brother and slayer of Osiris, who founded, it was held, the Ancient Egyptian state, and Ahriman, the cosmic foe of Ahura Mazda, the protective and universal deity of Zorastrian Persia. In these cases mundane enemies became the accomplices of the cosmic foe, as the Hyksos were of Seth for the Ancient Egyptians or the barbarians were of Ahriman for the Zorastrian elite of the early Persian Empire.[30]

The mobilization of Christian Europe in the Dark Ages against the Islamic foe precipitated the transition to feudalism. The alien negative moment, which the feudal nobility was successfully able to prevent, was an Islamic occupation and subjugation of Europe. It consolidated its hold by resisting Viking and Magyar invasions and then maintained a fragile unity, always liable to be broken by internal dissensions, in assuming the offensive during the crusades against Islam under the leadership of the Papacy.

The great advance of the medieval period culminated in the internal creativity and divisiveness of the Renaissance and Reformation.[31] The

---

30. The most notorious practitioner of existential enmity to date has of course been Adolf Hitler, whose credo in this regard is expressed by the following: 'the art of leadership consists of consolidating the attention of the people against a single adversary and taking care that nothing will split up this attention.... The leader of genius must have the ability to make different opponents appear as if they belonged to one category', A. Hitler, *Mein Kampf*, tr. James Murphy, Hurst and Blackett, London, p. 110. Different opponents need to be identified as tools of a 'Great Satan', Khomeini's designation for the United States. The process of stigmatizing a foe as the source of all evil comprises his 'satanization'.

31. Protestantism as a revolt against medieval Christianity in the name of the Pauline Kerygma recapitulates the thematic of the latter's original existential enemy, Islam, which rejected Christianity in the name of their common semitic-monotheist roots. Calvinism, in particular, forlornly imitates those Judaic features prominent also in Islam: its militaristic fervour (the jihad), its migrationism (the Hijra), its theocraticism (the imama), its predestinarianism and its austerity. See the stimulating work by Patricia Crone and Michael Cook, *Hagarism; the Making of the Islamic World*, Cambridge University Press 1977, pp. 139–45.

Reformation involved the successful rejection of papal authority by much of the uplands of Switzerland and Transylvania, the offshore north and dyke-strewn Holland – those areas where resistance to retaliation could be more effectively organized; while Germany, France and Central Europe became the battlegrounds, yielding the Counter-Reformation its major successes. The secession of inaccessible regions of Europe from its common religion gave each half of the ideological divide an existential enemy against whom to mobilize its populations, imperial and tradition-alist on the one side and increasingly nationalistic and bourgeois on the other. The emergence of capitalist nations in the north was facilitated by the execration of popery, while the persistence of absolutist monarchies in the south was complemented by the heresy-hunting of the time.

Existential enmity has become associated with another form of self-identification, in a dialectic in which nationalism has arisen as the inter-mediary moment. As well as the negative foil of the enemy, societies have often invoked in critical founding moments an avatar of their existence in a charismatic idol or model. Nations have formed around the twin ideas of an enemy in a heroic struggle and a heroic martyr or leader; England in the Hundred Years War and Joan of Arc; the Papacy and the Tudor monarchs; Spain and William of Orange; world imperialism and Lenin and Castro. The more assertive a society in struggle, the greater the idolatry of its leader, whether Hitler, Mao, Stalin, Kim-il-Sung, Ho Chi Minh, de Gaulle, or Khomeini. Just as the existential enemy has its biological origin in the struggle for existence, so existential idolatry, or a cult of personality, has its roots in the 'aping' of the leader in the dominant hierarchies of primate social groups, such as our own. The existential enemy personifies the vampire of reason or the threat to a society's self-identity and the existential idol personifies its desired self-identity in the struggle for existence. They both, thereby, enter into the service of the ruses of reason, which issue from this struggle.

Societies can take as their existential idol not only individuals or institutions, but also other societies which they strive to emulate. This can impart a greater dynamism to their development and induce a mimicry of the idol, either effective and even superior to the original or, in a subjective colouring, as a caricature of it, depending on their respective natural endowments and their objective possibilities. Thus, Germany took England as its model in the nineteenth century, albeit with a strong undertone of hostility. Japan has taken the US as its charismatic idol in the postwar world and largely succeeded in surpassing it in economic vitality and modernity, while its continued dependence on the latter geopolitically remains clear. It is even possible for the existential enemy to become the existential idol, as has the USA for the USSR under Khrushchev and perhaps today, even if an idol only in certain narrowly defined terms.

The state, then, needs to be understood as carrying out three basic sets of functions:

1. The pre-emption or reparation of social (indeed sometimes cosmic) destruction by nature (or the gods), by other societies; and by internal lawlessness; employing its monopoly of violence. The rule of law (including cosmic law), its command over pre-emptive or reparative forces and its consequent powers of authority as the apex of the mode of security; hence its character as custodian of the realm of necessity.

2. The pre-emption or reparation of violent class struggle and social cleavages and the execution of creative tasks, whether those of the ruling classes or status groups or society at large; hence its character as the executive committee of the ruling classes and status groups and as custodian of the province of necessity in the realm of freedom.

3. Frequent mediation between an existential enemy personifying the vampire of reason in the domains of necessity and an existential idol in those of freedom; hence its character as the hallowed and legitimate custodian and avatar of social or national existence.

6. The International Mode of Security

As has already been related, international modes of security can obtain among blocs of countries. This can occur in two different ways, either from imperialism, as with the Roman or British Empires, or when a religious or ideological-cum-political struggle has developed, as between the Islamic world and medieval Christendom or today between NATO and the Warsaw Pact, which is also the product of a geopolitical imperialism.

While empires may be defined in the first place as international modes of security, this does not prejudice explaining them as the outcomes of economic or other levels of social existence. A higher-order definition can also be given in terms of whatever is in fact being secured, indicating the peculiarity of an individual imperialism's dynamic, such as commercial imperialism or the security imperialism of the USSR (the Warsaw Pact comprising the outworks of the Russian socialist state's security in the West). In the case of a more voluntary participation by independent nation-states in a common military bloc, such as NATO and SEATO, the international mode of security may be further defined in terms of the common bond of its members, a liberal-democratic capitalism being secured in the former case and capitalism of whatever political complexion in the second.

The very security character of an empire or an international organization, such as NATO, can compel it to take the offensive against other empires or blocs antagonistic to its raison d'être and its existence. Defining both NATO and the Warsaw Pact as international modes of security, therefore, with their own peculiar aspects, need not prejudice a broader examination of the origins of the Cold War or a judgement as to which of the two is the more aggressive protagonist within it. The interplay of the economic, the geopolitical and the ideological in instigating different imperialisms is a complex subject requiring an analysis sensitive to the peculiar conditions of each historical epoch.[32]

Modes of security, then, can exist on both the international and national (or local) levels. Moreover, the immediate explanation of the character of local modes of security can lie in facts about their geopolitical location amid some conflict between international modes of security, as with the adhesion of certain states to capitalism or socialism today. The complex interaction between international and more localized modes of security can only be understood in terms of the different forms which the struggle for social existence has assumed in different historical epochs.

---

32. See Giovanni Arrighi, *The Geometry of Imperialism*, Verso 1978, for a highly original and perceptive analysis of Western forms of imperialism.

10

A Summary of the Argument

The philosophy or theory of history has long tended to concentrate upon the significance of either cultural or material factors in promoting social change. The modern debate has centred on whether ideas of a cultural kind – religions, value systems, political creeds – or forces and structures of material production or geopolitical power have predominated in influencing the course of history. The former position has been espoused by Hegel, Weber and Toynbee; the latter by Marx and his followers and geopolitical theorists and historians. In addition, there has been a rich vein of historiography which has given attention to the relationship of societies to their geographical and demographical endowments, notably the Annales school in France. These perspectives have not been mutually exclusive and several historians have combined motifs from different sources of inspiration, Jones and McNeill, for instance, integrating environmental and geopolitical concerns into their works.

It has been argued above by contrast that these different approaches need to be synthesized within a wider framework of thought than each presupposes independently or severally. This problematic consists of the perennial interplay between creation, preservation and destruction on every social level. Human groups cannot be understood solely in terms of the creative properties of their economies, societies and civilizations (to take the triad which gave the Annales journal its subtitle) or even of their environments as well; they also undergo the insistent impact of destructive forces, from which the former can help to preserve them.

In the first place, societies are obliged to be prophylactic and recuperative with regard to various rapacious natural forces: of hunger, thirst and exposure of their members, by provision of basic necessaries; of disease and individual death, by medicine and reproduction; and of entropy and erosion from the elements, by environmental management, particularly after agricultural settlement. Pressure from other societies, themselves subject to these assaults and tempted to mitigate them at others' expense, need to be withstood by defensive preparations and social cohesion. Indeed, tendencies towards internal fragmentation and secession have to be prevented from undermining social or territorial integrity in the face of either pressures from without or those, such as overpopulation, from within. In the process, a wide range of cultural activities becomes mandatory: the acquisition of knowledge concerning the destructive powers in contention and the creative powers capable of being harnessed to meet them; the maintenance of public morality and law to enforce discipline and loyalty; and the education of offspring into the above requirements. However successful these activities may prove to be, extinction remains inescapable for the individual members of a society; and religious forms of consolation and compensation can become necessary to ensure that the above requirements are adequately met, at least in certain circumstances. For a religion, once installed, can become indispensable to satisfying certain types of social necessities, so assuming a decisive role in social life, of which more soon.

Homo sapiens as a whole with its vaunted rationality encounters as its deadliest enemy the very nature that gave rise to it, which, unless adequately propitiated, can drain its life-blood away; the rapacity of nature in its incessant vicissitudes and demands comprises the predator or vampire of the reason realized by homo sapiens and its civilizations. Yet, not only do human groups form the prey of nature, they can quite rationally subject other species and each other to conquest and rapine, indeed subordinate strata within them to the oppression of others. The vampire of reason is ambivalent in its appearance, sometimes being incarnate in the predatoriness of nature, its voracity towards humanity, and sometimes that of human predators towards their victims, including their own kind; however, as even the Mongols eventually learned in China, it is more rational for a system of exploitation within a society to preserve, and even improve the conditions of, the subject population in order to guarantee and maximize surplus-generating powers. The vampire of reason in its human guise within settled societies is generally, therefore, not destructive of human lives, but of their freedom.

Nature is by no means uniformly hostile to human civilizations, indeed furnishes them with a fount of resources capable of being transformed into objects of practical or pleasurable use. Likewise, contacts between societies are far from being invariably destructive, permitting an exchange of goods, persons and ideas to flourish. Even wars and natural disasters can have creative repercussions, destroying outmoded institutions and societies and transmitting new artefacts, creeds and information across hitherto impenetrable barriers of social custom and ideological and political control.

Similarly, the oppression of some social strata by others is not necessarily incompatible with considerable self-autonomy and scope for freedom on the part of the exploited, excepting such cases as gang slavery and child labour. Peasants and tradesmen have sometimes been only lightly taxed and in return have reaped certain benefits from belonging to a settled or civilized social order, not least freedom from arbitrary violence and access to towns and cultures that would have been historically impossible without some oppression.

Societies in fact are not exclusively defined either by their contention with destruction or by their many-sided creativity. In the first place, they are obliged to inhabit a realm of necessity, the sphere within which they contend with their destruction and that of their members. This requires activities on every social level from economics and defence to demographic, environmental and cultural self-protection. In addition, they inhabit a realm of freedom, the sphere within which they are free from such requirements. Again, this can assume the form of varied activities on every social level, including the provision and enjoyment of luxuries and leisure or art and knowledge. The realm of freedom, however, as well as that of necessity can contain those activities of aggression against other societies in warfare and oppression and those structures of domination within which social exploitation takes place.

It might seem anomalous to maintain that religious movements and institutions and exploitation or oppression can inhabit both the realm of necessity and that of freedom, contrary to the Marxist procedure, whereby religious institutions are confined to being superstructural and exploitation to being basic in the realm of necessity.

The *realm* of necessity, however, possesses its own *province* of freedom, within which there is scope for choice and change in meeting the requirements of social life. Food must be eaten and defence provided, but cuisines and security arrangements can vary widely. Religions and places of worship may not have been essential in earlier epochs for social existence, but may have offered highly effective ways of satisfying requirements that were, such as the need for consolation for death and destruction, the need for deterrence against wrongdoers and for discouragement of rebellion or secession, and the need for sanctions for marriage ties, military loyalty and reciprocal social bonds; as well as providing some protection for travellers, commerce and towns and refuges for the victims of violence and treason. These and many other facets of religious life were highly suitable to fulfilling various functions in the realm of necessity, even while the extravagances of religious art and mysticism embellished the realm of freedom. Different cuisines and systems of defence and religious belief can comprise unnecessary but sufficient conditions of insufficient but necessary conditions of communal existence, or social usin conditions.

They are unnecessary in themselves because no one of them has to be selected, but are sufficient to satisfy necessary conditions of social life, which are themselves insufficient on their own to bring it about.

Conversely, the *realm* of freedom contains its own *province* of necessity, that set of its component activities which are necessary for the realization and enlargement of its existence, namely the provision and protection of a surplus-generating system, whether a tribute-paying empire or a hierarchical social order or indeed both.[1] There are things that need to be done in order to accomplish those that do not have to be done. They are unnecessary and insufficient in themselves for a realm of freedom, but are necessary components of sufficient conditions of such a realm; that is, they are insufficient but necessary components of unnecessary but sufficient conditions of a realm of freedom, or social inus conditions.

The provinces of freedom and necessity in their respective realms interact with these realms themselves. Thus, the province of freedom in the realm of necessity is capable of being transformed by developments within the realm of freedom itself, notably by the emergence of nuclear weapons from the subatomic investigations of modern physics. Expansive epochs are often characterized by a perpetual transformation of their physical conditions of existence, as the technology and ideas of the time prove to have unexpected repercussions. Similarly, the province of necessity in the realm of freedom can be disrupted by unforeseen events in the realm of necessity, as pertinently today with the spread of AIDS and its impact, not just on mortality rates, but on sexual mores.

The two examples cited of these influences reveal the wide scope of the interplay between the realms and provinces of freedom and necessity, ranging from economic and military affairs to sexual and ideological ones. Every social level is partly within the realm of necessity and its accompanying province of freedom and partly within the realm of freedom and its attendant province of necessity. In certain epochs the former pair predominated over the latter and in others the latter over the former. Indeed, historical epochs can be distinguished by whether they are dominated by destructive and preservative forces or by preservative and creative ones, depending on the power and incidence of these dimensions of social life and the responsiveness of societies to the challenges besetting them. Nevertheless, even in the direst epochs, the realm of freedom is never quite extinguished, while in expansive ones the realm of necessity

---

1. Just as religion does not exclusively inhabit the realm of necessity, so oppression does not the realm of freedom in so far as it facilitates peace and the taming of arbitrary violence in the realm of necessity, as in the Roman Empire for its non-slave population, and in so far as basic necessities are unequally distributed.

can still pose grave problems, as notably in our own with its droughts, famines, wars and plagues.

Over the long run, there has been a strongly upward movement, despite many setbacks, whether in production and wealth or life-expectancy and population. Yet the advance and diffusion of productive technology and of ecological knowledge and medicine has been accompanied by the development of more powerful techniques of warfare, such as nuclear weapons.

The development of new destructive forces by nature and mankind explains why periods of expansion and economic growth, in which the *domains* of freedom come to the fore, alternate with those concerned with security, in which the *domains* of necessity prevail.[2] Thus the high Middle Ages with its thrusting outward in the crusades and its economic dynamism were succeeded by the great crisis of feudalism in the fourteenth century, characterized by soil erosion, famines, the Black Death and the destructive warfare of the time, in which large armies and bands of freebooters devastated the countryside of continental Europe. In our own epoch, however, the development of armaments of such destructivity as nuclear weapons has paradoxically rendered them rationally unusable in the advanced industrial zone and permitted a continuation of growth; its growth crisis today is quite different in scale from the retrogression of past crises, such as that of feudalism.

The chief reasons for the secular primacy of the realm of freedom over that of necessity to date can only be understood in terms of the interaction within them of various social levels. Those physical activities of either realm which involve contending with or exploiting nature's possibilities – such as economic production, demographic reproduction and environmental protection – comprise components of what can be termed the mode of livelihood. Societies subsisting in nature are obliged to develop not just their productive and reproductive powers, but also pre-emptive and reparative forces to minimize nature's destructive forces by harnessing its creative ones, as in medicine and environmental maintenance. The creative and destructive powers of nature vary widely in their incidence and character across the globe and through time, depending on the historical geography and animal-cum-human demography of different regions. This necessitates different responses. In riverine or coastal areas, dams and dykes, drainage systems and locks and bridges and ports become crucial for ensuring survival and conveniences, while in land-

2. The domains of freedom comprise the realm of freedom and the province of freedom in the realm of necessity within both of which alternatives emerge; while the domains of necessity comprise the realm of necessity and the province of necessity in the realm of freedom within both of which exploitation and disasters take place.

locked ones wells and aqueducts, fuel deposits and roads and vehicles suitable for the terrain are vital both for necessaries and luxuries. The various regions of the world, moreover, are characterized by different threats from microparasites and animals and different hazards of climate and geology. Furthermore, nature varies not only in space but in time, whether under the impact of human societies themselves, as with much soil erosion, or due to its own fickleness, as with ice ages and many floods and droughts. The formative influence upon an economy's character and performance, therefore, derives from the environment to which its technology must adapt. A more basic level of social existence than the development of the productive forces in relation to modes of production, to which Marxism gives pride of place, is the development of the productive, pre-emptive and reparative forces in relation to historical geography and demography, fundamental referents for an authentic historical materialism.

The different modes of subsistence cited by Smith – agriculture, industry, pastoralism and commerce – can be combined in any given society to compose a certain mode of livelihood. Yet it is not only the imperatives of livelihood that demand human existence within society, but those of security against internal dissension or other societies. Societies possess modes of security within which a measure of protection from violence, indigence and arbitrary dispossession can be guaranteed. They provide insurance not just for property, but for human life itself.

In many cases in earlier and even in later civilizations the relevant mode of security consisted of a religious world-view and set of institutions, such as Hinduism and its caste system in India, where political dominion and demarcations often shifted in uncertain fashion within an unchanging Hindu society. The mode of mundane security or political life employs the panoply of law, administration and coercion to enforce protection of person and property and civic discipline; while the mode of magical security or religion deploys the codes of salvation and sanctity to confer its own forms of order and authority. In earlier civilized societies religious or magical modes of security provided crucial sanctions for political or mundane modes of security, nearly all of them developing theocratic forms of state. The harsh exigencies of life with its inexplicable threats from nature or the outer world were alleviated by extramundane compensations and controls.

Modes of security are not, however, exclusively concerned with the requirements of the realm of necessity. They also inhabit the province of necessity in the realm of freedom. For Marxism the political and religious levels are superstructural and determined in their character or at least their course by the requirements of the economic base or the relations of production, the latter corresponding to the development of the productive forces. But, in fact, the modes of mundane and magical security have more than a relative autonomy with regard to the economic base; they can determine the nature of the property regime and can deflect the economic development of societies for centuries into quite different paths, even when they share the same modes of livelihood and fundamental technology.

Thus, the agrarian civilizations of medieval Europe and the Arab world were distinguished from each other in a fundamental manner by their respective modes of security. Feudal Christendom comprised a peculiarly decentralized zone of communities, linked together by the common bond of the Papacy and the Christian church. Its essential principle of operation lay in an exchange of protection and conditional landownership, whether by lord or peasant, on the one hand for service, military service by the lord and his vassals or labour service by the peasants, on the other. The Arab world after the conquests of Islam was periodically organized into regional states under the various caliphates and kingdoms of Baghdad, Egypt, Morocco and Spain; while its property systems were characterized by an absence of private ownership of land, which remained in the possession of caliphs, monarchs and sheiks. A ruling caste of soldiers and tax collectors battened upon village communities retaining considerable social independence. No symbiosis of protection, landownership and military service took place such as characterized feudal Europe and Japan. The dividing line between these divergent political systems and property regimes was decided by the fortunes of battle, not the requirements of economic development; southern and central Spain and the Balkans escaped feudalism for centuries and entered into the Muslim world because of the Moorish and Turkish conquests of the early and high Middle Ages.

A concomitant of this direction of causation between geopolitical and religious levels and economic affairs is that status, or the degree of protection afforded to various groups in the community, such as soldiers and priests, can determine the nature of class rather than the reverse. This, indeed, was the usual pattern in the pre-capitalist world. The agents of the caliphate, for instance, were a ruling class only in so far as they collectively controlled the productive forces; they constituted originally a ruling status group, whose share of the surplus extracted from the peasants and merchants was legitimated by their position in the hierarchy of rank. In the case of feudal Europe, the fusion of the modes of security with the relations of production allowed lords to enjoy a conditional landowner-ship, albeit one which could be abrogated by their liege-lords or superiors in the rank hierarchy. Status here directly fashioned class relations, indeed determined them in conjunction with the division of labour entailed by the predominantly agrarian mode of livelihood; peasants were subjected wherever they lacked arms or upland retreats.

This is not to deny that in the modern period with the triumph of capitalism a different type of social development emerged in which productive development and property systems did eventually become decisive in forming much of the political and religious levels of existence. But this could only occur because of the earlier construction of absolutist nation-states with their strong enforcement of general security. The dynamic of pre-capitalist hierarchical societies was twofold, one form generally residing in the accumulation of surplus by war and tribute, taxation and rent in their domains of freedom and the other in that of means of security in their domains of necessity, that is, security not only for the population and its territory but for the surplus-generating system itself or the property regime dominant in the realm of freedom's province of necessity. It has been under capitalism that the dynamic of the realm of freedom has become continuously expansive, assuming the form of the accumulation of capital and the development of the productive forces for reasons shortly to be considered. In pre-capitalist societies the modes of security, as the main means of surplus-extraction, whether from other societies or the underlying population, tended to determine the course of economic development; many ancient and Asiatic societies of domination invested their surplus not primarily in developing their economies beyond the provision of indispensable public works, in particular means of communication and transport, but in elite consumption and in accumulating means of security, such as castles and weapons and temples and tombs.

The development of pre-capitalist societies and the eventual transition to capitalism can be understood in terms of the struggle they necessarily waged for their social survival. Human societies are subject to a struggle for social existence, much as social animal groups might be in the wild.[3] They must contend in their domains of necessity with the destructive forces of nature and of other societies. Their modes of livelihood (and component modes of subsistence) and their mundane and magical modes of security are at stake in the struggle; and those that fail to perform adequately tend to be replaced by more effective variants, as hunter-gathering, animism and primitive tribal organizations were slowly dislodged across the globe by agriculture and settled theocratic states. This is strongly reminiscent of the eclipse of the early hominids by proto-

---

3. The existence of animal group selection has been disputed recently by many biologists for reasons discussed above, see pp. 75–6. These reasons, particularly the supposed absence of genuine non-genetic altruism among animals, do not obtain for human beings.

human groups. Increasing sophistication in the means of production, destruction contention and destructive abilities enabled some to prevail over others.[4]

The struggle for social existence encompasses the influence of conscious choice and change as well as unconscious changes, unlike kin natural selection in the wild, as of ant and bee colonies. For there exists, as we have seen, a province of freedom in the realm of necessity, wherein different methods can be selected, either consciously or by elimination of the unsuccessful, in performing essential tasks. Moreover, a society's realm of freedom can influence the province of freedom in its realm of necessity, as modern science has done with engineering and military technology, deflecting social structures into novel solutions, albeit ones then tested by insistent pressures from the struggle for existence.

These pressures account for the fact that, among the activities which unfold in the realm of necessity, some have greater urgency and priority than others for at least individual societies. Language and public morality, education and cultural conservation are as essential to a society's survival as economic or security activities, but the latter are generally more insistent and so more efficacious in directing social change. The former are finally essential to society because of their indispensability to the latter, while the reverse is not the case. The requirements of economic and geopolitical life are not only immediate, but shift with the vagaries of nature and the dispositions of other societies, while cultural mores are not, at least immediately, concerned with survival and are often transmitted from generation to generation without disturbance. The disasters which can befall a society from inadequate means of livelihood and security, such as drought, floods, famine, depopulation, invasion and disintegration, are more likely to occur and when they do so are more likely to require urgent attention than those ensuing from ignorance, amorality and poor communications (given the largely spontaneous reproduction involved in acquiring knowledge, morality and language). Moreover, the latter are most to be avoided by reason of leading to the former, while the

---

4. To postulate the existence of such group selection among human communities, as Carr-Saunders termed it, might seem to involve a return to Social Darwinism. But the unit of selection in question is not the individual organism but the group, and does not concern their individual survival attributes. Social Darwinism, indeed, is a misnomer for the emphasis upon continuing individual selection in human history, which the Social Darwinists desiderated.

This does not preclude the fact that the struggle for existence can unfold within, as well as between, societies; social forms can compete with each other, not only within a feudal or capitalist society, but also in a society in crisis or undergoing a breakdown, such as Rome in the third century A.D. or late Ming China. Even individual selection remains in a qualified way in feudal warfare and capitalist competition and in such institutions as the mandarinate in China.

former are primarily to be avoided on their own account.

There is one significant exception to this rule and that is the disasters which supposedly accrue from defaults in religious rites. Religious observances and institutions provide a primary security, once they are accepted by their believers and elite beneficiaries as being indispensable to their salvation and privileges. This contrariness has allowed them to influence historical development in decisive ways, as with the religious wars and human sacrifices of the Maya and Aztec societies; although with the qualification that this has only occurred for so long as their struggle for social existence has not exacted lethal penalties for counter-productive activities. Creeds that are extravagant in terms of their material and metaphysical investments tend to be eliminated in favour of less irrational ones, as were the Maya and Aztec religions in time.

The struggle for social existence has changed its character in the course of history. From being a brute competition between hominid hordes it has evolved into a complex interaction between increasingly sophisticated societies and their natural or human enemies or potential enemies. Whatever the origins of civilized societies and states, their continuous existence necessitated institutions capable of quelling internal disorder and secession, resisting foreign invasion and providing necessaries and surplus goods, while contending with the vicissitudes of geographical and biological nature. They proved variously successful in these tasks, depending upon the character, strength and persistence of the forces opposing them and upon the prescience and vitality of their responses. Yet all early civilized societies eventually succumbed to some disaster or another.

In the process of this long struggle civilized states could be vanquished by barbarians; useful, indeed precious, knowledge could be lost, as with the destruction of the Alexandrian library; and valuable material advances, such as Roman roads, be abandoned. In generally expansive epochs, such as our own, the eclipse of one zone by another need not be incompatible with a general advance. For one society or zone of societies can lead for a while and then transmit its ideas and capacity for leadership to another, better placed to exploit new technologies, as the United States was with the railways and steam engines initiated in Britain. In pitting societies against each other even destructive epochs of history have released or stimulated potentialities for greater development than would have been possible within the older structures. The decline of the Roman Empire eventually permitted the emergence of a multi-centred and vigorous European zone of societies, while relieving the barbarian pressures upon China, which in the Dark Ages of Europe made great advances in technology, science and civilization. Even in the Dark Ages themselves agricultural productivity began to recover and develop as technologies which had been ignored in the technological conservatism of Roman times were generalized across Europe, such as the watermill and the millboard plough.[5] The losses to culture from the fall of the Hellenistic world and Alexandria did not preclude the more resilient ideas of material activity from surviving and spreading. The remarkable dynamism of European Christendom in the Middle Ages created a decentralized economy capable of nurturing market relations and the growth of capitalism, itself capable of ushering in the modern world. It is inconceivable that such progress would have been possible had Europe still been ruled within the imperial grasp of Rome. The vampire bat of Roman forms of exploitation, in Sainte Croix's phrase, was incompatible, as he eloquently shows, with the long-term amelioration of the conditions of the peasantry and townsfolk upon which the dynamic of Western Europe's economic life was to be premissed. The vampire of reason in its predatory Roman shape was to be defeated in a creative wave of barbarian destruction, a ruse of the reason expressed in the general struggle for social existence.

In any form of struggle for existence, whether it be between species, societies, social forms, capitalist firms, technologies or ideas, a reason and rationality can develop and spread. Reason here is definable as an ever more complex and expansive order, permitting greater freedom from destruction and free creativity. The ever more complex and expansive cognitive order attained by the advance of science is the example usually given of discursive or theoretical reason; and scientific advance itself is the typical instance of rationality, or the possession or exercise of reason. The order in question here consists of an increasingly successful adaptation or correspondence of scientific hypotheses to the world which they are designed to illuminate. This instrumental rationality has its biological counterpart in the natural selection of species promoting ever more complex forms of life.[6] It also possesses a near equivalent in practical reason, such as is embodied in technology, wherein an increasingly complex and pervasive order of correct solutions to practical problems has been achieved. It has been the argument of this work that a further instance of rationality derives from the increasingly complex and

---

5. This is not to deny the extent of retrogression in economic life during the Dark Ages when trade contracted drastically and Roman roads fell into neglect.

6. The evolution of species has been punctuated by periodic crises during which intensified competition has led to a simplification and diminution in number of life forms for a while; this has not been incompatible with, but has on the contrary accelerated, the long-run trend towards greater complexity and pervasiveness, much as capitalist crises have done with the trend towards more complex and pervasive forms of production and consumption. The recurrent employment of Occam's Razor, therefore, in favour of the simpler among competing hypotheses, is compatible with an ever greater complexity of knowledge, since successive sets of hypotheses have an ever greater generality.

expansive order manifested by successive forms of social organization, promoted by the struggle for existence between societies. For this has made them increasingly responsive to the requirements of the realm of necessity and to those of the related province of necessity in the realm of freedom, or in other words to the advance of destruction avoidance and free production or creativity in the *domains* of necessity. Societies have been able to become so responsive partly by harnessing the advances of theoretical and practical reason to achieving such goals and partly by rendering themselves increasingly suited in their organization, ideals and beliefs to the exploitation of the science and technology involved.

However, societies have also developed increasingly powerful means of destruction, not only by perfecting weaponry, but also by unleashing destructive developments in nature, such as pollution and new micro-bacterial infections. These forms of destruction have threatened the very order at the heart of the progress of rationality. They constitute the vampire of reason in the negative sense of being corrosive of human, or indeed natural rationality. This very destructiveness has, however, had its creative side. By exposing weaknesses in social organization and dispositions it has contributed in the long run to their rectification, whether within the society so exposed or, if insufficiently resilient, in its supersession by superior forms.

The struggle for social existence, then, promotes new powers of destruction as commonly as it does those of self-survival and creation. But the very destruction involved has so far merely served to promote more effective forms of social organization, more effective that is in terms of the rationality required to improve humankind's powers of self-survival and creation. The great cataclysms of history have in this sense been recuper-ated for the species as ruses of reason, being the occasions for accelerating historical progress, as with the world wars of the last two centuries proving instigators of social revolutions and reforms.

Even when the vampire of reason assumed the form of Mongol destruc-tiveness, its baleful consequences were accompanied by creative develop-ments: the construction of a Eurasian-wide empire allowed ideas and goods to cross the continent, bringing Chinese inventions and wares to Europe and European ones to China. Even the pestilence which the Mongols carried in their train, the famous Black Death, was to play a decisive role in terminating serfdom in the West and resolving the crisis of the feudal economy.

This perspective on history can be accused, as was Hegel's, of inter-preting human sorrows and catastrophes as mere occasions for species advance. Sufferings of course possess far more significance than this. Yet the callousness of the ruse of reason is no sure argument against its existence. The rational progress manifested so far, however, is now threatened by nuclear and other perils far more dangerous than any that have existed hitherto. There can be no guarantee that the cunning of reason will continue to prevail.

The conception of a universal progress stemming from the very failures of individual societies and of a beacon of advance being passed from one civilization to another closely resembles that of Hegel's philosophy of history, not only with the ruse of reason, active above the heads of particular agents, but with its world-historical individuals and societies as landmarks in the development of the world spirit or Logos. Indeed, the emanations of the struggle for social existence, not in spite but precisely because of its Darwinian connotations, can be seen to be reminiscent of aspects of Hegel's argument. In the form it assumes in human history, the struggle for existence allows a growing role for ideas. Ideas can survive destructive forces more successfully than their physical embodiments, as Marx acknowledged when he implied that the cognitive, not the physical development of the productive forces, was the driving force of history. Not only can ideas be transmitted or communicated more easily through space, they can also prove more resilient in the face of invasion and catastrophes. This is especially the case with practical ideas, which conquerors are usually and rationally quite ready to adopt from their victims. Even if cultural notions have been suppressed, sometimes savagely, practical ideas have been put to good use, as have roads and available implements, under secure empires of domination.

Instead of species and their characteristics being the subject of selection and ever more complex advance, societies and general ideas, whether of livelihood, security or free speculation, compete with each other within an abrasive nature, promoting a comprehensive advance, not only by the elimination of the less successful, but by conscious invention and imitation and learning from the misfortunes of others. This parallel structure of argument is not so surprising when it is remembered that both Hegel and Darwin were inspired by the same source, the 'political economy' of Smith and Malthus. The hidden hand of the capitalist market-place demonstrated the possibility of the ruse of reason for Hegel, while Malthusianism stimulated both Darwin and Wallace to their contemporaneous discoveries of natural selection. In each case an apparently blind interaction can be given its own implicitly teleological or functional explanation.

The ruse of reason inherent in the general advance of the struggle for social existence, indeed, not merely echoes but has been further advanced by the hidden hand of capitalism. As Marx himself foresaw, the network of capitalist competition, ushered in by the West, has brought whole nations under its sway across the globe, not only within but against it. The struggle has assumed military and ideological as well as economic and demographic forms, both in earlier centuries and today.

The arch-opponent of the historicism of Hegel and Marx, Karl Popper, has objected that the development of scientific ideas is unpredictable and, given their immense power in influencing the future and the importance of prediction in scientific thought, this makes general ideas about history impossible to confirm. Yet he himself had earlier suggested that the succession of scientific conceptions has a dynamic, that of their continuous improvement through the refutation of successively more comprehensive and less fallacious theories. He has also suggested the parallel between this version of cognitive development and Darwin's principle of natural selection. Nature is the arbiter, whether of species or scientific theories, and their internecine struggle promotes forms increasingly better adapted to it. The inveterate foe of dialectics has thereby laid his theory open to being interpreted as an account of the ruse of reason or impersonal hand at work to improve knowledge. Indeed, it is not only scientific, but also religious, political and other ideas which are open to refutation and general improvement in this way. Given Popper's premiss of the immense power of ideas, an ameliorist philosophy of history can be adduced from his own argument.

In actuality it is not only ideas of all kinds, but also social institutions and groups which are subject to natural selection. The negativity of nature in its many forms, whether as corrosive of homo sapiens and its environments or of human groups and their beliefs or of technological and scientific theories, comprises the vampire of reason, which has, nevertheless, through its very success in eliminating species, societies, forms of society and ideas so far been cheated of a final victory by the ruses of reason or cunning of history, which its devastations incite.

The speculative philosophy of history cannot realize its own potential until its claims have been checked through a critical appraisal of their implications for historiography and sociological enquiry. The increasingly complex forms of the struggle for social existence, for example, need to be analysed in terms of the findings and arguments of historians concerning the respective types of society that have succeeded each other in the past; the modes of argument deployed in historiographical and sociological debate would need to be considered. A critical, not merely speculative, philosophy of history remains to be elaborated.

Index

Key concepts are in italics

Afghanistan 66, 71, 90, 175
Africa
    North 56, 73, 98, 121, 126 n20, 140, 151
    pre-colonial 10, 180, 181
    sub-Saharan 33, 52, 108
agriculture
    and basic needs 100
    effect of environment on 45, 78
    as mode of livelihood 55, 56, 79–84 *passim*, 119, 123, 189, 206, 208
    and technological progress 121, 122, 151
AIDS 101 n90, 204
Althusser, Louis 107
Anderson, Perry 90–91, 121
Annales school 8 n7, 201
anthropology 40, 106
Arabia 163
    and caravan trade 75, 96, 96 n83
    influence of Islam on 97, 97 n86, 98, 98 n87, 140, 155, 156 n27, 157
    as tribal society 73, 99, 122, 156
Aramaeans 85
armed forces 64, 65, 65 n40, 98 n87
    see also militarization; warfare
arms race 62, 83, 100, 147, 153–4
Arrighi, Giovanni 199 n32
Aryans 7, 85, 191
Athens 7, 86, 191
Aztec civilization 104, 171, 172–3, 180–81

Balkan peninsula 59, 84, 90–91, 207

Bentham, Jeremy 161 n32
Berkeley, George 18 n6
Berlin, Isaiah, *Two Concepts of Liberty* 185 n15
biology 16, 38–9, 42, 54, 75, 76, 96, 161, 164, 211
Bloch, Marc 85, 119, 125, 127, 128, 183, 184 n14
Boneparte, Napoleon 63, 68
    period of 67, 153
Braudel, Fernand 46–7, 50, 59 n31, 93
Buddhism 154, 184
Bulliett, Richard W. 96 n83
Byzantium 89, 97, 153

Cambodia 29
capitalism
    and 'hidden hand' 24, 137, 158, 161, 164, 213
    influence of geography on 9, 52, 66, 130, 150, 211
    and knowledge 133, 134
    Marxist theorization of 2, 59, 110, 114, 115, 129, 195
    military factors and 92, 93, 106, 119, 120, 123, 124, 127, 198, 199
    and realm of freedom 113, 155, 159
    and realm of necessity 30, 30 n20, 31, 77 n59, 125
    religious factors and 175, 197
    and social order 44, 81, 163, 188, 189, 193, 194, 208, 209 n4
    and state power 7, 72, 147

Germany 9, 61, 62, 63, 64, 65, 68, 72, 73, 107, 145, 146, 163, 194, 197
Geyl, Pieter 67
Gibbon, Edward 174
Giddens, Anthony 180
glaciation 2, 19, 45–6, 78
Gould, Stephen 38
Great Britain 52, 54, 66, 68, 72, 107, 163, 172, 172 n12, 183, 195 n28, 210
  see also under specific countries
Greece, Ancient 7 n3, 36, 72, 85, 86, 107, 127, 131, 132 n26, 148, 151–3, 163, 182, 191, 210
greenhouse effect 46 n13, 178

Hall, John, *Powers and Liberties* 44 n12, 97 n85
Hebrews 85
Hegel, G.W.F. 1, 2, 13, 24, 24 n17, 32, 33, 105, 106, 136, 139, 158, 160, 160 n31, 161, 163–4, 201, 212, 213, 214
Hinduism 43, 62, 90 n75, 154, 155, 168–70, 186, 206
historical materialism *see under* materialism
Hitler, Adolf 63, 65 n38, 176, 196 n30, 197
Hobbes, Thomas 8, 11, 18, 42, 174, 177, 178, 179
Holland 57, 64, 66, 67, 90, 117, 154 n24, 163, 183, 197
hunter-gathering 78, 79, 80, 83, 151, 189, 208
Hyksos 7, 85, 191

idealism 1, 15, 25, 32, 135, 136, 138–43 *passim*, 148, 150, 158, 160
imperialism 6, 7, 12, 23, 67, 68, 71, 72, 73, 81, 116, 119, 123, 124, 132, 132 n26, 145, 170, 173, 174, 194, 197, 198, 199, 199 n32
India 7 n3, 10, 43, 44, 47, 48 n17, 62, 70, 85, 88, 89, 90, 90 n75, 122, 133, 155, 169 n8, 206
Industrial Revolution 48, 51, 81 n64, 82, 92, 117, 121, 124, 130, 133, 133 n27, 139, 148, 153
industrialization 29, 30, 81, 81 n64, 82, 84, 92, 107, 119, 134, 145, 149, 189, 194
industry 7, 83, 84, 89 n74, 122, 123, 145,

189, 195 n28, 206
inus conditions, concept of 29 n18, 30 n21, 66, 66 n41, 93, 132 n26, 140, 204
Iran 85, 98, 122, 174
Iraq 124
Ireland 68
Iron Age 7, 85, 86, 191
Islam 94, 96, 96 n83, 97, 97 n86, 98, 98 n87, 130, 139–40, 155, 156, 166 n1, 171, 174, 174 n18, 175, 176, 184, 196, 196 n31, 198, 207
Islamic society 57, 90, 90 n75, 94 n80, 99, 121, 123, 195
Israel 124, 176, 176 n20
Italy 63, 68, 132, 133, 148, 163, 195

Japan 7, 31, 47, 64, 66, 71, 80, 81, 82, 84, 90, 92, 106, 119, 123, 127, 128, 130, 131, 133, 145, 146, 163, 180, 194, 196, 197, 207
Jones, E.L., *The European Miracle* 10 n10, 201
Judaism 90 n75, 97, 175, 175 n19, 176, 184

Kant, Immanuel 18 n7, 160, 160 n31, 161, 167, 168
Kassites 7, 85, 191
Keynes, John Maynard, *The General Theory of Employment* 161 n32
Khaldun, Ibn 56, 74
Khmer Rouge 29
Khomeini, Ayatollah 174, 196 n30, 197
Khrushchev, Nikita 197
Korea 62, 66, 68, 148

Lacoste, Yves 12 n2, 13 n3, 56 n29, 74, 85, 126 n20
Lamarck, J.B. 38, 77 n59, 147, 156
Landes, D. 117
Lange, Oscar, *Political Economy* 53, 54
leisure 158, 162
Lenin, V.I. 29, 30, 158, 197
Lessing, Gotthold 142
Lévi-Strauss, Claude 137
liberalism 184, 185, 185 n15, 186
livelihood, mode of 55–6, 83 n66, 123, 199, 206
  agrarian 172, 192
  economic factors of 64, 65, 87, 91, 118